Innovation, Transformation, and War

D1572711

INNOVATION, TRANSFORMATION, AND WAR

Counterinsurgency Operations in
Anbar and Ninewa, Iraq, 2005–2007

JAMES A. RUSSELL

STANFORD SECURITY STUDIES

An Imprint of Stanford University Press
Stanford, California

Stanford University Press
Stanford, California

© 2011 by the Board of Trustees of the Leland Stanford Junior University.
All rights reserved.

No part of this book may be reproduced or transmitted in any form or by any means, electronic or mechanical, including photocopying and recording, or in any information storage or retrieval system without the prior written permission of Stanford University Press.

Printed in the United States of America on acid-free, archival-quality paper

Library of Congress Cataloging-in-Publication Data

Russell, James A. (James Avery).
    Innovation, transformation, and war : counterinsurgency operations in Anbar and Ninewa, Iraq, 2005–2007 / James A. Russell
        p. cm.
    Includes bibliographical references and index.
    ISBN 978-0-8047-7309-6 (cloth : alk. paper) —
    ISBN 978-0-8047-7310-2 (pbk. : alk. paper)

    1. Social Counterinsurgency—Iraq—Anbar (Province).   2. Counterinsurgency—Iraq—Ninawá.   3. United States—Armed Forces—Iraq.   4. Tactics.   5. Iraq War, 2003–.
I. Title.

    DS79.764.A63R87   2011
    956.7044'342—dc22   2010030489

Typeset at Stanford University Press in 10/14 Minion

Special discounts for bulk quantities of Stanford Security Studies are available to corporations, professional associations, and other organizations. For details and discount information, contact the special sales department of Stanford University Press.

Tel: (650) 736-1782, Fax: (650) 736-1784

New Orleans, LA.
February 2011

CONTENTS

(On-line figures illustrating the text are listed in the Appendix
on pages 253–54; the figures themselves may be accessed at
http://www.sup.org/itw)

New Orleans, La.
February 20th

ACKNOWLEDGMENTS

I strongly opposed the Bush administration's decision to invade Iraq and still believe that the invasion represented a strategic blunder from which the United States may never fully recover. I had a deep sense of foreboding in the spring of 2001, when, as a civil servant working on Persian Gulf regional policy at the Defense Department, I watched a new caste of political appointees arrive in the department's policy secretariat. During the 1990s, I had worked as a civilian for Republican and Democratic administrations in the Defense Department and had no problems supporting the regional policy of either party. That changed after the election of 2000, when the civilian policy secretariat became stuffed with right-wing ideologues. Many of these appointees had strong opinions about what to do in the Gulf—opinions that I thought were dangerously misguided. As the Iraq country director from 1996 to 1998 in the policy secretariat, I had directly participated in operationalizing the policy of containment that in many ways was deeply unsatisfying but which drew upon a successful strategic template that had successfully protected and furthered America's global interests for over half a century. Today the policy of containment looks like a bargain when measured against the human and monetary costs associated with the U.S. invasion and occupation of Iraq.

More than a decade of working on Gulf-related security policy had induced in me a certain caution before the war about believing the obviously facile claims of supposed "experts" who minimized the military challenges that awaited us in Iraq. By 2004 and 2005, veterans of the Iraq war began appearing in my classrooms in the Department of National Security Affairs at the Naval Postgraduate School, where I had successfully decamped to in the summer of 2001. The accounts from my students seemed only to confirm what looked like an unfolding strategic debacle in which incompetence at the highest reaches of our national command authority had placed our men and women in uniform in an extremely difficult military situation.

In 2006, I decided to write a book about their situation. My then neighbor and colleague Professor Harold Trinkunas wandered into my office one day after learning of my plans and urged me to think about writing the book in conjunction with getting a Ph.D. With the help of my good friend Wyn Bowen, I subsequently entered the doctoral program in War Studies at King's College, University of London. During the development of my dissertation research, Wyn linked me up with Professor Theo Farrell, who subsequently provided invaluable guidance and support as I developed the ideas of military innovation presented in this book.

I started out thinking I would be writing about the U.S. military failure in Iraq. That changed after being invited by Tom Travis and Ted Cavin to the Joint Center for Operational Analysis at the Joint Forces Command in late 2006. During the visit, I heard a presentation by Kelly Musick (a JCOA analyst) about the emergence of so-called counterinsurgency best practices by U.S. forces conducting military operations in Anbar Province during the summer and fall of 2006. The presentation came as press reporting suggested that local security had greatly improved in Anbar with the turning of tribal leaders against Al Qaeda in Iraq, or AQI, as it was then called. I decided to write a book that attempted to document and explain the emergence of these best practices. This book tells part of the story about how American ground forces fought the insurgents in 2005 and 2006 and tries to chronicle the process of adaptation and innovation exhibited by the units covered in these pages.

The JFCOM analysts were surprised at the emergence of these best practices in 2006—as was I. Up until this period, U.S. military tactics seemed focused on conventionally oriented military operations, and our ground forces did not seem to be adapting to the insurgency inside Iraq that had gathered momentum throughout 2004 and 2005. Ironically, by late 2006, just as American units in Anbar were mastering counterinsurgency tactics and full-spectrum operations, it became clear that the Bush administration had lost confidence in its military leaders in Iraq. During late 2006, as we were defeating the Sunni insurgency in Anbar, the Bush administration developed a series of policy options that later resulted in the decision to increase the number of troops in the spring of 2007. Many books document what happened next: the promulgation of new joint counterinsurgency doctrine in December 2006, the increase in troop numbers, and the appointment of General David Petraeus as senior military commander in Iraq are widely seen as turning the tide on the battlefield against the insurgents. This book has little to add to that story and instead focuses on tactical-level battlefield operations before the surge, as brigade and company commanders struggled to adapt their balky organizational structures to the demands of fighting an insurgency. The story that emerges in these pages suggests that the established popular narrative of what happened to the U.S. military in Iraq is much more complex than generally believed. Evidence from the cases examined here suggests that adaptation and innovation in the field led the Defense Department's rear-echelon efforts to reorient the organizational capacities of American ground forces toward irregular warfare and counter-insurgency.

Many friends and colleagues helped me along the way. Colleagues in the Department of National Security Affairs at the Naval Postgraduate School provided moral and intellectual support as I slogged my way through the research. I particularly thank Daniel Moran, Don Abenheim, Doug Porch, and Jim Wirtz for their friendship and support. I particularly benefited from an ongoing two-year conversation with my good friend and colleague Daniel Moran about the many strategic and military issues addressed in these pages. It is certainly the case that his brilliance and insightful analysis helped me try to organize my own thinking on the complicated issues covered in this book. I also found willing and supportive help from the units that I focused on in this research. Nick Marano, Dan Zappa, V. J. Tedesco, Charles Webster, Michael Shields, Mark Freitag, Sean MacFarland, Scott Wuestner, Bill Keyes, William Jurney, Rick Somers, Matt Albertus, Dale Alford, Ed Matthaidess, John Gronski and others were of great assistance in helping me to understand the intricacies of tactical-level operations conducted by their units in Iraq. I should also mention a group of NPS students that participated in a series of seminars I taught in 2007 and 2008 as I refined my own thinking on military innovation. As always in these classes, I learned as much from my students as they did from me and the course readings. Ray Mattox, Pete Rodgers, Bobby Davis, Daniel Hancock, Doug Thies, Kyle Phillips, Brad Fultz, Ferdinand Hafner, Todd Anderson, Bryan Wilson, Dennis Faulkner, Chris Stelle, Bill Duggan, Mark Munson, and Jason Howk all helped to enliven classroom discussions about the issues presented in this book. Barry Zellen also provided invaluable editorial assistance in the preparation of the manuscript.

I must also mention two people whose indelible imprint is felt at least by me in the pages that follow, even though they had no direct hand in the preparation of the book. Colonel John Greenwood, USMC (Ret.), gave me my first job out of graduate school as assistant editor at the *Marine Corps Gazette* in the early 1980s. The experience of working for Colonel Greenwood undeniably set me on the path that led to the writing of this book, which in some ways represents a full circle journey in which I have, after twenty years, returned to thinking and writing about the same kinds of tactical-level military issues that I first encountered while working under Colonel Greenwood's insightful tutelage. After leaving the *Gazette*, I went to work for Llewellyn King as a reporter for *Defense Week*. While I didn't realize it at the time, working as a reporter for King was to become one of the most important experiences of my professional life. The skills developed working as a journalist at *Defense Week* established a firm foundation for all of my subsequent professional endeavors working in the Office of the Under Secretary of Defense for Policy and then later at the Naval Postgraduate School. The research and writing for this book draws heavily on the skills that Llewellyn King carefully cultivated in all his reporters—and I am eternally grateful to him for giving me the chance to develop the skills that continue to serve me well to this day.

Last but not least, I would be remiss if I did not mention the inestimable support of my loving wife, Julie Carson, who helped keep me focused on the project by kicking me out of the house on the weekends so that I could finish this book.

Innovation, Transformation, and War

1 INTRODUCTION

The United States stormed into Iraq in March 2003 boasting the world's best-trained and -equipped military. Using a host of technologies and new weapons that had been integrated into its force structure over the preceding decade, the invasion force made quick work of its adversary in a march on Baghdad that took only three weeks.[1] The invasion unveiled a "Shock and Awe"[2] campaign of rapid dominance packaged under the ostensibly new paradigm of "effects based operations."[3] The invasion framed the impressive application of combined arms conventional military power that routed Saddam's armies and delivered U.S. forces into downtown Baghdad in three weeks. The invasion force applied a new generation of sensors, standoff munitions, and digitized command and control systems to great effect during the invasion against a marginally competent enemy.[4] The invasion seemed to confirm to many the primacy of U.S. global military power.

As is now widely known, however, the actual invasion of Iraq represented only the opening phase of the war. Unfolding events gradually drained away the initial sense of optimism over the removal of Saddam and the defeat of his army as the security environment inside Iraq deteriorated over the summer of 2003. By the winter of 2003–4 it became clear that, while Saddam's army had been defeated, armed resistance to the invading and occupying force had only just begun. While the U.S. political leadership tried to discount and marginalize the initial appearance of Iraqi resistance groups in the summer and fall of 2003,[5] the American military gradually became aware that it was immersed in a full-blown insurgency—a kind of warfare for which it had failed to prepare.[6] The American military slowly came to the inescapable conclusion that the methods and equipment for defeating Saddam's Army wouldn't work against increasingly well organized and adaptive insurgent groups. The U.S. military either had to adjust or face defeat.

This book addresses a discrete, but arguably vital, part of the U.S. war in Iraq in Anbar and Ninewa Provinces during 2005 through early 2007—a period when the United States clearly faced the prospect of battlefield defeat and strategic disaster. It focuses on counterinsurgency, or COIN, operations by a series of Army and Marine Corps battalions operating in a variety of environments during this period. The book seeks to answer one central question: how did the units examined in the pages that follow adapt to the growth of the insurgency during this period? The book presents evidence suggesting that the units successfully innovated in war—a process that drew upon a complex series of forces that enabled the units to transition successfully from organizations structured and trained for conventional military operations to organizations that developed an array of new organizational capacities for full-spectrum combat operations.

The research for this book adds an interesting dimension to the established popular narrative of America's counterinsurgency campaign in Iraq. That narrative contains several elements. The first is that military success magically materialized after President Bush sent an additional 20,000 troops to Iraq (the so-called surge) in the spring of 2007. The second is that military success materialized only after General David Petraeus decisively reoriented American battlefield tactics toward COIN, once he assumed command of U.S. forces in Iraq during the same period. The third is that improved battlefield performance directly followed the promulgation of new counterinsurgency doctrine in December of 2006.[7] While each of these narratives is correct in an overall sense, they are also incomplete and present only part of the story of how America's ground force decisively reoriented itself toward irregular warfare in Iraq. Evidence presented in this book suggests that by the time President Bush announced the "surge" and Petraeus was named to "rescue" the COIN campaign in the spring of 2007, the units in the following case studies had already built successful COIN competencies and were experiencing battlefield successes—most dramatically in Anbar Province in the fall of 2006. Importantly, in Anbar, at least, these were not ad hoc unit innovations made to no strategic effect. In Anbar, it is clear that the wartime innovation process *did* produce strategic effect and proved instrumental in the defeat of the Sunni insurgency, as will be addressed in Chapter 4. The units examined in this book showed an ability to adapt and innovate in the field dating from late 2005 with little direction from higher military and civilian authorities. None of the units examined herein received what could be considered command-level guidance from the headquarters level on how to structure their counterinsurgency operations.[8]

It is clear that the commitment of additional troops in 2007 proved instrumental in improving the security situation throughout Iraq and most particularly in Baghdad, just as it is clear that the appointment of Petraeus—a leader committed to COIN—represented an important signal of America's commitment to the new methods of fighting the insurgents. It is equally clear that the promulgation of new doctrine helped to systematically enhance the preparation of incoming units to conduct counterinsurgency, just at it is clear that the manual for the first time provided senior military leadership at Multi-National Forces Iraq, or MNF-I, with a template around which to structure and direct a national-level counterinsurgency campaign. While the promulgation of new joint COIN doctrine in December 2006 unquestionably helped to better train and prepare incoming units that subsequently arrived as part of the surge in the spring of 2007, it does not explain the improved battlefield performance of the units studied here in the eighteen preceding months. This book argues that it is somewhat misleading to assert that the new doctrine suddenly and systematically enhanced battlefield performance that had been notably lagging. This book presents evidence suggesting that tactical momentum (particularly in Anbar Province—the epicenter of the Sunni insurgency) had been building for the previous eighteen months largely as a result of innovation exhibited at the tactical level by a number of Army and Marine Corps units.

Prior to the appointment of General Petraeus as military commander in February 2007, U.S. military commanders in Iraq, Tampa, and Washington had not systematically re-examined the nation's approach to fighting the war. Within Multi-National Forces Iraq (MNF-I), there was debate in late 2006 over the desirability of increasing the number of U.S. troops on the ground but little examination over the overall approach.[9] In early 2006, however, a drafting team headed by Conrad Crane and Jan Horvath working under General Petraeus at Fort Leavenworth feverishly prepared a new counterinsurgency manual—an effort that in itself happened because of the recognition that deploying forces needed a new doctrinal template to prepare them for COIN operations in Iraq.[10] This book has little to add to the already told story of the preparation of the new manual and the important impact of the new doctrine on military operations in Iraq after the manual's publication in December 2006. This book instead chronicles the parallel search for solutions to the insurgency that proceeded on an ad-hoc basis at the tactical level in several U.S. units fighting the insurgents during the same period that the team worked to develop the new COIN manual. These parallel searches for solutions to the tactical and operational problems in fighting the insurgency were loosely connected in that the team preparing the new manual was generally aware of the tactical experiences of U.S. units fighting the insurgents. The team preparing the new manual certainly knew of the ad hoc, tactical innovation process, as can be seen in certain sections of the doctrinal manual.[11] In the field, however, brigade and battalion commanders received little in the way of headquarters-level guidance or information from the team writing the new doctrine or from other higher headquarters on how to conduct counterinsurgency operations. In the cases studied here, it is clear that the improved battlefield performance of certain American units during 2005–6 occurred in the absence of, and not because of, competent top-down direction from the highest reaches of the civilian and military hierarchy. As recounted in several well-known summaries of the period, the White House, State Department, Defense Department, Joint Staff, the Central Command, and MNF-I appeared incapable of jointly formulating and directing the execution of a unified strategic plan in Iraq that linked the application of military force to clearly defined political objectives.[12]

During congressional testimony in October 2005, then Secretary of State Condoleezza Rice described the U.S. military strategy in Iraq as "clear, hold, and build." Whatever those terms meant, they had never been communicated in any operational form to the military prosecuting the counterinsurgency, and senior military commanders had no idea what she was talking about.[13] Rice's approach seemed to draw upon an article in the journal *Foreign Affairs* by Andrew Krepinevich in which he called for an "ink spot" strategy which recommended that U.S. military forces stop focusing on killing insurgents and instead shift to providing local security for the Iraqi population.[14] On the military side, ideas had surfaced independently in the summer of 2005 that units should structure their operations along a number of simultaneous Logical Lines of Operations, or LOOs, to apply their capabilities across the full spectrum of the combat environment.[15] President Bush echoed Rice's words in October 2005 without input from those prosecuting the war. In November 2005, the White House released a *National Strategy for Victory in Iraq* that repeated the "clear, hold, and build" approach, though there is no evidence that this document provided the basis for a military strategy that was communicated to forces fighting the insurgents.[16] If anything, the White House gave conflicting messages on military strategy throughout the period. In a speech at the Naval Academy on November 30, 2005, President Bush described the U.S. approach somewhat differently from clear, hold, and build, telling cheering midshipmen: "We will continue to shift from providing security and conducting operations against the enemy nationwide to conducting more specialized operations targeted at the most dangerous terrorists. We will increasingly move out of Iraqi cities, reduce the number of bases from which we operate, and conduct fewer patrols and convoys."[17] In December 2005, Bush repeated the mantra coming from MNF-I Commander General George Casey, telling an audience at the Woodrow Wilson Center in Washington DC: "As Iraqis stand up, we will stand down."[18]

While political leaders appeared confused over military strategy, senior U.S. military commanders with responsibility for Iraq operations articulated a relatively consistent set of objectives. MNF-I Commander General George Casey and the Central Command's General John Abizaid pursued an approach from 2004 through 2006 that sought to turn over responsibility for local security to the Iraqis as quickly as possible.[19] Casey and Abizaid believed that the insurgent violence was directed primarily at the U.S. occupation. Both believed that U.S. troops represented an "antibody" to Iraqi culture and society and that lowering the profile of U.S. troops by consolidating them at a few isolated military bases would reduce insurgent violence. Neither saw the insurgency as a complex, tribal, ideological, and sectarian battle for political power and influence between a variety of different groups with competing objectives. To his credit, Casey clearly realized that American units needed to build COIN competencies, although he refused to embrace or operationalize a national-level campaign plan that reflected general principles of counterinsurgency. In August 2005, he commissioned Colonel William Hix, who headed the MNF-I strategy office, and Kalev Sepp, a COIN expert at the Naval Postgraduate School, to survey U.S. units to determine their COIN proficiency. The survey found that 20 percent of units in the field were demonstrating COIN proficiency; 60 percent were struggling to reorient themselves; and 20 percent of the units showed little COIN proficiency at all. Interestingly, the survey found the younger officers more flexible and interested in exploring COIN capacities than the senior battalion and brigade commanders.[20] There is no evidence that Casey ever used the study to argue for enhanced COIN training with either the Army or Marine Corps back in Washington. Casey's establishment of the COIN Academy in Taji, Iraq, in late 2005, however, demonstrated his awareness that U.S. units needed to reorient themselves away from traditional conventional-style military operations and reflected his lack of confidence that the lack of preparation for COIN could be remedied in predeployment training.[21] The academy conducted five-day courses to familiarize incoming U.S. commanders with the tenets of COIN theory. The curriculum drew upon the writings of David Galula and other noted COIN theorists.[22] The academy played to mixed reviews, however, and the administration of the facility eventually was turned over to retired military officers with little background or expertise in COIN. The MNF-I command emphasis during this period of the war overwhelmingly remained on building up the Iraqi Security Force, or ISF, and conducting "decisive" military operations like that which happened in November 2004 in the assault on Fallujah. Once the Iraqis became capable of independent operations, both Abizaid and Casey sought to withdraw U.S. forces to several major operating bases and then withdraw them from the country altogether—as quickly as possible. Neither Casey nor Abizaid ever promulgated a nationwide campaign plan to counter the emerging insurgency as it gathered strength and momentum in late 2003 and 2004.[23] In the summer of 2005, Colonel Hix's office finally produced an overarching campaign plan that formalized the approach of building up the ISF. The plan, however, did not emphasize the core COIN principles of local security and population protection.[24] Many officers in the field felt a disconnect between Casey's emphasis on demonstrating "progress" in developing host-nation military capabilities and the difficult realities of standing up a new ISF in places like Anbar Province. Some within the MNF-W staff felt pressure to generate indicators showing unrealistic progress in the development of the ISF so that Casey could realize his objective of extricating the United States from Iraq as quickly as possible.[25] A PowerPoint briefing slide describing Casey's campaign dated June 12, 2006, did not refer to local security, the insurgents, or the need for the United States to adopt a new approach to COIN.[26] During the summer of 2006, Casey unsuccessfully pushed a plan in the interagency in Washington to draw down U.S. forces in Iraq from fourteen brigades to five or six by the end of 2007.[27] Growing increasingly skeptical of Casey's approach, the White House formed an ad hoc group to review U.S. strategy in the fall of 2006 that provided three options for a revised Iraq strategy. In January 2007, President Bush chose the group's option to increase troop strength.[28] In the spring of 2007, as General Petraeus took over command, the focus on building up the ISF had not changed substantially. In a briefing prepared for Petraeus by MNF-I deputy commander General Ray Odierno, dated February 8, 2007, the emphasis remained on setting the conditions "for the ISF to emerge as the dominant security force."[29]

The disconnect between battlefield commanders and the confused national level leadership adds another interesting twist to the problems facing tactical commanders responsible for structuring field-level operations. All the cases examined in this book show that the search for tactical solutions to the problems presented by the insurgency proceeded for the most part without interference from higher headquarters at MNF-I or any other headquarters elements that might have imposed solutions that dictated battlefield tactics, such as the Central Command in Tampa, Florida, or the Joint Staff in Washington, DC. Moreover, there is no evidence that the political leadership in the Defense Department or other executive branch agencies sought to impose solutions at the tactical level—although General Casey clearly faced political pressure from Secretary Rumsfeld to avoid "Americanizing" the war. Despite the pressure on Casey, however, no school solution materialized à la Vietnam that allowed systemic biases at senior levels to impose themselves on commanders leading engaged forces. Ironically, the lack of a school solution can be explained partly by the lack of a doctrinally approved joint approach to fighting an insurgency before December 2006, when the Army and Marine Corps jointly released a draft of *FM 3-24 Counterinsurgency*. While the Army had released an interim doctrinal manual, *FMI 3-07.22, Counterinsurgency Operations* in October 2004, the manual applied only to Army units and contained no guidance on structuring COIN operations at the "joint" level. The interim manual generally emphasized the kinetic side of COIN, focusing on destruction of the enemy's forces—as opposed to full-spectrum operations.[30] These limitations mitigated the manual's impact in Iraq, since most military units were faced with a requirement to master full-spectrum operations and conducted tactical operations as joint task forces that incorporated units and organizational components from across the Department of Defense. Unconstrained by an established COIN doctrine, and impelled by desperation to find anything that worked, brigade commanders and their subordinates covered in the following case studies received wide flexibility to structure their operations to fight the insurgency. As a result, commanders and their supporting organizations freely cycled through a series of actions that helped reduce the effectiveness of insurgent operations directed at their units.

The case studies in this book chronicle an iterative process of organically generated tactical adaptation and innovation that unfolded over time in a distinctive progression. The process began in what could be described as tactical, ad hoc adaptation in which individual leaders reacted to local circumstance by cycling through different ways of employing their units and equipment on the battlefield. Some of these adaptations succeeded and others failed. As leaders identified successful adaptations, the process gathered momentum and new organizational standard operating procedures emerged that became more widely adopted by military units fighting the insurgents.[31] Organizational innovation then manifested itself through the emergence of a series of new standard operating procedures that collectively resulted in fundamental changes to the ways in which the units examined herein fought the insurgents. As these innovations produced success on the battlefield, they eventually fed into more formalized military doctrine that followed later.[32] While execution of the innovation process happened in the field, it is clear that the process involved many actors throughout the military chain of command. Individuals, units, and headquarters elements stretching from Anbar to Baghdad, Fort Leavenworth, the Pentagon, and beyond searched for solutions to the problems being encountered on the battlefields of Iraq. The argument in this book is that this process was led largely from the field during this discrete period of the war.

BATTLEFIELD INNOVATION AND COUNTERINSURGENCY AMERICAN STYLE

This book argues that the collective momentum of tactical adaptation documented in Chapters 3, 4, and 5 can be characterized as organizational innovation. The term "innovation" is defined as the development of new organizational capacities not initially present in these units when they arrived in Iraq and that had only tangential grounding in established capstone doctrine. This definition could be regarded as encompassing only short-term, situational tactical adaptation. This book, however, argues that tactical adaptation can serve as a way station along the route toward more comprehensive innovation. In the cases examined here, multiple tactical adaptations occurred iteratively over time that eventually produced new organizational structures and new organizational capacities built in war that fundamentally changed the nature of organizational output delivered over the course of the units' deployment. This definition of the concept of innovation suggests that innovation per se need not be permanent, or enshrined in new doctrine in order to be considered as innovation.

The new capacities built iteratively over time changed the way these units fought the insurgency. This book's case studies detail a process of wartime innovation that manifested itself as a series of organic, bottom-up procedures developed within the battalions and brigades fighting the insurgents. While the innovation process developed organically, that process drew upon information and enabling processes nested in a variety of sources outside the units themselves. Innovation occurred within the units through the fusion of the information and enabling processes that ultimately produced new organizational outputs. Basic capstone doctrinal grounding in military operations proved to be a fundamental building block for the innovation process. Previous experiences in Iraq and Afghanistan helped shape the innovation. Non–institutionally blessed sources of information on COIN theory and history were consciously drawn upon by units as they intellectually reoriented themselves toward full-spectrum operations. A variety of digital domain platforms helped units freely pass information and lessons learned back and forth, which helped the process of adaptation and innovation. The innovation produced new organizational capacities that shaped successful military operations across the spectrum of kinetic and nonkinetic operations to reduce insurgent-generated violence. Wartime innovation in the cases studied here flowed from agile, flexible, decentralized organizations that featured flattened and informal hierarchical structures. Throughout their deployments, each of the units covered in the following case studies demonstrated significant learning capacities that proved central to the innovation process. The case study narratives built on primary source data present a picture of military organizations acting in ways that are contrary to the popularly accepted view that military organizations function as bureaucratically inclined, hierarchically structured organizations slow to respond to changes in the external environment. In the cases studied here, the exigencies of wartime produced much different organizational behavior.

The American wartime experiences chronicled in this book are historically significant given the previous and disastrous experiences of the United States in fighting irregular war in the post–World War II era. At first blush, the comparisons between Vietnam and Iraq seem attractive. The military fought both wars in the context of strategic confusion, in which the relationships between military operations and strategic objectives appeared unclear. As shown by the case studies in this book, however, the U.S. military experience in Iraq bears little relationship to the historical experiences of the Vietnam War—at least insofar as the adaptive and innovative capacities of America's military institutions are concerned. Moreover, unlike Vietnam, the Army and Marine Corps *did* institutionally embrace COIN competencies and eventually produced doctrine as evidence of that institutional commitment. Evidence presented in the pages that follow suggests that certain American ground units (both Army and Marine Corps) in Iraq evolved into flexible, adaptive organizations taking advantage of twenty-first-century human and technological capacities. The units examined in the following pages proved to be technologically advanced, complex organizations with a highly educated and trained workforce that embraced environmental complexity and searched for optimal solutions to operational problems. The organizations covered in this study did not satisfice—or take the path of least resistance—in their search for solutions to the tactical problems posed by the insurgency in Iraq.

By 2005 various U.S. brigade and battalion commanders, as illustrated in the case studies that follow, began independently to change their approach on the battlefield, embracing requirements for a COIN campaign tailored to the Iraq environment. That change was required is not in question—many observers have cogently chronicled the U.S. ground forces' initial stumbling attempts to adapt to the insurgency in 2003 and 2004.[33] The units covered in this book built new innovative core competencies within their organizations, drawing upon such factors as: (1) digitally based communications and data systems that seamlessly passed information on a continuous basis between units preparing for their deployments; (2) imaginative battlefield leadership that delegated authority, welcomed the concept of distributed operations, encouraged the free flow of information throughout the organizational hierarchy, and freely changed their organizational structures in the field in order to apply their capacities across the spectrum of kinetic and nonkinetic operations; (3) the use of advanced technologies and analytical methods to combat insurgent networks; and (4) a continuous education process in which units kept seeking information and expertise from many different sources to aid in their tactical decision-making processes.

The emergence of American COIN competencies in the field adds an interesting twist to another of the popular narratives of the period. Prior to the Iraq war, the Bush administration initiated a process called "transformation" to reform the Defense Department's sprawling military and civilian bureaucracies. This process overwhelmingly featured top-down direction from the Defense Department's civilian leadership to executing organizational elements. Then Secretary of Defense Donald Rumsfeld's now well known micromanagement of the Central Command's war plan reflected an attitude that civilian management could and should wrench hidebound military bureaucracies around to a new way of fighting. Rumsfeld's new way of war, however, had little to do with counterinsurgency and activities he derisively referred to as "nation-building." Rumsfeld insisted on fewer troops than initially wanted by military commanders and sought to make the invasion an advertisement for a new American way of war featuring precision guided munitions, speed of movement, and effects-based operations.[34] The irony of the argument in this book is that the U.S. military indeed transformed itself during the Iraq war, though not in the ways envisioned by Rumsfeld. Prior to December 2006 and the promulgation of the new doctrine, the most important part of the transformation occurred not in the invasion but in the counterinsurgency campaign afterward, and not through top-down direction but through ground-up, organic processes in which tactical units eventually embraced and mastered the very nation-building skills that Rumsfeld sought to avoid.

MILITARY DOCTRINE AND ORGANIZATIONAL INNOVATION

The process of organically generated military innovation described here suggests that lack of an established doctrinal approach to COIN did not constrain units in the following case studies from becoming proficient in irregular warfare. The argument presented here is that formalized doctrine played an important but ultimately only a tangential role in structuring the COIN operations of the units examined herein from late 2005 through early 2007. The Department of Defense defines doctrine as "[f]undamental principles by which the military forces or elements thereof guide their actions in support of national objectives. It is authoritative but requires judgment in application."[35] To be sure, definitions of this concept have evolved throughout the twentieth century for American military institutions. The current definition followed a healthy debate over the degree to which doctrine represented concrete rules and techniques to be applied on the battlefield, versus a view that doctrine represented only a guide for action with significant leeway delegated to unit commanders in structuring combat operations while in contact with the enemy.[36] In his analysis of relationships between the formation of doctrine and the organizational experiences in the Marine Corps in the early twentieth century, Keith Bickel pointed to the existence of "formal versus informal" doctrine. Formal doctrine represented formalized institutional knowledge promulgated in doctrinal manuals used for training forces. Informal doctrine, by contrast, exists in parallel to formalized doctrine in the form of professional journal articles, personal letters recounting battlefield lessons and experiences, and field orders that come to represent a body of knowledge that, Bickel argues, finds its way into formalized form.[37]

Scholars typically examine and analyze changes in military doctrine, viewing these changes as an important indicator in assessing the degree of innovation in military organizations.[38] This is understandable. Changes in military doctrine are easy to identify since, first and foremost, these changes must be written down. Doctrine's explicit character does not, of course, guarantee its institutional effect. Not all doctrinal changes succeed in changing real-world military behavior. Those that do manifest themselves as a host of observables that provide evidence of a new outlook and new practices in the areas of training, unit organization, and tables of equipment—all of which can be observed and analyzed directly.

In the case of the United States and most other advanced militaries, twentieth-century military doctrine demonstrates a reasonably logical progression of an approach to warfare that has sought to apply firepower against the enemy in successively more complicated ways at successively greater distances.[39] The U.S. Army's Airland Battle doctrine, introduced in 1986, reflects this progression.[40] Indeed, the application of combined arms on twentieth-century battlefields reveals an iterative and evolutionary process as successful modern militaries slowly mastered the capabilities offered to them by the integration of advances in indirect fire and precision-guided munitions, communications, intelligence, and the ability of units to fire and maneuver effectively in coordination with other combat arms.[41]

In Iraq, however, analysis of Army and Marine Corps doctrine as it existed before 2003 provides little indication of how these organizations would fight an insurgency. Indeed, prewar capstone military doctrine emphasizing traditional conventional military operations that focused on fire and maneuver proved to be of little use in fighting the insurgents in Iraq. Importantly, however, while the specific tactics, techniques, and procedures (TTPs) might not have been used, the processes of unit command and coordination established by capstone doctrine provided a procedural roadmap over which the innovation process flowed. Over the period studied in this book, battlefield commanders in the following case studies drew upon established doctrinal processes to construct altered organizational structures with new TTPs to apply new COIN competencies appropriate to Iraq's environment.

While the execution of the battlefield innovation process happened within the units in this study, it would be a mistake to characterize that process as strictly either "bottom up" or "top down." The processes of wartime innovation in the units studied here did not result solely from factors within the unit, nor was the process prompted solely by top-down processes featuring the articulation of a new military doctrine, whether created by forceful civilian intervention from above or by dynamic senior military leadership at the headquarters level. The innovation process exhibited by the units in the following case studies was dialectical in nature and drew upon a complex series of forces from both within and outside the units that fused together in ways to produce organically generated change—change that eventually "pulled" tactical practice, institutional innovation, and (finally) authoritative doctrinal pronouncements along behind it.

Established doctrinal processes as described in foundational capstone doctrine like the Army's *FM 3.0 Operations* provided a framework and common understanding for the units as they responded to the insurgency. The Marine units also drew upon their established doctrine to help provide a framework to structure their COIN operations. All of the units examined in this book exhibited firm grounding in doctrinally bounded processes and applied those processes to the problem of COIN in Iraq. Instead of being hampered by rigid bureaucratic organizations bound up in red tape,[42] wartime experiences in Iraq show that networked, informal, and cross-functional organizations sprang up over the course of military operations that fused disparate organizational elements, both military and civilian, into a synergistic whole applied to great effect against the enemy. In many respects, the organizations responsible for combating the insurgency proved to be very unbureaucratic in their behavior. These organizations produced the tactical flexibility *and* innovation that fundamentally changed the way that U.S. forces fought the insurgents. These changes, which encompassed a wide array of kinetic and nonkinetic activities, dramatically reduced the military effectiveness of insurgent operations in the cases examined in this work.[43]

The U.S. military experience in Iraq has not proven to be a replay of the military experience in the Vietnam War. During Vietnam, the U.S. Army refused to adapt itself institutionally to the combat environment created by its enemies, despite being directed to do so by President Kennedy, and despite undeniable evidence that its operations were not defeating the Viet Cong insurgency.[44] While certain organizational components like the Marines (Combined Action Platoons in I Corps) and Special Forces (Civilian Irregular Defense Group in the Central Highlands) explored innovative approaches to fighting the counterinsurgency in Vietnam, these changes never received institutional support at what would now be called the "joint" level, and slowly withered away as the Army doggedly pursued more conventionally oriented military operations.[45]

As of this writing, U.S. forces have ceased combat operations in Iraq. This book does not argue that the American use of force in Iraq will produce a stable, peaceful, and democratic government or society there. It also does not argue that the improved military capacities exhibited by U.S. military units "won" the war or even that these capacities were primarily responsible for the reduction in insurgent violence in Iraq. As in all forms of warfare, the political dimensions of the armed struggle inside Iraq perhaps proved to be the most important factor framing the U.S. struggle with the insurgents during this period of the war. In Anbar Province, for example, the growing disaffection of nationalist-oriented insurgents with Sunni extremists during the period of this study provided a vital political backdrop that created a political opportunity for U.S. military units. National-level political developments in Iraq during the period were equally important in pushing Iraqi nationalist oriented insurgents into a closer relationship with the U.S. military. The point that needs emphasizing is that improved American COIN competencies represented one—albeit an important—element in a complex series of factors that led to the improvement of security inside Iraq. One unfortunate result of the American military experience and the supposed success following the increase of forces in 2007 is the widespread and largely unsupported assertions proclaiming that the increased troop levels achieved some kind of "victory" in Iraq. This is a dangerous and incomplete reading of history and forms part of an argument asserting that well-executed tactics supporting supposed principles of counterinsurgency can somehow magically produce victory. This is again a dangerous and misleading reading of the circumstances of the war in Iraq as it is elsewhere in places like Afghanistan.

History may judge that U.S. military adaptation and innovation did not happen fast enough to keep pace with evolving political circumstances within both Iraq and the United States. One of the wider implications of this book is that leaders need to consider the adaptive and innovative abilities of their military organizations in the decision-making process used to decide when to apply force in pursuit of strategic objectives. As much as political and military leaders want to believe that their military organizations can accomplish national objectives in a variety of different operational environments, the reality is that these institutions cannot seamlessly and effortlessly transition between dramatically different scenarios and demonstrate immediate effectiveness across all spectrums of combat. When the sequences of organizational adaptation and innovation become desynchronized from overarching political realities governing the war, the state applying force can face problems in achieving its objectives no matter how adaptive and innovative their military institutions may be. Whatever the strategic and political outcome in Iraq, it should not obscure the organizational flexibility that eventually unfolded at the tactical level in certain units fighting the insurgency. This organizational flexibility produced wartime innovation that fundamentally changed the conduct of the war against the insurgents in the years preceding the promulgation of formal, joint doctrine.

MILITARY INNOVATION AND GRAND STRATEGY

Why weren't America's armed forces ready to fight an irregular war when they arrived in Iraq? There certainly was no shortage of national-level guidance suggesting—even directing—the advisability of developing competencies to fight a counterinsurgency. In the five years following the September 2001 attacks, the Bush administration promulgated an enormous variety of documents intended to provide strategic guidance to the nation's civilian and military organizations. Indeed, no U.S. administration in history has ever released such a flood of paper explaining different aspects of the nation's grand strategy.[46] In addition to explaining the nation's global interests and objectives to the public, this collection of documents effectively provided the "commander-in-chief's intent" to military organizations for their use in tailoring their resources, plans, and programs to achieve the nation's objectives. These organizations were expected to translate political and strategic guidance into military actions, or outputs, that addressed the objectives articulated at the strategic level. This collection of documents arguably subjected U.S. military institutions and their associated civilian bureaucracies to their most far reaching changes since the end of World War II.[47] Then Secretary of Defense Donald Rumsfeld characterized these changes as "transformation," a process that was meant to fundamentally alter the management and operational activities of all elements of the Defense Department's sprawling civilian and military bureaucracies.

The 2001 and 2006 *Quadrennial Defense Reviews* particularly emphasized the need to reorient these diverse organizations away from "traditional" Cold War state threats to meet the challenge of coping with irregular warfare, disruptive attacks by adversaries wielding dangerous new technologies, and catastrophic attacks by sub- and nonstate actors wielding mass-destructive weapons.

Other Defense Department internal studies echoed the call to build irregular warfare competencies in the same period. Soon after the Marine Corps and Army blasted their way into Fallujah in November 2004, the Defense Science Board released a report titled *Transition To and From Hostilities* that called for the Defense Department to build new organizational competencies to manage stabilization and postconflict reconstruction activities following the conclusion of conventional military operations.[48] As the Army and Marines swept through the towns on the Iraqi-Syrian border in November 2005, the Defense Department published DoD Directive 3000.05, *Military Support for Stability, Security, Transition, and Reconstruction (SSTR) Operations*, which formalized acceptance of the Defense Department's portion of the postconflict mission. The new directive operationalized National Security Presidential Directive 44, *Management of Interagency Efforts Concerning Reconstruction and Stabilization Operations*, which gave the State Department primary responsibility for coordinating governmentwide efforts to mount reconstruction activities in war-torn countries like Iraq.[49]

It seemed reasonable to expect that military organizations would respond vigorously to such presidentially directed change, particularly when supported by explicit follow-on implementing instructions from the Secretary of Defense to his military departments.[50] But as has been chronicled elsewhere, it is clear that the U.S. military remained unprepared for the kind of warfare it encountered in Iraq—despite ample official warning for two years prior to the invasion.[51] When the Iraq war began, U.S. Army *Field Manual (FM) 3-0, Operations*, provided the doctrinal principles guiding the application of force by the main U.S. ground component.[52] The manual's core concepts were rooted in maneuver warfare and the associated theoretical elements of applying "combat power" to defeat an enemy. Only two out of the twelve chapters (Stability Operations and Support Operations) focused upon nonmaneuver warfare issues, and only one and a half pages of the entire document even mentioned the term "asymmetry."[53] Prior to September 11, 2001, irregular warfare, terrorism, and insurgency were of scant concern to the U.S. Army. And despite the putatively galvanizing effects of Al Qaeda's attacks on that day, President Bush proved no more successful than President Kennedy, forty years before, in generating the institutional change called for by new strategy documents oriented toward the conduct of irregular warfare.

CASE STUDIES: COIN OPERATIONS
IN ANBAR AND NINEWA PROVINCES, IRAQ

The research presented here employs a case study methodology that examines a range of different unit types conducting COIN operations in Iraq over the period from July 2005 through March 2007: three active-duty Marine Corps battalions; an Army brigade consisting mostly of National Guard units; an Army armored brigade composed mostly of active-duty units; an active-duty Army armored battalion; an active-duty Army cavalry group; and an active-duty Army brigade that had just fielded its new Stryker wheeled vehicles. The cases in this research are qualitative comparisons between disparate organizational structures. Indeed, it would be virtually impossible to conduct case study research of the kind presented here between identical organizations. This is because each of these units functioned as joint task forces that included many disparate organizational (both military and civilian) elements, so it is perhaps a misnomer even to identify each unit by military department. But for purposes of the analysis, this book identifies each unit according to the service that constituted the bulk of the unit's combat manpower. In addition to different services, the cases cover units with different operational backgrounds and training. The Marine Corps infantry battalions, for example, greatly differed in their organizational structure and training from an Army armored battalion. Moreover, the Army light infantry units covered here—the Stryker-equipped units—differed significantly from their Army armored brethren and the Marine Corps light infantry. The cases are also comparative studies of units at different stages of the force modernization process taking place under the rubric of "transformation." Both of the Army light infantry units were in the midst of the transformation process, fielding an array of new equipment intended to allow them to fight differently on the battlefield. The rest of the units could be considered as "legacy" force structure units with organizational structure, equipment, and training that had not changed significantly since the end of the Cold War, if not before. There are other differences in the cases. The units had different types of equipment, different manning and organizational structures, and, most important, each unit faced different wartime environments. Despite these differences, however, the case study methodology remains a useful instrument to document the process of wartime innovation.

Each of the case studies demonstrates significant variation in its innovation processes. The across-the-board variations in the innovation process—even between similarly structured units—reinforce the argument that the innovation process did not result from top-down direction but came instead from dialectical processes that supported organic, internally generated responses to the battle-field environment. These processes were both top-down and bottom-up, so to speak, but supported a process of innovation that happened organically within the units of this study. The cases are also taken from units operating in different locations, different time periods, and different combat environments. This varia-tion further strengthens the test of the argument that the innovation processes happened independently within the units. The search for COIN competencies led to some striking similarities in the development of these competencies, but the processes for competency development differed widely among the cases.

The selected cases will illustrate the complexity of the issues being addressed in this book's research questions.[54] Each case study will highlight different as-pects of the dialectical learning process by U.S. military units in Iraq. The cases are thus bounded by time period and geographic area, and all focus on the ac-tual conduct of counterinsurgency operations, albeit in different locations and in different circumstances. The case studies are intended to capture the inter-action between and among the environment, the enemy, individual decision-making, and organizational processes that produced actions on the battlefield. The cases draw upon multiple sources of data that are intended to build a chain of evidence surrounding the research questions and the hypothesis describing the process of organic change and innovation in Iraq. The case studies will be presented as narratives, drawing upon evidence gathered from interviews, press reporting, military unit after-action reports, internal government documents, and scholarly articles. Evidence presented in the cases then will be inductively evaluated to determine if there are generalizable inferences that can be drawn about the processes of battlefield innovation.

Relying on primary source data to compile the case studies brings certain risks. Indeed, there is a likelihood that the data is systemically compromised by the built-in biases of the providers of the information. All military units for obvious reasons seek to portray their actions in the best possible light. Promo-tions and future career assignments can depend on perceptions of how their units performed in combat. This study addresses this bias by drawing exten-sively on secondary source reporting that describes the operations of the units covered in the cases. The secondary source reporting serves as a cross-check to confirm the accounts of events and unit actions provided by members of units, both in interviews and in their internal documents extensively used in this book to construct the empirically built cases.

Organized insurgent resistance to the U.S. occupation first emerged in Anbar in what became known as the "Sunni Triangle," an area in western Iraq bounded by Al Qaim on the Iraq-Syrian border, and the cities of Ramadi, Fallujah, and Baghdad. The security environment in Anbar deteriorated steadily throughout the summer and fall of 2003.[55] A toxic mix of unemployed Iraqi Army personnel, former Baathist leaders, an entrenched and independent tribal structure, and mostly foreign Sunni Islamic extremists produced a variety of insurgent groups that, while having different political, social, and religious orientations, were at least initially unified in their opposition to the U.S. occupation.[56]

By the spring of 2004, Fallujah and Ramadi had effectively become hostile enemy territory for U.S. forces. Following the brutal killing of U.S. contractors in Fallujah in April 2004, Marine Corps units assaulted the city. After objections by Iraqi leadership, the assault was terminated and the insurgents returned.[57] The city was assaulted again in November in what amounted to a repeat of the April operation—except this time the city was conquered and occupied.[58] The Fallujah attacks, however, had little impact on the strength of the insurgency elsewhere in Anbar, except that fighters that fled before the attack ended up in other parts of the province.

The first cases describe military operations by two Marine Corps battalions and an Army cavalry group operating on the Iraq-Syrian border in 2005 and 2006. I argue that these units independently built a series of COIN competencies during their deployments that dramatically improved local security throughout their area of operations. The innovation process featured the following: a move to distributed operations and decentralized authority; adaptation of the combined action platoon concept to local circumstances; application of law enforcement procedures to combat insurgent networks and the innovative use of technologies and software as part of that effort; and organizational flexibility in responding to the increased flow of intelligence information that flowed from a variety of collection sources. The collective force of these innovations completely reoriented the operations of these units during their deployment toward COIN operations that included a variety of task functions that, at the time, had not been tried in the field.

The second case addresses military operations in and around Ramadi from July 2005 through March 2007. By the time the 2nd Brigade Combat Team of the 28th Infantry Division (2/28) arrived in Ramadi in July 2005, the city was fully in the grip of a variety of insurgent groups.[59] This case will cover operations in Ramadi, focusing on the operations of 2/28 from July 2005 to August

2006 and the transition to 1st Division, 1st Armored Brigade (1/1), which conducted operations from August 2006 through early 2007. The summer of 2006 saw 1/1 change battlefield tactics in Ramadi from those pursued by 2/28. In addition, 1/1 integrated a host of new lethal and nonlethal initiatives in Ramadi.[60] The change in tactics in the fall of 2006 coincided with the so-called tribal awakening in which the Sunni tribal sheikhs in Ramadi rose up against Al Qaeda in Iraq (AQI). Cooperation between 1/1 and the tribal sheikhs gathered momentum throughout the fall of 2006 and winter of 2007.[61] By early 2007, the security environment had dramatically improved in Ramadi. Improvements in Ramadi gradually cascaded throughout the rest of the province through the spring of 2007. By the time of 1/1's departure in mid-2007, attacks mounted by Sunni extremist groups had declined dramatically and Anbar was cited by many as a "success" story.[62]

The process of organizational innovation in Anbar involved a definite progression of iterative tactical adaptation between 2/28 and 1/1. During the summer of 2006, 2/28 had begun the process of trying to isolate insurgent areas in Ramadi through greater controls over ingress and egress routes to and from the city. Under 1/1's tactical scheme, unit personnel were slowly dispersed throughout Ramadi in combat outposts (COPs) that provided local bases from which to conduct foot patrols, which improved local security and built relationships with city residents on a block-by-block basis.[63] As the COPs increased in number through late 2006 and early 2007, 1/1 simultaneously re-energized efforts to stand up the local police force, convincing local tribal leaders that their members would not be sent to other parts of Iraq. Each of these iterative steps reinforced the other and built momentum over time that marginalized the insurgents.

The third innovation case examines prosecution of the COIN campaign in Mosul, a city of 1.7 million people in Ninewa Province in northern Iraq.[64] Experiences in Mosul did not resemble the cataclysmic events in Anbar that resulted in the Fallujah operations, but the environment was nonetheless very difficult for U.S. forces. In the fall of 2004, 3rd Brigade, 2nd Infantry Division (3/2) deployed into northern Iraq in relief of the 101st Airborne Division. The transition saw a decrease in combat troops from nearly 20,000 to 5,000. Insurgents took advantage of the reduced combat presence, and attacks dramatically increased throughout 2004–5.[65] In November 2004, Mosul had to be reoccupied by U.S. forces. In August 2005, the 172nd Stryker Brigade Combat Team (SBCT) arrived in Ninewa, inheriting a vibrant and lethal insurgency, limited local participation in police forces, and a "train-and-equip" program for the Iraqi Security Force that had stalled.[66] Over the next twelve months the 172nd SBCT conducted counterinsurgency operations that dramatically reduced insurgent operations against U.S. forces and greatly improved security throughout Ninewa Province.[67] The story of the 172nd SBCT shares some of the elements of the Anbar case: development of nuanced situational awareness through extensive outreach to the local tribes; gradual standup of indigenous police forces; and the slow but steady increase in ISF capabilities.

The Mosul case features major differences that flowed from the use of the Stryker brigades, which were some of the first "transformed" units in the Army. The Stryker units featured an integrated command and control system that was supposed to improve situational awareness. This system, called "blue force" tracking, linked all deployed vehicles into a single network. Personnel in the Stryker could communicate with other vehicles and headquarters elements via classified e-mail, which was linked to intelligence and sensor feeds. These capabilities were fused together in what amounted to an ad hoc network, integrating intelligence and command and control nodes at higher headquarters with the tactical units conducting counterinsurgency operations.[68] The network involved participants from a wide variety of civilian and military organizations.

The structure of the innovation process in the Mosul case is similar to that of Anbar in that it began as a series of small, iterative steps that built momentum over time. In Mosul, however, the process unfolded differently in part because of the different characteristics of the Stryker brigades and the capabilities they brought to the battlefield. These capabilities bounded the process of tactical adaptation in interesting ways that emphasized the transformational technologies used by the brigade. These technologies were harnessed to great effect—aided by informal social networks within the Stryker brigades and the myriad outside organizations involved in the counterinsurgency campaign. The role of these informal networks in the process of innovation will be highlighted in the case study.

CHAPTER ORGANIZATION

The next chapters will discuss the following:

Chapter 2 will provide the theoretical framework surrounding the issue of change and adaptation in military organizations. It will also survey relevant literature on organizational behavior that I believe is particularly germane to the research question and hypothesis.

Chapters 3, 4, and 5 will present the case studies. Each chapter will present the empirical data assembled from which inferences will be drawn.

Chapter 6 will conclude this book, drawing inferences from the case studies using inductive analysis. It also will determine the relevance of the inferences to prevailing theories that describe the sources of wartime military innovation. It will then analyze the implications of the findings for strategy and policy.

2 THEORIES OF MILITARY INNOVATION

The idea that militaries adapt to changing battlefield conditions is neither startling nor new, being in many respects implicit in the idea of strategic interaction itself and in the universal ambition of military organizations to outdo each other in combat. A rich literature exists that seeks to explain how and why militaries fight the way that they do, and what causes them to change that behavior on the battlefield.[1] It is not surprising that much of this literature views military innovation as the result of a process that flows from the top of the organizational structure down to its executing elements—although the arguments covered in the next section emphasize different independent variables as affecting this fundamental process. Military institutions are, after all, arms of the state and are charged with its protection. These institutions are also undeniably hierarchically structured organizations—structures that have existed since the dawn of organized warfare. In mature democracies, authority to protect the state is delegated from the state's political leaders to its military institutions.[2] Within these institutions, the military leadership uses the delegated authority to operationalize the political leadership's objectives through a series of plans, policies, and programs that are in turn delegated down the organizational hierarchy for implementation. Authority logically flows from the top down in this system, a process that involves two closely related elements: (1) the military objectives and priorities of the state as defined by its political leaders based on their perception of threats to the state, and (2) the internal organizational steps taken by military institutions to execute the wishes of the political leadership. These two steps in part explain why scholars addressing innovation in military organizations assign causality for that innovation to factors either external to the state or internal to the state. A similar divide is also reflected in much of the theoretical literature in international relations and security studies.

International relations theorists in the "realist" tradition argue that states respond rationally to threats to their security, carefully weighing the costs and benefits of various courses of action to protect the state. Under this argument, the behavior of organizations charged with protecting the state generally is consistent with this overarching priority.[3] As the realists see it, threats to state security invariably stem from factors external to the state, such as rivals in the anarchical international system seeking power and influence. In response to external threats, states arm themselves and build military organizations to protect the state and to serve as instruments to exercise influence over friends and rivals in their own quest for power. In this argument, the actions of military institutions flow more or less logically. As leaders of the state perceive threats to state security, they direct military institutions to act in ways that address the threat and protect the state; and when they perceive those threats to state security to be undergoing change, they consequently direct military institutions to take steps to address the new threats. These steps, in turn, produce innovation by military organizations.

A variant of this approach accepts that military institutions act in ways to protect the state, but assigns a more pronounced role to inter- and intraorganizational processes in explaining the ways in which these institutions execute the wishes of their political masters. This approach argues that a state's pursuit of security cannot be fully understood without grasping the role that its own internal organizations play in shaping its behavior, as well as the impact that organizational characteristics can have on the process of delivering outputs that respond to external threats.[4] Military innovation is thus seen as being affected by the important intervening variable of organizational and bureaucratic behavior. This latter explanation is linked to the "bureaucratic politics" approach of understanding state behavior pioneered by Graham Allison, Morton Halperin, and others.[5]

This book aims neither to resolve the differences between these arguments nor to determine whether internal or external explanations are superior. However, it does recognize that the actual application of state military power on the battlefield undeniably happens through military organizations structured as complex, hierarchical bureaucracies. As a consequence, altering organizational performance on the battlefield undeniably means changing the behavior of large, complex organizations. As emphasized by Stephen Peter Rosen, "[No] one has yet explained how nations can wage war under modern conditions without operating with and through the huge bureaucracy that is the American military. The problem of military innovation is necessarily a problem of bureaucratic innovation."[6] Or, one could reverse Rosen's logic and argue that bureaucratic innovation (and, ipso facto, bureaucratic resistance to innovation) is necessarily a problem for military innovation.

Prevailing wisdom in the literature on bureaucracy and organizational behavior argues that military organizations—like most entrenched bureaucracies—are change-averse. That is to some extent a function of the institutional maturity of most, and certainly of the best, military organizations, which over time develop established behaviors and habits of thought that inhibit innovation in the name of preserving traditional values and practices that have proven their worth in the past. The military departments in the United States (Army, Navy, Air Force, and Marine Corps) provide the quintessential example of this phenomenon.[7] These organizations are all mature, entrenched bureaucracies that consume more than half a trillion dollars annually by some estimates—more than the military spending of most of the rest of the world combined.[8] Some argue that these organizations are motivated primarily by the need to preserve their budgets, organizational identity or "essence," traditional missions, weapons programs, and the institutional values that are central to their respective identities.[9] These core values effectively constitute a series of bureaucratic imperatives that drive risk-averse and change-resistant behavior and, in parallel, a thirst for money that seems forever unquenched.[10] It is fair to say that the U.S. military departments all exhibit this sort of behavior—particularly when it comes to their cherished weapons programs. The Air Force, for example, has successfully convinced its political patrons in the executive branch and the Congress to pay hundreds of billions of dollars for the F-22 fighter despite the fact that most advanced states have given up on the idea of building advanced combat aircraft. In other words, it is difficult for the Air Force to argue that the new capabilities represented by the F-22 are necessary as a response to a tangible external threat. Alas, the Air Force is not alone. For its part the Navy continues to spend billions of dollars on huge new aircraft carriers while simultaneously emphasizing the central doctrinal importance of maritime security—a mission wholly unsuited for these large platforms. In both cases (the F-22 and aircraft carriers), these platforms are believed central to institutional identity and values—despite their questionable relevance to the security environments in which they will operate.[11] These are only two obvious examples of the powerful role played by organizational imperatives in shaping institutional behavior. Needless to say, instituting dramatic change and innovation of any sort in entrenched military bureaucracies is hence believed to be extremely difficult.

In the United States, the political calendar adds another intervening variable that also influences the process of organizational innovation. U.S. military institutions are sophisticated domestic political actors that service a variety of stakeholders and constituencies with a diverse array of interests—not all of which are in agreement. For example, the Congress occasionally forces the military departments to purchase unwanted equipment because of the interest of the Congress in defense spending in their districts.[12] The need to service their diverse stakeholders provides an added shaping factor that militates against dramatic changes in organizational behavior and action by military institutions. The need to service these multiple constituencies promotes a "lowest common denominator" approach as entrenched bureaucracies consider the prospect of change. Further, when institutional leadership confronts any unwanted "new" defense strategy requiring dramatic change, it realizes that the new strategy may last only as long as the current administration remains in office.[13] The four-year presidential election cycle thus provides military bureaucracies with a systemic incentive to delay any unwanted organizational, programmatic, or other actions required by the execution of the new strategy. Simply put, military bureaucracies in the United States are skilled at waiting out their political masters in order to preserve cherished programs and budgets.[14]

The debate over the relative importance of external and internal determinants of state behavior, the impact of these determinants on organizational behavior, and the subsequent sources of battlefield innovation is germane to this book. In assigning causality to the process of innovation within military organizations, scholars typically look at military doctrine as a vital indicator in judging whether internal or external factors are shaping their battlefield performance. As noted in Chapter 1, military doctrine reflects formalized institutional knowledge often gained from historical experience that sets important parameters for preparing military organizations to fight. Doctrine represents the institutional operationalization (or not) of the wishes of its political and organizational leadership for its executing arms on the battlefield. Doctrine is hence believed by some to be an important indicator of institutional learning and military innovation. One school of thought emphasizes the importance of the security environment and the subsequent calculations that political leaders make to protect the state and further its influence and power over rivals.[15] A second school emphasizes processes and variables that are internal to the state itself, which produce institutions and supporting military doctrine that shape the way military organizations fight.[16] While these contending approaches may point to the impact of different independent variables on the character of military doctrine, both essentially agree that institutional performance and innovation are strongly influenced by factors that start at the top of the organizational hierarchy and work their way down to the executing elements. "Top," in this context, means senior leadership of military organizations, as well as organizations that can lie outside the military chain of command but that exercise influence over institutional behavior.

DOCTRINE AND MILITARY INNOVATION

The hypothesized process of field-generated military innovation in this study suggests that the lack of a specific, approved joint COIN doctrine did not hinder the innovation process. When matched against the experiences of the units covered in this study, the mainstream literature on military innovation demonstrates shortcomings.[17] A finding from this analysis is that the distinctions and treatments in the literature between tactical adaptation, institutional and organizational innovation, and military doctrine need to be recast to acknowledge a more complex series of relationships between the concepts. The literature in security studies is partially responsible for this intellectual rigidity—treating innovation and tactical adaptation as different though related concepts. Innovation is generally regarded as a higher-order concept than adaptation, which is more tactical in nature. Doctrine operates above both these levels, though it is thought to infuse the conduct of military organizations at the operational and tactical levels.[18] Rosen is skeptical that military doctrine provides a good indicator of innovation in military organizations. He makes no mention of doctrine in his definition of military innovation, which he defines thus:

> A change that forces one of the primary combat arms of service to change its concepts of operation and its relation to other combat arms, and to abandon or downgrade traditional missions. Such innovations involve a new way of war, with new ideas of how the components of the organization relate to each other and to the enemy, and new operational procedures conforming to those ideas. They involve changes in critical tasks, the tasks around which war plans revolve.[19]

Rosen argues that innovation happens mostly in peacetime. He emphasizes the role played by intrabureaucratic forces within military organizations that pit professional communities against each other in the battle for limited resources. The internal friction between these communities generates a kind of creative and healthy ideological and intellectual struggle. Organizational leaders emerge from this process that protect their respective communities and provide the intellectual and political space to pursue new ideas on how best to secure military victory. Rosen believes that these senior military leaders play a predominant role in directing the process of peacetime organizational innovation. He places less emphasis on the role of outside civilian intervention.[20]

Uncertainty surrounding the impact of doctrine on military innovation is shared by others. Theo Farrell offers a definition of military innovation that tries to capture not just changes in doctrine but also changes in other aspects of military organizations, such as "changes in the goals, actual strategies, and/or the structure of a military organization."[21] Jeffrey Isaacson, Christopher Layne, and John Arquila also tie military innovation to something other than doctrine, offering that military innovation "is manifested by the development of new war-fighting concepts and/or new means of integrating technology. New means of integrating technology might include revised doctrine, tactics, training or support."[22]

Alan Beyerchen draws upon complexity theory in developing a sequence in which innovation happens as the end result of a process that starts as invention,[23] which is followed by research and then development—and includes complex feedback loops at all stages of the process.[24] Beyerchen argues that military innovation can be divided into three overlapping phases: technical change that can result from new equipment that is used at the tactical level; operational change in which a series of new procedures are developed to field new equipment; and broadly based technological change that provides a new set of parameters, or context, for military operations at the strategic level. Beyerchen suggests that innovation occurs as a cascading series of best practices that can lead to something called "diffusion." He states: "Adaptation is primarily associated with the innovation phase, while the introduction of new military doctrine is in general closely associated with the diffusion phase."[25]

Williamson Murray frankly doubts whether the sources and processes of military innovation can be described with any confidence. Murray argues: "The process of innovation within military institutions and cultures, which involves numerous actors, complex technologies, the uncertainties of conflict and human relations, forms part of this world and is no more open to reductionist solutions than any other aspects of human affairs."[26] Murray believes that military innovations which have the "greatest influence are those that change the context within which war takes place."[27] He believes there are two types of innovation: evolutionary and revolutionary. As suggested by the term, evolutionary innovation happens slowly over time but can cumulatively lead to dramatically different results in battle. Revolutionary change, he argues, happens mostly as a result of top-down leadership. He argues that Britain's creation of an integrated system of air defense that broke with previous doctrine governing the envisioned use of airpower represented an example of revolutionary innovation.[28]

None of these definitions by themselves seems satisfactory, although all in a sense are right. All these definitions of military innovation involve common elements: changed standard operating procedures; different relationships between and among combat arms; the blending of combat and noncombat capabilities to achieve battlefield "effect"; and the eventual development of different missions for military units not previously envisioned in doctrine. These phenomena interact with each other in complex and unpredictable ways to produce innovation.

The literature on organizational behavior offers contributions that can disentangle some of these definitional uncertainties. Returning to first order principles in theories of organizational behavior, March and Simon suggest that organizational innovation starts off with individuals as a problem-solving activity, which, under certain conditions, can then generate new organizational procedures.[29] March and Simon offer the straightforward proposition that "[t]he rate of innovation is likely to increase when changes in the environment make the existing organizational procedures unsatisfactory."[30] The clarity of this statement seems entirely appropriate to describing the process of military innovation and change while in contact with the enemy.

The definition of organizational innovation in war used in this book seeks to balance these competing concerns by emphasizing the overlapping relationships between the concepts and the observable process that organizations move through as tactical adaptations collectively produce new procedures that fundamentally change the conduct of military operations. This book agrees with those arguing that specific military doctrine per se presents a weak independent variable in directly driving the process of military innovation. Doctrine, however, is important to the innovation process. The cases in this study show that doctrinal processes helped shape organizational innovation by providing an underlying framework for units as they developed new organizational capacities to suit the COIN environment. Established doctrine provides parameters for all military units and informs their organizational structure, their table of equipment, their manning competencies, their training cycle, and their operational planning cycles. These doctrinal processes proved important for all the units in this study and channeled the innovation process in the direction sought by the organizational leadership.

INNOVATION IN WAR

Much of the literature on military innovation focuses on actions of military organizations in peacetime. Part of the purpose of this book is to address the paucity of work on military innovation in wartime during the contemporary period,[31] and to provide scholars with new analytical avenues and hypotheses to assess the sources and processes of wartime innovation. The prevailing view is that organizational innovation in war is extremely difficult. The German strategist Carl von Clausewitz believed that the circumstances of conflict made it difficult for militaries to develop a coherent situational awareness on which to base rational decisions, noting: "The difficulty of accurate recognition constitutes one of the most serious sources of friction in war, by making things appear entirely different from what one had expected."[32] Clausewitz believed that the friction of war made simple problems complex, and "the apparently easy so difficult."[33] The lack of reliable and accurate information during war made it difficult to subject wartime decisions to a structured, rational decision-making process. As emphasized by Clausewitz, the wartime environment is thus characterized by a structural uncertainty that has been described by many as the so-called fog of war. Clausewitz famously stated: "War is the realm of uncertainty; three quarters of the factors on which action in war is based are wrapped in a fog of greater or lesser uncertainty."[34]

Rosen usefully addressed the tension between peacetime and wartime innovation and change. He drew a clear distinction between improved mission performance that flowed from organizational learning, based on feedback and use of intelligence, and organizational innovation in response to enemy action on the battlefield. Rosen argued that while many believe that innovation happens more easily in war than in peacetime, genuine battlefield innovation is in fact extremely rare. Rosen agreed that organizational learning is possible in wartime but believes it is usually limited to improvements in the ability of military units to conduct established missions. He argued that innovation in wartime is related to how military organizations measure their effectiveness. He noted that "the definition of the strategic goal, the relationship of military operations to that goal, and indicators of how well operations are proceeding can be thought of as *strategic measures of effectiveness* for the military organization."[35] In other words, wartime innovation won't happen unless and until military organizations perceive themselves as being ineffective, which involves reaching judgments about the degree to which military operations are achieving the desired strategic effect. Rosen argued that innovation in war won't happen unless the institutions are provided with indicators showing that they are failing on the battlefield. "When military innovation is required in wartime, however, *it is because an inappropriate strategic goal is being pursued, or because the relationship between military operations and that goal has been misunderstood* [emphasis in original]."[36] Rosen believed that innovation in wartime is thus symbiotically tied to measures of organizational effectiveness.

The finding from this analysis is that scholars must note more closely the forms and sources of military adaptation and innovation that occur in wartime, compared with those that occur in peacetime.[37] In peacetime, change is more likely to be stimulated by the senior civilian and military leadership through an ostensibly rational process by which authority is delegated down through the chain of command, from the President to his Secretary of Defense, who in turn delegates implementing authority to his military departments.[38] Those departments in turn produce top-level military guidance, which provides an explicitly structured roadmap through which units can pursue their tactics, techniques, and procedures. It is on this basis that doctrine is promulgated, equipment bought, and training structured, so that, in theory, military units arrive in the field ready to pursue their mission in ways that are consistent with the requirements and the wishes of their political masters. This book argues that the wartime environment in Iraq tilted the organizational balance of military institutions toward internal, organically driven change and innovation. The nature of this process necessarily reverses, or at least challenges, the peacetime process. In wartime, established peacetime relationships may change, in practice if not on paper, as authority is decentralized down to the tactical level—where authority to act and make decisions on courses of action happens outside the conference rooms of Washington, DC.

MILITARY INNOVATION AS A TOP DOWN PROCESS

In his landmark work *The Sources of Military Doctrine*, Barry Posen made one of the first systematic attempts to explain the relationships between grand strategy, military doctrine, and the behavior of military organizations in combat.[39] Using battles fought at the outset of World War II as case studies, Posen sought to explain variations in the military doctrine and the resultant ways of fighting between the militaries from France, Great Britain, and Germany. Nesting his explanatory framework in realist and neorealist international relations theory, Posen argued that military innovation stems from intervention by civilian political leadership that forcefully wrenched military institutions into activities that address the new threat. In his case studies, Posen showed that each of these states perceived its strategic circumstance somewhat differently, which, in turn, led to different military doctrines and defense postures. France's military posture, for example, was essentially defensive in nature—a product of the country's strategic circumstance and the desire of its leadership to forestall another German invasion of its territory. On the other hand, Germany's military posture and supporting doctrine emphasized an offensive, aggressive scheme of operations that reflected its leadership's appreciation that the country was bordered by two powerful, hostile states. In the interwar period, Germany built an army and scheme of operations designed to quickly defeat one of those adversaries before turning to the other. Posen argued that the process of innovation in these states was assisted, or facilitated, by the emergence of dynamic "maverick" senior military officers. These officers provided civilians with the technical knowledge and substantive expertise needed to help flesh out and implement the ideas of the civilian leadership. Posen found little evidence in his case studies of internally generated doctrinal and organizational innovation within the military institutions themselves. This led him to conclude that:

> military organizations will seldom innovate autonomously, particularly in matters of doctrine. This should be true because organizations abhor uncertainty, and changes in traditional patterns always involve uncertainty. It should also be true because military organizations are very hierarchical, restricting the flow of ideas from the lower levels to the higher levels. Additionally, those at the top of the hierarchy, who have achieved their rank and position by mastering the old doctrine, have no interest in encouraging their own obsolescence by bringing in a new doctrine. Thus innovation should occur mainly when the organization registers a large failure, or when civilians with legitimate authority intervene to promote innovation.[40]

His findings fit within balance-of-power realist and neorealist international relations theory, which argues that states exist within an anarchical, self-help system in which they all seek to maximize their influence and power over rivals.[41] Consistent with realist theory, Posen argued that civilian leaders are constantly evaluating threats to state power—as opposed to entrenched military leaders, who are generally risk-averse and oriented toward maintenance of the institutional status quo, even at the risk of failing to adapt to external change. When the civilian leadership perceived that the strategic environment had produced new threats that changed the state's strategic circumstance, those leaders directed change in the state's military institutions—for the most part successfully in the end. One of Posen's strongest case studies illustrating this point was his analysis of the role played by senior civilians in forcing the Royal Air Force (RAF) to place more emphasis on fighter defenses in England during the interwar period. Posen's military maverick, Air Marshall Sir Hugh Dowding, emerged to work with the civilian leadership in spearheading efforts within the RAF to build the capacities of Fighter Command during the 1930s. With the support of the civilian leadership, Dowding overcame internal opposition within the RAF that wanted instead to focus upon strategic bombing. Dowding's efforts proved crucial to building an integrated system of air defense that positioned the RAF to defeat the Luftwaffe in the Battle of Britain in the summer and fall of 1940—a turning point in the war.[42]

Deborah Avant has offered a variation on Posen's argument for top-down battlefield innovation, placing more emphasis on intergovernmental organizational relationships as sources of both resistance and support for military innovation. While agreeing with Posen that political leaders play important roles defining threats to the state, she emphasizes the role that factors internal to state institutions play in shaping military doctrine and battlefield performance.[43] Avant employs institutional theory to explain how militaries are likely to respond to different operational environments. Institutional theory posits that governments act in ways that reflect the priorities of their system of internal organizational incentives.[44] Institutions seek mainly to preserve their influence and prestige, according to the theory. Avant's approach draws upon the principal-agent literature to build her argument,[45] which focuses on the delegation of authority between organizations to take advantage of the task specialization and knowledge asymmetry provided by specific communities in a contractual relationship.[46] Avant suggests that, just as a patient contracts with a doctor, and a client with a lawyer, based on expectations of knowledge and expertise, military organizations similarly act as agents for their political masters (principals). These principals in turn establish a reward system to induce desired behavioral norms and competencies and, if necessary, behavioral changes in their military agents.

Under this theory, military institutions respond to their principals' needs by taking steps to ensure that they can meet the needs specified by the principal. They do this by establishing an internal system of incentives in the form of promotion policies that reward performance in the competencies desired by the principal. This ensures that the organization as a whole continues to receive the patronage and rewards of the political leadership, which, in the U.S. case, are provided in the form of money (and lots of it). If the reward system becomes mismatched with demands of the operational environment, organizational performance will inevitably suffer. Avant argues that the U.S. Army failed in Vietnam because its internal reward system remained focused on fighting the great conventional battle in Europe against the Soviet Union. Counterinsurgency competencies needed to succeed in Vietnam were not deemed important to institutional survival and hence were not developed.[47] As noted by Avant, promotions within the Army during the period came not through demonstrating skills fighting the Viet Cong. Instead, the institutional incentive system remained structured to reward competence in what was deemed the more important mission of preventing the Soviet Army from overrunning Europe. According to her argument, the Army could have succeeded in Vietnam if its internal incentive system had been reoriented to reward competency in counterinsurgency. She concludes that the institutional leadership in the Army decided against this course of action because of its institutional preferences for fighting conventional war—competencies for which it was assured of receiving the continued patronage of an important principal (the U.S. Congress).

Despite their differences, however, both Avant and Posen implicitly assume that the outputs of military organizational structures reflect the choices of leaders exercising authority in a process that is essentially top down and that functions rationally in accordance with the nature of the hierarchy. They subscribe to Kurt Lang's straightforward proposition that "[t]he hierarchical structure exemplified by the military chain of command postulates a downward flow of directive."[48] For example, Posen suggests that military institutions will inevitably reflect the wishes of their political masters. While he acknowledges that military institutions are by nature conservative and resist change, he proposes that forceful civilian leadership will ultimately reorient military doctrine and organizational capabilities in the ways sought by the civilian leadership. Avant's main difference with Posen is that she recasts the nature of the relationship between the military and the civilian leadership. Avant also adds Congress to the mix, because of the instrumental role it plays in maintaining the military's external reward system. With ultimate control over money, Congress exerts a powerful additional influence on the principal-agent delegation by effectively introducing an additional layer of principal influence over the agent's actions. Avant agrees with Posen that military institutions are change-averse but, using principal-agent theory, suggests that military institutions invariably will act to protect their institutional survival by keeping their external benefactors happy. When the benefactors decide to alter or change the nature of the principal-agent relationships, she argues that this incentive system guarantees that the institutions will change to ensure continued access to money and patronage. Avant operationalizes the institutional behavior by looking at internal promotion policies, which are meant to build core competencies to ensure that the institution's role in the contractual arrangement can be fulfilled.

Stephen Peter Rosen has taken a different approach in explaining the behavior of military organizations. He emphasizes the peacetime role of intrabureaucratic dynamics within military institutions in shaping the development of new organizational capabilities for the battlefield. He agrees with Avant that the internal system for managing promotions within the military service can be an important determining factor in shaping the direction of military change. But while Posen and Avant argue that civilian intervention is critical in the process of military innovation, Rosen believes that military institutions will innovate on their own and need not depend on outside intervention to stimulate the process.[49] As previously addressed in Chapter 1, Rosen points to the emergence of internal leaders within military institutions that attract resources and talent in the development of new ways of fighting. Rosen argues that the internal winners of the intraorganizational process, in turn, direct the process of organizational innovation.

Each of these arguments emphasizes different factors as being critical to the process of military innovation. Importantly, however, all three assume that authority flows down the governmental hierarchy in a reasonably predictable process and that organizational output will be characterized by a degree of consistency with the wishes of senior authority—whether that authority stems from within the organization or some other related institution.

IRAQ AND TOP-DOWN EXPLANATIONS OF MILITARY INNOVATION

What would these arguments predict about the American military's performance in Iraq after Saddam Hussein was toppled and the insurgency gathered momentum in 2004 and 2005? In some respects, the Iraq war appears tailor-made to test Posen's argument regarding the role that civilian leadership's perceptions of the strategic environment play in shaping the doctrine and force structure of its military organizations. President Bush and his senior civilian leadership clearly judged that the 9/11 attacks represented a broad change in the security environment that constituted a fundamental and dramatically new threat to the state. Reflecting this belief, the Bush administration released a bevy of strategy documents describing the new threats and called upon military institutions to realign their capabilities to address them. As part of its case, the Bush administration continually asserted after 9/11 that the United States was in fact engaged in a war "that is irregular in nature"—the so-called long war.[50] Parroting the verbiage of the 2001 *Quadrennial Defense Review (QDR)*, the 2006 *QDR* emphasized that the adversaries in the conflict "are not traditional conventional military forces, but rather dispersed, global terrorist networks that exploit Islam to advance radical political aims."[51] These adversaries also allegedly sought unconventional weapons to mount mass casualty attacks. Adapting the entire Defense Department organizational structure to conduct irregular warfare constitutes one of the main "fundamental challenges" facing the entire defense and interagency establishment, according to the QDR.[52]

Posen's argument initially appears to fit closely the situation in the United States between the 9/11 attacks and the invasion of Iraq. Civilians believed that threats to the state had changed dramatically, which necessitated that military institutions change their doctrine and way of fighting.[53] Virtually all the Bush administration strategy documents called for the nation's military to prepare for terrorism, irregular warfare, and counterinsurgency—exactly the kind of environment that would emerge in Iraq after Saddam's overthrow.[54] Other circumstances of this period also seem to strongly support Posen's argument. During preparations for the Iraq invasion it seemed clear that strong, aggressive civilian leadership was exercising exactly the kind of strong control over military institutions suggested by Posen's argument. The civilian leadership clearly forced the military into a war for which it lacked enthusiasm.[55] But not only did the civilian leadership force a war on a reluctant military, it also forced the military to substantially alter its invasion plan by reducing the number and types of troops for the operation. As has been chronicled elsewhere, Defense Secretary Donald Rumsfeld sought to unveil a new American way of war in the invasion that emphasized speed, maneuver, and long-range precision-guided munitions—all capabilities applied under a systems-based scheme of warfare known as "effects-based operations." After initially opposing Rumsfeld's ideas, the military eventually produced an invasion plan that met Rumsfeld's demands. The invasion force's quick advance into Baghdad seemed to confirm Rumsfeld's vision of a new American way of war by a "transformed" U.S. military. As chronicled in this book, however, the critical part of the "transformation" process came not during the invasion but afterward, in the chaos that ensued after Saddam's armies had been defeated.

Posen's argument would suggest that the military should have produced a new doctrine or directives to align its capabilities with the threat environment as defined by the civilian leadership. Interestingly, that actually happened in 2004 and 2005 when the Defense Department produced a *DoD Directive 3000.05, Military Support for Stability, Security, Transition, and Reconstruction (SSTR) Operations* that assigned specific responsibilities to the military departments on the battlefield after the conclusion of conventional military operations.[56] Moreover, and most important, new doctrine did eventually emerge through the efforts of General Petraeus and his team of experts at Fort Leavenworth—the epitome of the top-down processes that Posen believed to be central to military innovation. Prior to the appearance of the new doctrine, however, these top-down processes had little direct impact in the field. This is perhaps unsurprising, since the promulgation of the directives happened as forces were engaged with the enemy. Predictably, none of the military officers interviewed for the case studies linked their actions on the battlefield to the directive. The irony of *DoD Directive 3000.05* is that despite the fact that the State Department received ultimate responsibility for postconflict reconstruction activities, in Iraq the postconflict reconstruction mission fell to battalion and brigade military commanders, who actually executed the mission reasonably well, as chronicled in this book's case studies. In Iraq, at least, the real intent of the directive—to transfer postconflict responsibilities to the State Department—went unrealized at least in the period studied in this work.

It is difficult to apply Rosen's framework to the Iraq situation because the United States has ostensibly been "at war" continuously since the 9/11 attacks and the invasion of Afghanistan a month later. To the extent that claims about a perpetual "war on terror" are taken seriously, Rosen's argument about the peacetime sources of military change don't technically apply to the period covered in this book. While Rosen is reluctant to point to doctrine as a source of innovation, he generally believes that militaries will employ their combat arms on the battlefield in ways that reflect past practice—unless there has been peacetime innovation. Rosen believes that innovation in war won't happen until the institutions charged with prosecuting the war are presented with evidence that their approach is not achieving the desired strategic objective. He argues that this "evidence" takes the form of indicators of military effectiveness that demonstrate battlefield failure. Innovation will happen in war when new strategic measures of effectiveness are developed to better match military operations and strategic objectives, according to Rosen. Applying this argument to the U.S. military experience in Iraq is problematic. As previously noted, the United States had no operative doctrine around which to structure counterinsurgency operations in Iraq, and thus had no established metrics through which to judge the strategic effectiveness of military operations. In fact, there was widespread confusion about the strategic objectives associated with the Iraq invasion and the role that military forces were supposed to play once Saddam had been removed.[57]

Confusion on this critical point emerged in the contentious hearings during the September 2007 congressional testimony of General David Petraeus, commander of the Multi-National Forces-Iraq, and Ambassador Ryan Crocker, U.S. ambassador to Iraq.[58] The Petraeus testimony drew upon a series of quantitative metrics meant to represent organizational "effects" that were supposed to demonstrate the positive impact that had resulted from increased troop levels in Iraq. His testimony centered on the presentation of data that measured weekly attack trends, trends in ethnic and sectarian violence, arms caches found, employment of improvised explosive devices (IEDs) against U.S. forces, and attacks against U.S. forces. The data all demonstrated decreasing trend lines in each category and suggested a causal link between organizational outputs and the operational environment in Iraq. Critics of the testimony suggested that the data, while interesting, had nothing to do with real "strategic effect." They argued that the only meaningful strategic measure of effectiveness centered upon the process of political reconciliation in Baghdad, by which a unified and inclusive national government capable of administering the country must be created. Unsurprisingly, neither Crocker nor Petraeus could offer any metrics to measure this effect and satisfy their critics. The logic of Rosen's argument suggests that, absent an agreed set of new metrics of effectiveness, the military would adapt tactically to its environment but would produce no lasting institutional innovation, and no fundamental departures from the ways in which combat arms were habitually applied on the battlefield. I argue that this prediction was not borne out in the units analyzed in this study.

Avant's argument matches up poorly against the U.S. battlefield performance in the Iraq war. Avant's principal-agent argument predicts that battlefield performance depends on the internal incentive structure within the military—a structure that reflects the institution's contractual obligation to its civilian masters (principals). Her approach would argue that direction from the civilian authorities to prepare for irregular warfare would be insufficient to change battlefield performance unless the internal incentive structure was also aligned to reward competence in irregular warfare. It is true that neither the Army nor Marine Corps had altered or changed its internal system of promotions to reward competency in counterinsurgency, despite requests from the political leadership to develop these competencies after 2001. In fact, one could argue that the internal rewards system changed in ways to reward competence in conventional military operations that emphasized transformation-type capabilities—the opposite of irregular warfare competency. If anything, the internal reward system was altered prior to the war to reward performance in the kinds of competencies that Rumsfeld sought in the military. Rumsfeld clearly exerted unprecedented influence over senior military department promotions in an attempt to instill a new brand of leadership that embraced his concepts of modern war.[59] Avant's argument would correctly predict the performance of the U.S. military force in the invasion, but it breaks down once the Army and Marine Corps start to confront the insurgency. Absent a changed internal incentive structure, engaged institutions should resist widespread adoption of irregular warfare competencies developed through experience in Iraq; but that is not what the record shows. I have found that in Iraq, the Army and Marine Corps eventually *did* develop exactly the kinds of core competencies they needed through battlefield experience over time, and applied these competencies in ways that bore little or no relationship to the system of internal rewards in each of the institutions. In Iraq, the institutions developed exactly the opposite kinds of competencies initially called for by their civilian master. In other words, the development of these competencies bore no direct relationships to the personnel incentive structures. In this respect particularly it is worth repeating: Iraq was and is not a replay of Vietnam.

ALTERNATIVE EXPLANATIONS FOR WARTIME INNOVATION

The case studies presented in the following chapters will suggest that arguments focusing on top-down processes of military innovation present an incomplete picture of the American battlefield performance in Iraq. If these explanations do not suffice, then how is the performance of the U.S. military to be explained? What are some alternative explanations that offer a more convincing framework than the top-down arguments? This book argues that a complex, dialectic process of organically executed innovation unfolded over an extended period in a process led from the field by units engaged with the enemy, and this unit-level innovation preceded the formation of the U.S. military's new COIN doctrine by many months. That the prevailing top-down theories of military innovation attach little emphasis to organically generated innovation is somewhat surprising. Explaining military performance in war by pointing to the dynamic flexibility of military organizations that draw upon bottom-up processes certainly is not unknown. Indeed, there is a literature composed mostly of empirical studies chronicling many well-known cases of wartime innovation in military organizations.[60] These works suggest important insights that can help develop a more comprehensive understanding of the complex and dynamic processes that ultimately enable military organizations to innovate in war, often in the absence of, or prior to, the emergence of new doctrines at the top levels of the command or politico-military decision-making structures.

Bruce Gudmundsson's account of the gradual evolution of German infantry tactics in World War I offers a compelling portrait of a military organization constantly searching for tactical innovation to break the military stalemate on the Western Front.[61] By the end of the war, the German infantryman bore little resemblance to his 1914 counterpart. By 1918, German infantry formations operated as combined arms units, were armed with a more diverse array of equipment, were trained in many specialized tasks, and were capable of complex fire and maneuver coordination. Decisions on battlefield tactics were made at comparatively low levels of command—a precursor to modern day decentralized, distributed operations. Gudmundsson points to the strong role played by education in the German military system that established an officer- and noncommissioned officer corps well schooled in the art of military tactics, combined with the confidence to execute them on the battlefield. A similar process unfolded in the British Army, in which disastrous tactics used during the first two years of the war were discarded and replaced with similar storm trooper–type tactics being developed by its German adversary. Contrary to popular perception, the British fielded a tactically proficient, skilled army by the end of the war capable of complex fire and maneuver tactics.[62]

The evolution of German infantry tactics during the war laid the groundwork for the development of the blitzkrieg in the interwar period, in which mechanization allowed it to overcome the physical limitations of its soldiers in fighting the war of deep maneuver and encirclement with which it perpetually (and unsuccessfully) sought to break the Western Front stalemate in World War I.[63] While doctrinally bounded by the concept of the blitzkrieg in World War II, the German traditions of decentralized operations backed by a strong junior officer and NCO corps continued in World War II.[64] In the latter stages of the war, German infantry tactics continued to evolve as its army disintegrated, creating ad hoc battle groups known as *Kampsgruppen* that proved particularly adept at delaying Allied armor advances with ambushes using the handheld *Panzerfaust*.[65]

The integration of Allied close air support with ground operations in Europe during World War II provides another compelling example of internally generated wartime innovation. General Pete Quesada, who headed the Army Air Force's IX Fighter Command, pioneered the development of complex procedures and solved numerous technical problems that confronted the Army Air Corps as it sought to provide tactical battlefield support to U.S. and Allied military units during the invasion of Europe and advance into Germany. Quesada achieved success in spite of a disinterested senior Air Force leadership that overwhelmingly supported the use of air power for long-range strategic bombardment. Quesada is credited with developing the use of microwave early warning (MEW) radar to direct pilots in real time to their targets. He also devised a system that married the MEW with a Signal Corps radio (the SCR-584) that effectively allowed ground-based personnel to act as ordnance targeteers for single-seat fighter bombers. The close "column-cover" operations between armored and air units used in the Allied breakout from the Bocage country in operations around St. Lo is widely considered one of Quesada's greatest innovations in the air-ground campaign. The IX Fighter Command built by Quesada to coordinate air operations in Europe proved in many ways to be a precursor to today's combined air operations centers utilized by today's Air Force. Quesada successfully fought against institutional opposition within the Army Air Corps to using aviation in direct support of ground operations as well as skeptical ground commanders in establishing tactical air power as a vital component in Allied combined operations in the European theater.[66]

A process of organically generated tactical adaptation and innovation is also described by Keith Bickel in the development of the Marine Corps's *Small Wars Manual*.[67] Bickel argued that the Marine Corps's experiences in the "small wars" of Haiti, Dominican Republic, and Nicaragua finally made its way into formalized doctrine through the efforts of an informal network of officers bent on sharing their experiences through professional journal articles, field orders, and interactions in the Marine Corps school system. Bickel characterized this process as "informal" doctrine, which preceded the promulgation of more formal institutional doctrine and which emerged over the opposition of senior leadership. The resulting *Small Wars Manual* enshrined the lessons learned in these early-twentieth-century engagements for future generations of Marine Corps officers. The relevance of Bickel's study to this analysis is the particular emphasis placed on the role of individuals in promoting institutional change. While Bickel focuses exclusively on doctrine as the important organizational output in his process of bottom-up change, his emphasis on the process of doctrinal formulation using "informal" channels is especially relevant to this study. As the cases examined in subsequent chapters demonstrate, it is clear that informal channels were vitally important to military units seeking solutions to the tactical problems posed by the insurgency. The Army Knowledge Online website, the companycommander.com site,[68] the use of blogs, simple e-mail, and a host of other digital-age means provided commanders with ample means through which to pass along lessons learned and shared experiences for incoming units. In Iraq, it is clear that these processes helped shape the training and battlefield tactics for incoming units that worked much more quickly than the process to promulgate new, formal doctrine.

Richard Duncan Downie and John Nagl argue that military innovation can function as a bottom-up process, provided that the military institutions are learning organizations.[69] Downie defines institutional learning as: "A process by which an organization (such as the U.S. Army) uses new knowledge or understanding gained from experience or study to adjust institutional norms, doctrine, and procedures in ways designed to minimize previous gaps in performance and maximize future successes."[70] Like many scholars, Downie believes that doctrine is an important indicator of military innovation which, he argues, accurately reflects institutional memory that can be altered or changed only in certain circumstances. Downie argues that no single factor alone can explain military innovation and emphasizes that innovation occurs through the systemic interaction of external factors, institutional influences, and the process of organizational learning.

Using case studies that examine the performance of the U.S. Army in Vietnam, the counterinsurgency program in El Salvador in the 1980s, and the drug war in the Andean Ridge, Downie finds that military innovation occurred only in those situations when external pressures, institutional factors, and the development of institutional learning were properly aligned to produce innovation as evidenced by new military doctrine. Drawing upon Downie's framework for institutional learning, Nagl examines the performance of the U.S. Army in Vietnam and the British Army in Malaysia. Nagl finds that the British Army succeeded in Malaysia because it was a learning organization and that the U.S. Army failed in Vietnam because it was not. The insights from Downie and Nagl are useful for our analysis here. The case studies in this book show that collections of rigidly structured, hierarchical organizations (called "task forces" in military parlance) displayed remarkable abilities to quickly change and adapt in wartime circumstances—displaying all the characteristics of learning organizations identified by Downie and Nagl as critical to wartime innovation.

In his book *Closing with the Enemy*,[71] Michael Doubler usefully packages many of these preceding concepts and applies them in his cogent analysis of the performance of the U.S. Army in the European theater following the Normandy invasion in June 1944. Doubler argues that the U.S. Army significantly improved its tactical abilities during the last nine months of the war, effectively mastering the combined arms doctrine that had been established at the outset of the conflict. Doubler emphasizes the immense impact played by the cumulative experience of fighting the Wehrmacht in North Africa and Italy in the preceding two years of the war—experiences that helped build the growing tactical competence of units as the war progressed. In one particularly illuminating case study, Doubler highlights two critical variables that stimulated tactical flexibility and adaptation leading to the breakout from the Bocage country in Normandy: (1) The Army institutionally encouraged the "free flow of ideas" and entrepreneurial spirit that flowed from the lowest levels to the most senior; and (2) the Army instituted no centralized control over the search for battlefield solutions and instead encouraged a decentralized, collective approach to solving tactical problems.[72] As noted by Doubler: "Senior leaders expected their subordinates to develop and execute solutions for overcoming the German defense instead of waiting for the staffs of higher headquarters to devise the very best answer to a tactical problem."[73] As part of this general approach, the Army gave battlefield commanders significant latitude in developing their own ideas on how to approach their particular tactical problems. Just as important, Army leadership proved receptive to innovative ideas that bubbled up from the tactical level. This receptivity led to modifications in the Sherman tank that gave it the ability to cut through the tough hedgerows of the Bocage.

Doubler's analysis supports the hypothesis presented in this work proposing a process of bottom-up military innovation insofar as he addresses the organic sources of tactical flexibility and innovation. As argued by Doubler, the breakout from the Bocage in Normandy resulted from a series of small iterative changes that stemmed from the adaptation of existing equipment to enable tanks to break through the hedgerows. This adaptation was supported by a more imaginative tactical placement of weapons and personnel to disrupt the German defenses once the hedge had been breached.[74] Doubler argues that particular tactical problems were solved throughout the campaign as part of a process through which the Army progressively improved its ability to fight in the ways envisioned by doctrine.

For purposes of this analysis, the preceding works on bottom-up military innovation develop a series of explanations that focus on the process of battlefield adaptation that I argue rises to the level of organizational innovation. The works highlighted in this section are very germane to the experiences of the United States in Iraq. This book hypothesizes that organically driven tactical change can accumulate over time and build a momentum all its own that can meet the standard identified by Rosen and others as innovation and which, in turn, can stimulate the development of doctrine.

The collective observations in the preceding works are consistent with Lynn Eden's research on the role played by "organizational frames" in structuring how organizations address problems and cycle through solutions.[75] While Doubler, Downie, and Nagl applied their frameworks to particular examples of military organizations in wartime, their work parallels certain aspects of Eden's exhaustive analysis of the Air Force's approach to solving the methodological problem posed by calculating blast damage from nuclear weapons. Eden argues that "during periods of organizational redefinition or upheaval, actors articulate organizational goals and draw upon existing understandings, or knowledge of the social and physical environments in which they must operate. This creates frameworks for action that structure how actors in organizations identify problems and find solutions."[76] The Air Force developed knowledge-laden frames built iteratively through the generation of new knowledge. This new knowledge then, in turn, infused new organizational routines. These new organizational routines mirrored, to some extent, the complexity of the problem confronted by the Air Force in developing methodologies for predicting the destructive power of nuclear weapons. Eden's argument shows the important role played by organizational frames that developed over time, which guided the institution through this complicated methodological problem. As will be demonstrated in the case studies in the following chapters, it is clear that the military organizations fighting the insurgents in Iraq built complex, knowledge-laden organizational frames to help guide their battlefield activities. The building of these frames through the process of organizational learning provided a critical building block for the process of wartime innovation in Iraq.

Here, it seems appropriate to note Chris Demchak's work on the impact of complex technologies on military organizations, which, along with the preceding works, makes an important contribution to this book's hypotheses on the nature and processes of organically driven wartime adaptation and innovation.[77] Demchak argues that as modern militaries like the U.S. Army adopt increasingly complex equipment, their organizational structures face a difficult, though not impossible, task of grasping the system's complexity. As Demchak argues:

> Complex systems have large knowledge requirements both initially and over time. When a system first begins to operate, it faces a universe of possible outcomes; many of these outcomes will predictably occur, and many will prove to be irrelevant. The outcomes constitute the "knowns" about the system—over time the largest category of outcomes. The set of "knowns" grows as the system runs, creating a learning curve that varies from system to system. For complex systems, it generally takes more time to accumulate enough knowledge to move significantly upwards on the learning curve.[78]

In other words, the problems posed by a system of technical complexity begets a kind of mirroring organizational complexity as the organization adjusts its standard operating procedures (SOPs) to the new system. This organizational complexity takes shape iteratively as SOPs become steadily more infused by knowledge generated through working with the new system. Demchak shows how Army maintenance units responded to the introduction of the M1 main battle tank by matching its system complexity with a similarly complex organizational structure.[79] Demchak effectively hypothesizes a kind of trinity that is again useful for this analysis: complex problems require complex organizational structures to develop complex solutions, all of which take shape iteratively as knowledge and understanding are accumulated over time.

Demchak's analysis demonstrates that Army units in the field using the M1 tank found themselves employing an extremely complex system that lacked a well-developed training and logistical infrastructure. Her research showed that military units infused with the "can-do" attitude adapted in the field to the problems and opportunities presented by the M1, in a process of organically driven change that depended on no textbooks or previously generated SOPs. As argued by Demchak, "Rarely discussed and even more rarely seen in print is the fact that local adaptations can change the true capabilities of the force. A multitude of minor variations appear in the tactical forces as each individual unit and section makes arrangements to accomplish its own missions. There merges an interconnected web of relationships and dependencies that work as long as the coordination and resource interactions are not significantly disturbed."[80] Demchak believes that this kind of organizational complexity is also extremely fragile, and she doubts its ability to function under the stresses of combat.[81] The analysis presented here suggests that Demchak is right to focus on the development of organizational complexity in response to the adoption of technically complex weapons platforms, but her predictions about the breakdown of these complex organizations in wartime is not borne out in Iraq. In Iraq, the structures of U.S. military organizations in many respects came not just to reflect the complexity of their own sophisticated technology, but also mirrored the complexities of the operational environment.

These preceding works, from admittedly disparate disciplines and with different analytical foci, nevertheless help us to understand the dynamics of organically executed organizational change in military institutions that will be described in the following case studies. Each, however, points to organizational processes through which iterative change and adaptation from low levels of the organization can dramatically impact organizational output. Bickel points to the important role played by informal networks as a tool promoting institutional learning. Downie and Nagl focus on organizational learning as a critical variable driving innovation. Doubler emphasizes the role that command atmosphere can play in creating a dynamic organizational process that frees the movement of information and ideas up and down the hierarchy. Eden points to the role that incremental increases in knowledge can have in forming "organizational frames" that help guide organizational problem-solving activities. Demchak suggests that organizations have a way of coping with complexity in systems that when combined with a military mindset can stimulate creative and adaptive solutions to problems in the field.

THE BEHAVIORALISTS AND ORGANIC INNOVATION

Underpinning much of the literature on organizational behavior is the idea that all large organizations, be they public or private, engage in rational and hence predictable actions. It is generally expected that organizational output flows predictably from a rationally conceived organizational structure. Organizational output, or action, is only the end product of a series of rational processes linked together in a causal, hierarchical chain. Dwight Waldo has defined rational action "as action correctly calculated to realize given desired goals with minimum loss to the realization of other desired goals."[82]

Max Weber offered the enduring "ideal" model describing the structure of modern bureaucracy that is used by organizational theorists as the standard by which variation in organizational behavior is measured. In what could be characterized as the "paradigm of the perfect," Weber's writings describe bureaucracy as the essence of modern industrial life, delivering repeatable, reliable, and efficiently produced output in a structured fashion. Weber held that bureaucracy "is superior to any other form in precision, in stability, in the stringency of its discipline, and in its reliability."[83] He believed bureaucracy to be "indispensable" to modern life and that "[t]he choice is only that between bureaucracy and dilettantism in the field of administration."[84] Bureaucracy had a number of enduring and attractive characteristics: (1) hierarchy and centralized authority in which "each lower office is under the control and supervision of a higher office";[85] (2) interaction between organizational components based on rules or regulations that create routinized interactions between and among organizational components; (3) rationalization of organizational function that allowed the specialization and division of labor—specialization based on knowledge, which in turn produced a personnel system based on merit and competence;[86] and (4) measurement of production and output through extensive records.[87]

Weber's theory is important for the purposes of this analysis because it predicts the genesis of what we would today call complex organizations. Weber foresaw that modern bureaucracies would become iteratively more specialized in their functions. He also foresaw the negative consequences within organizations that occur as functions became successively compartmentalized and decentralized. Such organizational structures would be difficult to alter and change. As is generally accepted, one objective of bureaucracy is in fact to make change difficult.[88] However, while bureaucracy largely succeeds as argued by Weber in structuring large and complex organizations to deliver predictable output, the functioning of these organizations invariably produces variation. It is the sources of variation that I believe are germane to my argument about the sources of internally executed adaptation and innovation.

In a sense, Weber did a disservice in leading the field of organizational behavior down a path to which it clings to this day—a path that seeks to explain the dysfunctional nature of bureaucracy and the reasons behind the variability in organizational output. Writing in the 1940s, Robert Merton delivered a not uncommon critique of bureaucracy, pointing out that the very strengths of the organizational structure (rationalization, specialization, span of control, and efficiency) gave rise to a host of other maladies.[89] Merton identified several problems: (1) organizations can be plagued by "trained incapacity" in which actions based upon training and skills that have been successfully applied in the past may result in inappropriate responses *under changed conditions*;[90] (2) the emphasis on predictability and efficiency could reduce organizational flexibility; and (3) devotion to rule-governed processes could lead to something called "goal displacement," by which "adherence to the rules, originally conceived as a means, becomes transformed into an end in itself."[91] The focus on the maladies of bureaucracy, while instructive, obscures the creative and dynamic processes that can be produced in bureaucracies under certain conditions.

Chester Barnard has described an enduring and competing vision to Weber in his work *The Functions of the Executive*.[92] Barnard believed that all organizations consisted of a cooperative social system that had important physical, psychological, and social limitations that essentially forced people into cooperation. He argued that organizations were by their very nature cooperative systems, and in fact they could not fail to be so.[93] He differed from Weber, who argued that relationships within organizations could be bounded by authority and the rules governing the interaction within an organization's specialized functional areas. Barnard suggested that, as social systems, all organizations were to some extent held hostage to intraorganizational social interaction. These interactions represented a powerful source of organizational productivity. Instead of seeking to limit the role of intraorganizational social systems like Weber, Barnard believed that these informal systems could be harnessed by managers and leaders in building productive and efficient organizations. Barnard emphasized the key role played by leadership that could marshal the human potential of informal social networks outside the formal organizational structure. Barnard's emphasis on the social component of organizations was backed by the Hawthorne experiments, which attempted to identify sources of organizational productivity.

Researchers at the Hawthorne plant of the Western Electric Company in 1927 isolated two groups of workers doing the same jobs and kept records on the productivity of the groups.[94] The experiments started out with the intention of measuring the impact of interior lighting on worker efficiency and productivity. One group had better lighting than the other group, and saw the intensity of the interior lighting increase over time. To the astonishment of the researchers, the productivity of both groups went up. While an academic debate over the rigor of the tests has raged over the years, the experiments found that separation of both groups from the larger workforce created strong social bonds within the groups that helped increase cooperation and productivity. The findings challenged the view, derived from Weberian ideas about scientific management, that workers could effectively be regarded as economic units of production that would operate in predictable ways in response to payment. The Hawthorne experiments demonstrated the powerful influence that informal social networks and relationships could exert upon organizational productivity. In interviews after the experiments, the workers reported that becoming separate from the broader organization made them feel special. The experiments revealed the powerful impact of human relations on the rational operation of the "system," suggesting that the discipline of behavioral sciences could be usefully applied to explain the sources of variation in the operation of large organizations. The experiments proved to be a precursor to further research on the impact of human motivation on the function of organizations. Maslow's theory of human motivation is perhaps the best known of these.[95]

Focusing on the human dimension as emphasized in Barnard's research remains relevant to this day and can be applied to the process of bottom-up military adaptation and innovation that is the chief concern of this study. As will be highlighted in the case studies, informal social networks operating outside the formal hierarchy proved to be extremely important sources of innovation and organizational productivity.

The so-called Behavioralist school of organizational behavior has several other useful insights into the sources of organic change. Herbert Simon accepted Barnard's essential point that organizations are socially constructed collections of individuals. Simon, however, sought to delve deeper into understanding human motivation and decision-making. Simon fervently believed that understanding human behavior was the first step in building a more coherent framework for organizational behavior.[96] In a series of works, Simon advanced a theory of "bounded rationality" that remains as powerful today as when he offered it up nearly sixty years ago. Simon argued that the process of human decision-making in organizations was bounded by a "triangle" of limits: (1) unconscious tendencies that affected the ability to perform the organizational task; (2) the role played by values in a decision-making process that might be inconsistent with the organization's objectives; and (3) the fact that individuals made decisions with limited knowledge of things that could be relevant to their tasks.[97]

Simon and March used the concept of bounded rationality as a baseline for a decision-making model which proposed that humans would invariably be drawn to satisfactory, rather than strictly optimal, alternatives as they solved problems. Humans would not, they argued, engage in an exhaustive analysis of alternatives in a search for perfect solutions. They described this phenomenon as "satisficing." The authors offered the following proposition: "Most human decision-making, whether individual or organizational, is concerned with discovery and selection of alternatives; only in exceptional cases is it concerned with the discovery and selection of optimal alternatives."[98] To illustrate the difference between optimizing and satisficing, they noted: "An example is the difference between searching a haystack to find the sharpest needle and searching the haystack to find a needle sharp enough to sew with."[99] As in the metaphor offered by March and Simon, the standards by which satisfactory outcomes are reached are also a function of the definition of the situation. The standards can go up or down, depending on the positive or negative experiences flowing from the chosen course of action.[100]

The journey toward constructing a series of hypotheses on the process of organic change and innovation has started with the actions of organizations in battle and moved steadily downward to the microlevel that looks at the decision-making process of individuals. There is one last stop before constructing a series of hypotheses on the nature of organic innovation and change.

John Steinbruner pushes the envelope of Simon's and March's thinking on the nature of human decision-making and the boundaries of human rationality that propel decision-making away from optimization. In his book *The Cybernetic Theory of Decision*,[101] he proposed an alternative to the "analytical paradigm" that, he argues, incorporates a rational, value-maximizing approach to decision-making. Steinbruner argued that individual decision-making is not necessarily driven by the logic of preference ordering and a vision of clear outcomes. Instead he argued: "The cybernetic paradigm suggests rather than the central focus of the decision process is the business of eliminating the variety inherent in any significant decision problem."[102] He advanced the proposition that decisions are aided by "servomechanisms," which act as regulators to keep the environment in balance for the individual, much as a thermostat keeps room temperature within a certain range. Such servomechanisms produce "strikingly adaptive outcomes in very complicated environments,"[103] of precisely the kind that armed forces confront on the battlefield. Steinbruner summarized the workings of the cybernetic decision-making process as follows:

> Roughly speaking, the mechanism of decision advanced by the cybernetic paradigm is one which works on the principle of the recipe. The decision maker has a repertory of operations which he performs in sequence while monitoring a few feedback variables. He produces an outcome as a consequence of completing the sequence, but the outcome need not be conceptualized in advance. The cook, in this model, does not construct the relative preference for sweetness or tartness for an average range of customers in baking his pies. Rather he follows established recipes and watches attendance at the restaurant and the rate at which his pies disappear.[104]

Steinbruner's cybernetic paradigm argues that the desire to control uncertainty trumps the rational pursuit of optimal objectives. He argues that individual decision-making confronts complex problems by segmenting complexity into constituent components, which can then be passed for decisions to other actors. Thus, complex problems lead to complex organizational structures as demonstrated in Demchak's work. Steinbruner applies his decision-making framework to workings of bureaucracies, proposing that the learning process in cybernetic organizations manifests itself in changed behavior rather than changes in outcome calculation. "Learning occurs in the sense that there is a systematic change in the pattern of activity in the organization. Over time, those programs and standard operating procedures persist that are successful in the limited sense which is pertinent; unsuccessful ones drop out."[105]

The literature reviewed in this section all bears in various ways upon the process of organic organizational adaptation and innovation. Doubler, Eden, and Demchak all tackle the issue of organizational change by treating the organization as the unit of analysis. All construct a series of related rationales that explain the process of organizational adaptation and innovation. I combine this analysis with a slice of organizational behavior literature that takes the unit of analysis down to the level of the individual—the irreducible component from which all organizations are built. Barnard, March, and Simon all offer insights on the importance of individual behavior and decision-making and the impact that human relationships can have on organizational behavior. Steinbruner brings the analysis full circle in his cybernetic paradigm, which relates individual to organizational decision-making. Like the other authors, Steinbruner offers an explanation for organizational dynamism and adaptivity that provides a stark contrast to the image of the rigid modern bureaucracy described by Weber.

IMPLICATIONS FOR THEORIES OF WARTIME INNOVATION

The arguments advanced in the literature reviewed above suggest a series of conditions that are necessary for hypotheses about the dialectical processes of organically executed organizational adaptation and innovation that will be tested against the experiences of America's armed forces in Iraq. This literature suggests a number of vital hypotheses. Organizational learning clearly is vital to the process of successful wartime innovation. It requires a number of critical supporting elements, including a two-way vertical flow of ideas up and down the hierarchy in which the top of the hierarchy accepts inputs from the bottom; a horizontal free flow of ideas between organizational structures; and organizational leadership that establishes a "culture" of learning and intellectual flexibility. "Outside" or external institutional pressure to change is also important—in this case, while U.S. military organizations did not immediately respond to the top-down direction to get ready for irregular war, the fact that they knew their civilian masters supported the development of these capacities certainly helped create an organizational environment to adjust and innovate. Feedback loops from the environment guided iterative changes in behavior that became operationalized by changed organizational SOPs. Knowledge acquired through the feedback loops populated organizational frames that informed the iterative adaptation of the SOPs that happened over time. The process of SOP evolution gathered momentum as learning increased over time and produced fundamental departures in organizational operations.

Organizational behavior literature suggests various tendencies of bureaucracies that will be tested in the case studies that follow: that innovation would be impeded by individuals and organizational elements seeking satisfactory as opposed to optimal solutions; that inter- and intraorganizational relationships between people are an important source of organizational productivity and dynamism, and also of adaptivity and innovation; that these relationships serve to break down hierarchy and flatten the structure of organizational authority and can be part of a process to create networked organizational structures across function and different domains of organizational authority; and that organizations can evolve and adapt to provide complex capacities that mirror the complexities of the operating environment.

The perspectives offered on organizational learning and organizational behavior suggest conditions under which battlefield innovation is possible. As noted in Chapter 1, this study argues that military innovation is first and foremost a process that manifests itself on the battlefield in the form of changed standard operating procedures (SOPs); different relationships between and among combat arms; the blending of combat and noncombat capabilities to achieve battlefield "effect"; and the eventual development of different missions for military units not previously envisioned in doctrine.

Accordingly, the next chapter will examine the wartime innovation process in the field of three units operating in western Anbar Province from the fall of 2005 through the summer of 2006: the 3rd Battalion, 6th Marine Regiment, or 3-6, and the 1st Battalion, 7th Marine Regiment, which operated in the area surrounding the city of Al Qaim along the Iraq-Syrian border; and the 4-14 Cavalry, which operated in the town of Rawah on the northern bank of the Euphrates River to the east of al Qaim. The next chapter will first present a summary of the insurgency in western Anbar and of the broader operational context that framed tactical operations by these three units.

3 WARTIME INNOVATION IN WESTERN ANBAR

Fall 2005–Summer 2006

On September 11, 2006, *The Washington Post* covered an intelligence report authored by a seasoned Marine Corps intelligence analyst who stated that Anbar Province in western Iraq had been "lost" to insurgents.[1] The news article quoted an unidentified Army officer, who, in confirming the details of the classified report, provided a searing assessment of the state of affairs: "We haven't been defeated militarily, but we have been defeated politically—and that's where wars are won and lost."[2] The classified report, authored by veteran Marine Corps intelligence officer Colonel Peter Devlin, provided a litany of disastrous failures by the United States in the three years following the invasion.[3] The report, quoted and summarized below, highlighted a variety of negative and, it stated, perhaps irreversible trends:

- The social and political situation had deteriorated so badly that U.S. forces were "no longer capable of defeating the insurgency in Al Anbar."
- The social order had completely collapsed, and "[v]iolence and criminality are now the principle driving factors" in daily life in the province.
- The Sunni tribal leadership had come to regard the Shia government in Baghdad as agents of Iran.
- The province had little prospect of attracting the investment needed to get the economy on its feet.
- Al Qaeda in Iraq (AQI) had become the "dominant organization of influence in al-Anbar Province, surpassing nationalist insurgents, the Iraqi Government, and the MNF [multi-national forces] in its ability to control the day-to-day life of the average Sunni." AQI had become "an integral part of the social fabric of Western Iraq," and the people of Anbar had come to "see it as [an] inevitable part of daily life and, in some cases, their only hope for protection against a possible ethnic cleansing campaign by the central government."

- Noting the steady increase of violence in the province, Devlin stated that "the insurgency has strengthened in the last six months. Insurgent groups are better organized, increasingly achieve effective operational security, have improved their capabilities to cache and distribute weapons, and have refined and adapted their tactics. Control of the criminal enterprise means the majority of insurgents are now financially self sustaining at the lowest levels."
- Devlin concluded that security and governance would continue to disintegrate in the province without a substantial influx of funds and the arrival of a division-size military force.[4]

Upon the report being made public, none of the senior military commanders in Iraq disavowed its contents or conclusions. Major General Richard Zilmer, the top Marine Corps officer in Anbar, stated: "I have seen the report, and I concur with that assessment."[5] The Multinational Corps Iraq (MNC-I) commander, Lieutenant General Peter Chiarelli, also endorsed the report's conclusions.[6] Chiarelli told reporters: "If you read the report, Pete is right on target. I don't believe there is any military strategy alone, any kinetic operations that we can run alone that will create the conditions for victory which we must have. I think the real heart of what Pete was telling us is that there are economic and political conditions that have to improve out at Anbar, as they do everywhere in Iraq, for us to be successful."[7]

As the Devlin report became public, further questions about the U.S. military commitment in Anbar arose when Chiarelli withdrew a battalion of 800 Army troops and their Stryker vehicles from the province. These troops rejoined 172nd Stryker Brigade Combat Team in Mosul and then redeployed with the whole brigade to Baghdad to help deal with the city's increasing sectarian violence. The Devlin report painted a bleak portrait of the political, military, and economic environment in Anbar three years after the invasion. Many commentators seized upon its gloomy assessment as a broader metaphor for American strategic failure in Iraq.[8] The military implications of Devlin's report seemed clear: after three years in the field, the U.S. Army and Marine Corps had not mastered the art of counterinsurgency and confronted institutional failure. While the insurgents had adapted their tactics, techniques, and operations to the environment—even reportedly becoming part of the social fabric of the province—the Army and Marine Corps had not demonstrated a similar adaptability. During the first two years of the war and into 2005, U.S. tactics remained focused on conventionally oriented fire and maneuver missions. Indeed, MNF-

I commander General Casey sought to consolidate U.S. troops at a few main operating bases isolated from the population as part of his plan to lower their visibility and turn responsibility for the war over to the Iraqis.[9]

This chapter covers the wartime innovation process of three units operating in western Anbar Province from the fall of 2005 through the summer of 2006: the 3rd Battalion, 6th Marine Regiment, or 3-6; the 1st Battalion, 7th Marine Regiment, which operated in the area surrounding the city of Al Qaim along the Iraq-Syrian border; and the 4-14 Cavalry, which operated in the town of Rawah on the northern bank of the Euphrates River to the east of al Qaim. The 4-14 had been detached from the 172nd Stryker Brigade Combat Team operating in Ninewa Province. The 3-6 was succeeded by 1-7 in the spring of 2006, whereas the 4-14 deployed into Rawah where there had previously been no sustained coalition military presence. The chapter starts with a summary of the insurgency in western Anbar and of the broader operational context that framed tactical operations by the units identified above. The case studies will be presented after this initial summary. During the fall of 2005, the U.S. tactical approach in Anbar began to shift away from conventional operations toward COIN-oriented operations. The evolution from 3-6 to 1-7 captures this process, as the 3-6 established a tactical approach that was subsequently embellished by 1-7. The 4-14 case also demonstrates a similar evolutionary process as the unit gradually developed and embraced its approach to COIN.

The insurgency had flourished in Anbar for a variety of reasons. The failure of local governance, coupled with the absence of any effective central government presence and the prioritization of public funds to non-Sunni regions, helped AQI to become a dominant political force in the province.[10] Devlin and others also identified U.S. and Iraqi troop shortfalls in the province as a critical contributing factor to what looked like an unfolding disaster. The lack of manpower hampered efforts to extend effective control beyond the walls of isolated American and Iraqi military compounds.[11] In the summer before the Devlin report became public, some observers described U.S. military tactics as "whack a mole," in which hastily assembled units ricocheted from one crisis spot to the next, mounting futile search and destroy missions designed to kill insurgents.[12] The emphasis on finding insurgents using conventional military tactics further highlighted problems created by the lack of combat troops in Anbar. The November 2004 assault on Fallujah highlighted U.S. limitations. To consolidate the two Army battalions and six Marine Corps battalions and their support elements for the assault, other parts of Anbar had to be denuded of troops. Military commanders lamented the approach that prevented them from remaining in one place long enough to build local relationships and apply the military and political tools at their disposal over an extended period.

The Devlin report's gloomy forecast mirrored a similarly gloomy—even desperate—mood in Washington, DC. By the end of the summer in 2006, it had become clear that President Bush had lost confidence in General Casey's leadership and his approach to the war. That fall he formed a group to review American strategy as a sense of desperation descended upon Washington.[13] Ironically, however, as national political and military leaders grappled with reorienting America's Iraq strategy, military commanders on the ground in Anbar had already refined their COIN approach and were making significant progress against the insurgents. In retrospect, the Devlin report represented rock bottom for the initial phase of the U.S. COIN campaign in Iraq. Even as his report hit the press and doom and gloom pervaded in the White House, a turnaround in the COIN campaign in Anbar had been slowly gathering momentum over the previous twelve months.

A mere seven months after Devlin's dire assessment, his report seemed largely forgotten. By the spring of 2007, many commentators openly stated that Al Qaeda had been defeated in Anbar. In April 2007, Marine Colonel John Koenig—the senior officer in charge of economic development in the province—confidently stated: "There are some people who would say we've won the war out here. I'm cautiously optimistic as we're going forward."[14] Various statistical indicators backed up the optimistic assessments. As an illustration of the dramatic change that took place over the last year, Anbar witnessed a 50 percent decrease in attacks between May 2006 and May 2007. A total of 400 incidents of violence occurred in May 2007, compared with 810 the year prior. Similarly, Ramadi experienced only 30 attacks in May 2007, as opposed to 254 in May 2006.[15] The situation in the Sunni heartland had improved so much that in October 2007, the U.S. representative to the United Nations, Ambassador Zalmay Khalilzad, reported that "the situation [in Anbar] province [is] largely stable and quiet, permitting reconstruction to take place."[16] Few argued with his assessment.

Observers pointed to a series of reasons behind the progress in the successful battles against Al Qaeda and other Sunni insurgent groups in Anbar in 2006 and 2007: (1) AQI overplaying its hand with the local tribal sheikhs through intimidation and brutal tactics leading to alienation and disaffection with AQI's cause; (2) AQI's disruption of the local black market revenue-generating activities by the Anbar tribal leadership, which helped further split the insurgency; (3) an improved range of counterinsurgency practices by the United States that, among other things, saw units dispersed throughout the Anbar urban areas in common operating outposts that provided improved situational awareness, local security, and better intelligence; (4) improved efforts to involve the local population in providing local security through membership in the Iraqi police; (5) realization by Sunnis that their political alliance with AQI held out no prospect for the recovery of their lost political authority and that a better relationship with the United States represented the only avenue to achieve this objective and to counter growing Shiite/Iranian influence in Baghdad; (6) realization by the United States that it had to back off its plan for a classically designed democracy administered by a strong central government and instead had to re-empower local elites; and (7) efforts by the central government in Baghdad to support local Sunni tribal leaders.[17]

All these factors reduced the effectiveness of the insurgents in Anbar over the 2006–7 period, perhaps most dramatically reported in the battle for Ramadi throughout the fall of 2006.[18] In retrospect, however, dramatic events in and around Ramadi in late 2006 and early 2007 represented the culmination of a series of actions throughout Anbar Province over the preceding two years in which the U.S. military took the fight to the insurgents, slowly but surely grasped the nuances of the complicated political and military environment, and made fundamental changes to their organizational SOPs to build a series of new COIN competencies. As previously noted, this book does not argue that success in Anbar can be attributed solely to U.S. military action, but it is clear that the tactical adaptation and organizational innovation of individual units played a significant part in that success. In Anbar, that innovation process unfolded over twenty-four-odd months of hard fighting. The crucial battle of Ramadi in late 2006 and early 2007 must be seen in the context of military operations ongoing throughout the province over the previous two years. During this period, U.S. military units continually cycled through a series of tactics, techniques, and procedures on the battlefield that saw growing competence of units in developing the appropriate balance between kinetic and nonkinetic operations; better development and integration of locally derived intelligence with operations; better use of information operations in the contested areas; and application of a systems-based analysis of the environment that helped operationalize the concept of effects-based operations. The story of this iterative, evolutionary, and organically driven process of innovation began unfolding in

Anbar after the Fallujah I and II assaults in 2004—both of which featured conventional-style military operations and, in Fallujah I, a failed attempt to train Iraqi military units to take on the mission of combating the insurgents.

THE END OF THE BEGINNING

Many of the elements of the counterinsurgency campaign used successfully by Marines and Army units in Ramadi during late 2006 and early 2007 were previewed during Operation Hunter and its aftermath—a series of operations that began in July 2005 in which U.S. and Iraqi forces swept the villages of western Iraq along the Syrian border—Husaybah, Al Qaim, and Ubaydi. In western Iraq, the Marine Corps and the Army began adapting and innovating as they sought a mix of institutional COIN capabilities tailored to the local environment. Out of the 2005–6 campaigns in western Iraq emerged a series of COIN best practices that would gradually appear throughout Iraq as the Army and Marine Corps slowly but surely wrenched themselves away from their institutional preference for traditional conventionally oriented operations. Units built their COIN best practices from the ground up, a process fostered by an innovative and creative officer corps, supported by their professional cadre of noncommissioned officers and executed by soldiers and Marines on the battlefield.

By late 2004, AQI had heavily infiltrated areas in western Iraq after being driven out of Fallujah. AQI naturally gravitated to the area to seize control over traditional smuggling routes into Iraq over the Syrian border—routes after the invasion that provided arms, men, and money for the insurgency. In 2004–5, Husaybah, a city of 30,000 along the border of Iraq and Syria in western Anbar province, was described by one military officer as "a Wild West Border town."[19]

The military footprint in western Anbar had been reduced as a result of the demands of conducting the Fallujah operations in March and November 2004. By mid-2005, Al Qaim, Husaybah, and the series of towns along the Euphrates River in western Anbar had become a center of AQI and insurgent resistance in western Iraq. By the summer of 2005, U.S. forces in western Anbar remained confined to three primary outposts: a Marine company in a heavily bunkered base called Camp Gannon in Husaybah; a squad protecting a communications tower just north of Al Qaim in an outpost called Khe Sanh, and battalion headquarters at Camp Al Qaim composed of two companies, an aviation detachment and logistics support elements. The combat power at Camp Al Qaim was limited by a requirement that one of its companies provide security at the sprawling Al Asad airfield. Camp Gannon, located on the outskirts of Husaybah, was a heavily fortified facility, and it routinely received mortar and sniper fire from insurgents that freely roamed throughout the area.

While AQI gradually seized control of many areas in western Iraq in 2004 and 2005, its presence in towns like Al Qaim did not go unnoticed by local residents. Over the period, a tactical alliance emerged between AQI and the Sunni insurgent nationalist groups bound together by their opposition to the occupation and the fears of growing Iranian Shiite influence throughout the country. Importantly, however, many of the foreign AQI insurgents remained outside the area's indigenous tribal and social structure—despite Devlin's assessment to the contrary. The Iraq-Syrian border region had long been controlled by the Albu Mahal tribe, one of the main Sunni groups composing the Dulaym tribal confederation in Anbar. The Albu Mahals were spread out along the Western Euphrates River Valley from Fallujah all the way to the Syrian border, with significant concentrations in Al Qaim, Hit, and Husaybah. While the Albu Mahals never enthusiastically supported Saddam, members of the tribe nonetheless gradually gathered under various insurgent nationalist groups opposing the occupation. While initially supportive of AQI in late 2004, by the middle of 2005 evidence appeared suggesting that the Albu Mahals (as well as other tribal groups) had become uncomfortable with the relationship.[20] In a pattern that would be repeated elsewhere in Anbar in 2006 and 2007, in what would later become known as the "tribal awakening," local tribes gradually came to object to AQI's heavy-handed, brutal tactics of intimidation, AQI's interference with their revenue-generating smuggling activities, and AQI's attempts to work its way into the social structure through marriage. By the middle of 2005, the Albu Mahals and the Albu Nimr tribe had established their own militia—called the Hamza battalion—to actively resist AQI in the area along the Iraq-Syrian border. In mid-2005, press reports indicated that the Hamza battalion was actively assisting U.S. forces with intelligence tips in Operation Matador in May 2005.[21] In response, AQI entered into an alliance with two rival tribes, the Karguli and Salmoni tribes, over the summer and finally drove the Albu Mahals from Al Qaim in September 2005.[22] In early September, AQI had taken over Al Qaim and posted a sign that read: "Welcome to the Islamic Republic of Qaim." The Albu Mahals would later join with coalition forces in a unit called the "Desert Protectors" in supporting the coalition offensives throughout the fall of 2005. They would be rewarded at the conclusion of the offensives and reinserted into their positions of power and influence by coalition forces. As the Marines reasserted control over Al Qaim, many members of the tribe found jobs with the newly reconstituted Iraq Army brigade and the police force. The assistance of the tribe in providing local security proved vital to reducing insurgent infiltrations into the city.

The terms and conditions of the relationship between U.S. military forces and the Albu Mahals would be repeated elsewhere in Anbar over the next twenty-four months as the so-called awakening process gathered momentum. Coalition forces adopted a laissez-faire attitude toward the tribe's revenue generating activities in exchange for help against AQI. The relationship would be solidified by giving the tribes important roles in the local government, police, and armed forces.

These local dynamics coincided with a growing operational focus on western Anbar by Multi-National Forces West (MNF-W, the coalition command whose area of responsibility included Anbar Province) after the conclusion of the Fallujah operations in late 2004. This increased focus was importantly bounded, however, by the need to control violence in Fallujah and Ramadi, the two main urban centers in the province. These priorities meant that the forces available to combat the insurgency elsewhere in the province were limited. In addition to operations conducted against insurgents in Ramadi (although those insurgents were characterized at the time as "criminals," unlike the "professional jihadists" that had controlled Fallujah),[23] others were executed in western Anbar to capture escaped Fallujah insurgents, and to prevent the infiltration of foreign fighters across the Syrian border.[24]

Through the spring and summer of 2005, MNF-W's focus shifted from eastern Anbar to the western Euphrates and towns such as Al Qaim, Hit, and Haditha, in which Abu Musab al-Zarqawi and the AQI leadership were believed to be hiding, and which also served as the logistical hubs for what was believed to be a robust foreign fighter infiltration network.[25] U.S. Marines conducted a series of operations in the western reaches of the province, temporarily occupying towns along the Euphrates in attacks such as Operation River Blitz,[26] Operation Matador, Operation New Market,[27] and Operation Sword.[28] These actions consisted for the most part of conventional-style clearing operations, with the units returning to their forward operating bases at the conclusion of the operations. During Operation Matador in May 2005, 1,000 Marines fought a frustrating week-long series of skirmishes with insurgents along the Iraq-Syrian border in an attempt to stem the flow of foreign fighters across the border. During the operation, local residents accused the Marines laying siege to Al Qaim of using indiscriminate mortar and artillery fire and air strikes, resulting in collateral damage and civilian casualties.[29] Fasal al-Goud, a former governor of Anbar that had sought help against AQI, leveled strong criticism of the U.S. tactics in Matador that, he said, only created more enemies. "The Americans were bombing whole villages and saying they were only after the foreigners," said al-Goud. "An AK-47 can't distinguish between a terrorist and a tribesman, so how could a missile or tank?"[30]

The U.S. military nonetheless claimed the operation was a success, citing 125 killed insurgents and the detention of 39 insurgent suspects.[31] Participants in the operation, however, were not so sure. Major Steve White, director of operations of the 3rd Battalion, 25th Marine Regiment commented: "It's an extremely frustrating fight. Fighting these guys is like picking up water. You're going to lose every time."[32] The approach to fighting the insurgents reflected the MNF-I command emphasis (coming from General Casey) on the "indirect approach," which emphasized lowering the U.S. military profile and boosting the capabilities of the Iraqi Security Forces, or ISF.[33] The approach on the battlefield also happened within a context in 2004 and 2005 that saw the consolidation of the U.S. military presence at larger bases at such sites as Tallil in southern Iraq, Al Asad in Anbar, Balad in central Iraq, and Qayyarah in northern Iraq. The consolidation of forces in these bases reflected the approach that sought to lower the visibility of U.S. forces and turn responsibility over to the Iraqis.

Consistent with the indirect approach, the 2nd Battalion, 7th Marine regiment mounted a ten-month effort to constitute combined action platoons of Iraqis and Marines around the city of Hit in Anbar, a city of 100,000 that lies halfway between Ramadi and Al Qaim.[34] After standing up the 503rd Iraqi National Guard Battalion in mid-2004, however, the unit disintegrated in fighting with AQI in October and could render little assistance to U.S. forces in their battles for control over the area with insurgents that had appeared in the area after the clearing actions in and around Falluja.[35]

Although attacks continued throughout Iraq at a high pace during the spring of 2005, some data provided room for optimism. Statistics revealed that attacks in April 2005 had actually dropped since January (22 percent, to forty per day), and U.S. casualties were at their lowest level in a year. In addition, at least anecdotally, Iraqi cooperation with the occupation was improving, with Iraqi civilians providing more intelligence to the coalition.[36] In addition, coalition leaders claimed that newly recruited Iraqi military and police forces would soon "be trained to take over counterinsurgency missions in most of Iraq."[37]

That hope, however, masked a growing unease by U.S. forces fighting the in-

surgency in western Anbar. Limited manpower, coupled with the intense security needs of Fallujah and Ramadi, ensured that the coalition could not maintain a sustained presence in the various towns of the region. In some towns
such as Rawah, Hit, and Haditha, there had been little sustained coalition presence at all during the war, and locals who had collaborated with the coalition
during the short interludes when the coalition was there had been threatened
or killed when those troops left.[38]

By the middle of 2005, military commanders described western Anbar as the
"epicenter of the country's deadly insurgency,"[39] and reporters labeled the Euphrates valley the "Ho Chi Minh Trail" of the war.[40] Despite the region's importance, the western campaigns were conducted by only three battalions of 2,100
Marines instead of the four battalions of 3,600 Marines that had occupied the
region a year before.[41] Despite hopes that the shortfall in coalition troops could
soon be filled by Iraqis,[42] that optimism was illusory, as it proved extremely
difficult to get trained Iraqi units to western Anbar and even more difficult to
recruit and retain local Sunnis in the various Iraqi security forces.[43] Despite
coalition assessments that they had killed enough insurgent leaders along the
border to reduce AQI's military capabilities,[44] the lack of sustained coalition
presence everywhere ensured that the insurgents could retreat when the Marines entered a town, but return and kill whoever had collaborated (or were
accused of collaborating) with the occupiers.[45]

Despite failing to capture or kill AQI leader Abu Musab al-Zarqawi, the various operations along the Syrian border in the spring of 2005 provided a glimpse
into the possibility of exploiting divisions between AQI and local Iraqis. During May 2005, Marine units operating along the border near Al Qaim reported
clashes between AQI followers and local tribes over the murder by AQI of a
local tribal leader, and their dissatisfaction with AQI's imposition of strict
rules banning such things as Western dress, smoking, and satellite television.[46]
At least briefly, the insurgency seemed in disarray, and coalition spokesmen
declared that "[t]his is not an expanding insurgency," because "the flow of
foreign fighters was ebbing," and suicide and vehicle bombings were decreasing.[47] Despite—or possibly in spite of—this self-proclaimed success along the
border during the summer of 2005, similar coalition operations in the region
were prosecuted throughout the fall, with continued sweeps of Anbar towns
in Operation Scimitar,[48] Operation Quick Strike,[49] Operation Sayyid,[50] Operation Iron Fist, and Operation River Gate,[51] designed to interrupt infiltration
of fighters across the Syrian border. In spite of—or possibly because of—the

coalition's emphasis on western Anbar, insurgent activity also increased in Fallujah and Ramadi.[52] The continued lack of a "consistent armed presence" by the coalition throughout much of the province ensured little cooperation by the locals against insurgents.[53] The largest of these operations was Operation Steel Curtain, which consisted of 2,500 marines and soldiers and 1,000 Iraqi troops.

The conventionally oriented military operations of the period that concluded with Operation Steel Curtain in November 2005 demonstrated a growing understanding that killing the insurgents or driving them from the area represented only the first phase of the "clear, hold, and build" COIN campaign that would eventually take hold throughout Iraq. Each of these phases came to be built on standardized best practices tailored to the local environments—best practices that eventually spread to other units elsewhere in the province, if not the rest of the country.

The planning for the last major conventional offensive of 2005, Operation Steel Curtain, demonstrated a grasp of effects-based operations—a recognition that the application of combat power had to take place within a wider social and political construct that sought to address and mitigate the potentially negative second order effects of those operations on the local population. Developments in the aftermath of Steel Curtain represented a critical turning point in the conduct of the counterinsurgency campaign in Anbar.

The 2nd Marine Division drew up an extensive "Joint Restricted No Strike Target List" in each of the towns in an attempt to prevent the targeting of mosques, schools, water towers, cemeteries, public buildings, water treatment facilities, areas of historical and religious significance, and hospitals. Sixteen of the sites were identified in Ubaydi, 29 in Husaybah, 26 in Karabilah, 9 in Ar Rabi, and 3 in Khutaylah. Destruction of any of the targets on the list had to be cleared by the Central Command. The operations were accompanied by a nonkinetic effects plan that featured loudspeaker broadcasts, radio broadcasts on AM frequencies, damage payments to residents whose property had been damaged, and extensive distribution of radios, handbills, and posters in the areas.[54] Four combat correspondents were distributed through the force, and a conscious effort was made to shape the reporting coming out of the event.

While the planning for the series of military operations in late 2005 demonstrated an increasing awareness of the complexity of the battle space, battlefield tactics adopted after the operations' conclusions proved far more critical to the long-term success of the COIN campaign in the area. In western Anbar in late 2005, U.S. battlefield tactics changed in ways that reflected a completely different appreciation of the environment and for the appropriate role played by U.S. military forces. While operations earlier in the year had featured conventionally oriented search and destroy missions like Operation Matador, incoming units in late 2005 realized that a new tactical approach would be necessary to tame the badlands of western Anbar. This period marked the beginning of the innovation process that built momentum throughout 2006 and 2007 in Anbar in the battle against the insurgents. The innovative approach to counterinsurgency operations in western Anbar proved to be a preview of what would come later in the eastern part of the province in 2006 and 2007.

3RD BATTALION, 6TH MARINE REGIMENT

At the outset of the fall 2005 clearing operations along the Syrian-Iraq border, the U.S. military footprint consisted of three main operating bases: Camp Gannon, Khe Sanh, and Camp Al Qaim. In July 2005 during his initial site survey of the area, Lieutenant Colonel Dale Alford, commander of the incoming Marine battalion, 3rd Battalion, 6th Marine regiment (3-6), which would be taking over operations in Al Qaim, realized that the isolated base areas in western Iraq had effectively ceded much of the border region to the insurgents—a blend of Baathist nationalists and AQI jihadists. Wherever the U.S. forces were not, the insurgents exercised control. Despite the dire situation, Alford confronted what was in many respects a familiar environment. He had seen many of the circumstances of western Anbar before in a storied Marine Corps career that had seen him involved in Haiti, West Africa, the Balkans—deployments that during the 1990s had come to be derisively referred to as "military operations other than war."[55]

The tactical approach to COIN taken by 3-6 in western Iraq was informed by Alford's vast experiences in fighting irregular war and by the battalion's previous experience conducting counterinsurgency operations in Afghanistan from April through December of 2004. Operating in a cluster of provinces in northeastern Afghanistan over eight months, the unit had performed a diverse array of tasks: fighting Taliban insurgents, training and integrating Afghan National Army units into its operations, providing security for provincial reconstruction projects, building organic intelligence capacities at the company level, and, establishing a sustained small unit presence in its areas of operations. All these lessons would be applied during the Iraq deployment, with the task of tactical execution falling primarily to the battalion's 350 noncommissioned officers who understood the unit's command priorities.[56]

Upon deploying the unit into western Anbar in September 2005, Alford immediately dispersed his forces out of the three main operating areas.[57] As Alford emphasized to his battalion on a nearly continuous basis: "It's the People, Stupid."[58] Alford framed the battalion's approach to conducting COIN operations by a simple objective: "[To] make the people choose us over the bad guys."[59] The dispersal of his forces out of their main operating bases represented the first step in his bid to establish a local presence to counter the insurgents. By the end of its first month, Alford had pushed the battalion into a variety of different outposts throughout the area. At the conclusion of Steel Curtain, 3-6 had further dispersed throughout the operational area into sixteen outposts in partnership with Iraqi security forces.

Using a Caterpillar D-9 bulldozer left behind by departing Army units, Alford's engineers built a series of platoon-size outposts that were jointly manned by 3-6 and the newly formed Iraqi 1st Brigade. These hastily prepared bases were rudimentary in nature but served as the instruments to quickly disperse the battalion and increase the presence of U.S. and Iraqi forces throughout the area. After shaping conventional military operations in the fall, 3-6 then launched the next phase of the clear, hold, and build approach. The next several months saw 3-6 focus on arriving at an appropriate balance of kinetic and nonkinetic tools to consolidate its control over the area. Alford established six command priorities for 3-6: (1) build up the Iraqi Security Forces; (2) establish combined action platoons to operate out of the combat outposts; (3) build and support the Iraqi police; (4) continue aggressive operations against the insurgents; (5) focus on civil affairs and reconstruction; and (6) build local governance and leadership.[60] These six objectives constituted so-called logical lines of operations, or LOOs, around which to structure the unit's operations during its entire deployment.

Each of the platoon-size outposts patrolled its local area on a near-constant basis to convince the local populace that the Iraqi-U.S. teams were there to stay and would not be returning to a large military base. Alford developed an innovative metric for each of his outposts—he requested all to report the number of meals that his personnel had eaten in local households. Alford kept track of his so-called eats on streets as one way to track the degree of local engagement by the joint U.S.-Iraqi team patrols.[61] Alford directed that most of 3-6's patrols to occur on foot, not in vehicles, as the unit began to execute the "hold" part of the plan. Alford intended the outposts to function as a variation of the combined action platoon model from Vietnam, with Iraqis and Marines living and operating together on a continual basis. The joint patrols proceeded to develop an intelligence reporting network built on local relationships. Each local network pooled its reports with the other combat outposts, giving the 3-6 battalion headquarters a fused and nuanced picture of the local environment. As the battalion moved to the "hold" part of the campaign, kinetic operations against the insurgents continued through joint Iraqi-U.S. actions aimed at border interdiction, river interdiction, snap vehicle check points, time sensitive targeting, and targeted raids.[62] As would be demonstrated in other units, none of the "clear, hold, and build" phases ever occurred as mutually exclusive operations. All phases happened simultaneously and were interrelated.

After the establishment of the combat outposts, 3-6 embarked on a series of initiatives to vest the tribal leadership into the system of local security.[63] The battalion embarked on parallel efforts to re-establish the local police force that had been decimated by AQI's campaign of intimidation and coercion. Alford subsequently sent 585 local recruits to the police academy in Baghdad for a two-week training course—a recruiting effort backed by the local tribal sheikhs. In addition, 3-6 placed contracts to rebuild four police stations that had been destroyed by the insurgents. The standup of the police force coincided with the building of a new Iraqi Security Force brigade—3rd Battalion, 7th Brigade—which drew largely from the local tribes in western Anbar. Through the first three months of 2006, the joint patrols and steady standup of the local police force gradually transformed the security environment in western Anbar and led to a reduction in violence. Sniping and IED attacks against the joint Iraqi-U.S. patrols declined dramatically in the spring of 2006. By the early spring, 3-6 began supplementing these efforts with civil affairs and reconstruction projects in the area. The battalion assigned civil affairs officers to work with the tribes on a daily basis to address such issues as electricity, water availability, sewage, schools, hospitals, roads, and garbage removal.

1ST BATTALION, 7TH MARINE REGIMENT

After the departure of 3-6 in the spring of 2006, 1st Battalion, 7th Marine Regiment, or 1-7, commanded by Lieutenant Colonel Nick Marano, deployed into the Al Qaim area and continued to consolidate the "hold" phase of the COIN campaign, building on the efforts of 3-6 to consolidate the gains in the counterinsurgency made in the fall of 2005. This was 1-7's third tour in Iraq (one of which was in Al Qaim), and Marano had extensive Iraq experience through his two prior tours working at the Marine Corps Marine Expeditionary Force, or MEF, headquarters in Anbar and at MNF-I in Baghdad. The prior experience of the unit and its commanding officer ensured that the organization possessed a high degree of situational awareness before it deployed into the area. Upon arriving in Al Qaim, Marano promulgated a new series of LOOs that related tactical operations with desired strategic effects. The LOOs were security, governance, economic development, communicating, and transition. Marano developed his LOOs independently through his own initiative, though he drew the approach from his previous experiences working in the Marine Expeditionary Force, or MEF, headquarters in Iraq at Camp Fallujah.[64]

Marano broke the LOOs down into more detail for each of the towns in 1-7's area of operation. The LOOs were "a bit ahead of the wave," according to Marano. These LOOs were adopted by Regimental Combat Team 7, which deployed into the Al Qaim region after 1-7's departure in the summer of 2006.[65] The LOOs reflected a clear and increasing grasp of the need to achieve the right mix of kinetic and nonkinetic tools to achieve the desired effect in 1-7's area of operations. The evolving approach of 1-7 throughout the spring of 2006 reflected a clear and steady development of core competencies that helped the unit arrive at an appropriate blend of organizational capacities in conducting its COIN operations.

The approaches of 3-6 and 1-7 reflected strands of continuity and the process of organizational innovation as the evolving tactics, techniques, and procedures, or TTPs, toward the COIN campaign in western Iraq gained momentum during late 2005 and early 2006. Upon deploying into western Anbar in the spring of 2006, Marano spread most of the battalion into the dozen-odd bases established by Alford in the fall of 2005. Marano sought to continue the process of pushing the unit out into remote areas and established additional combat outposts in western Anbar to consolidate the Marines' presence throughout the area. Despite his command's concerns that 1-7 was spread too thinly, MEF headquarters supported Marano's request to continue pushing the battalion out into more small outposts manned jointly with Marines and Iraqis.[66]

By June of 2006, 1-7 was spread out in more than fifteen outposts of varying size.[67] These outposts pushed 1-7 into the remote areas of Anbar Province along the Iraqi-Syrian border. The distance between the outposts created a communications and supply problem for 1-7. Given the dispersal of his battalion over such a wide area, Marano moved the unit to a concept of distributed operations, with significant authority for operations delegated down the chain of command to the company and squad level. He created four maneuver companies for the battalion to give his unit greater mobility and flexibility in responding to contingencies.[68]

As 1-7 further dispersed through western Anbar, it built on the progress of 3-6 in generating its own intelligence. By April of 2006, the locally oriented joint ISF-Marine patrols generated nearly 80 percent of the unit's intelligence.[69] The organic generation of intelligence that resulted grew dramatically during the spring and summer of 2006, overloading 1-7's standard S-2 complement of between four and six officers. By the end of its deployment, the 1-7 S-2 staff had grown to more than thirty analysts. The battalion's efforts to build organizational capacity to meet the demands for intelligence collection and analysis represented a critical component in its COIN operations. The 1-7 intelligence effort represented a multifaceted program built on a wide array of technologies, new software, and database programs, and perhaps, most important, a shared understanding throughout the unit of the importance of gathering data on a systematic basis to develop a nuanced understanding of the complex operational environment.

As a first step in building situational awareness, the unit organized a census and vehicle registration program for all the towns under its control in the spring of 2006.[70] Over the objections of Marano's headquarters at the regimental combat team, two vehicle checkpoints were established. Every vehicle had to be registered with the local police, and a color-coded sticker system identified the town from which the vehicle originated. The system allowed the joint patrols to clearly identify unregistered vehicles as well as vehicles that were not from the immediate patrol areas. The vehicle registration system represented one component of an areawide population census conducted by 1-7 throughout early 2006. Each town in the area was divided up into discrete named neighborhoods; each street received a name, and each house received a number to allow 1-7 and its surrounding units to have a common frame of reference for its respective areas. As part of the census, Marines went to every house in their sector and took a picture of the male head of household and identified family members. At the end of each week, the battalion held a leaders' meeting at which each unit presented a thumb drive with the census data to the battalion intelligence officer that was downloaded into a database maintained by the battalion S-2.

The census data proved critical to 1-7's operations throughout its deployment. Information gathered in the census, including the vehicle registration, was entered into a database called COPLINK, a law enforcement database and analysis software program used by the Phoenix Police Department that used artificial intelligence to draw upon multiple databases. Its appearance with 1-7 in Al Qaim was no accident. Marano's use of expertise from the U.S. law enforcement community happened as a result of a series of programs administered in the Pentagon. These programs sought to investigate the utility of building new COIN procedures that drew from the experiences of police departments around the United States. An organization called the Technical Support Working Group, or TSWG, convened a series of workshops in the summer of 2005 to familiarize experienced law enforcement officers from major metropolitan police departments with the COIN environment in Iraq and to determine whether their law enforcement experiences could be of assistance.[71] TSWG was one component of an ad hoc organization called the Combating Terrorism Technology Task Force, or CTTF, to support the Defense Department's efforts to fight the Global War on Terror (GWOT). A key function of CTTF was to coordinate DoD efforts to counter IED attacks in Iraq and Afghanistan. It was ready with funding to support any technologies or other means to support ground forces in Iraq.

The workshops found a receptive audience with the Marines and General James Mattis, who wanted to buttress the Marine Corps's already strong combat competencies in irregular warfare and counterinsurgency. He encouraged Marano and others to draw upon law enforcement expertise in preparing for their Iraq deployments.

A July 2005 workshop joined together police detectives from the Fairfax County Police Department, heads of the gang units from the Boston and Chicago police departments, as well as the deputy superintendents from these departments. Another member of the group was a detective sergeant from the Los Angeles Police Department (LAPD), Ralph Morten, who had recently traveled to Iraq to train Marines in tactical level skills to counter the IED threat. The attendees included several echelons of law enforcement skills, including senior departmental leadership, functional unit leadership—countergang units, as well as officers who engaged in daily enforcement operations and investigations. Supporting and guiding the discussions of the law enforcement officers was the Interagency Coordinator for the Joint IED Task Force, a Marine captain with extensive experience in Iraq and an expert on the insurgency and the IED problem. Additional participants included a former Navy Seal, a senior analyst from Defense Intelligence Agency (DIA), and a member of the Army Science Board.

The workshops helped build momentum within the Marines to investigate the utility of law enforcement training and TTPs for the COIN environment in Iraq. During 1-7's predeployment training, the unit worked extensively with a variety of police departments, including the Los Angeles and Phoenix police departments, to help the unit develop a policelike set of tactics, techniques, and procedures built around skills for observation, profiling, and questioning.[72] The training sought to make individual Marines comfortable with thinking about their jobs as being similar to that of a policeman on the beat. Marano believed that a gang warfare frame of reference might be useful in thinking through the tactical challenge facing 1-7 in Al Qaim—as had been highlighted in the summer collaborative workshops. The battalion drew extensively upon the expertise of Morten, a Los Angeles police detective that spent several months advising 1-7 in Iraq. Morten, a twenty-seven-year veteran of the LAPD, was regarded as one of the nation's top experts on suicide bombings after receiving several years of training by the Israeli police.[73] Morten connected the unit with contacts in the Pentagon to provide $2.5 million in funding for a partnership with Lockheed-Martin that developed into an initiative that 1-7 called "Project METRO," or Mobile Embedded Target and Reconnaissance Operation, which fused together the capabilities of the COPLINK database with new training based on tactical TTPs, and a suite of surveillance equipment provided by Lockheed-Martin Corporation.[74]

"Project METRO" fused together a series of disparate capabilities and technologies that shaped 1-7's approach to fighting in the COIN environment in Al Qaim in the spring and summer of 2006. The battalion staff inputted data gathered in the census and vehicle registration efforts into COPLINK and deployed sensors and cameras in areas identified through pattern analysis of attacks. All the information was queued to the battalion operations center to provide an integrated common operational picture that helped support all operations—both kinetic and nonkinetic. The suite of sensors and data processing capabilities lent itself to the new TTPs developed for 1-7's counterinsurgency operations. The surveillance helped monitor insurgent activity in remote areas, and information collected in the program greatly assisted in understanding the local insurgent networks. The unit installed overt and covert surveillance equipment throughout the urban areas and other areas with high IED activity. The centerpiece of the system was a series of police surveillance cameras installed throughout the border city of Husaybah, which had a population of 120,000.

Marano's regimental headquarters initially opposed the initiative because of the belief that Marano would use the equipment for force protection instead of counterinsurgency and counter-IED tasks.[75] Marano's lobbying at the head-quarters eventually convinced his superiors to let him try out his ideas. (The Marines subsequently developed something called GBOSS, powerful surveil-lance sensors mounted on towers inside base camp areas.)[76] The partnership with Lockheed Martin brought other surveillance equipment, such as acoustic recorders that were left inside target houses suspected of supporting insurgent activity. The system included something called a Wearable Intelligent Record-ing Environment (WIRE), a throat microphone and a small computerized per-sonal data assistant (PDA) that turned verbal observations into text. Fifty of these units were deployed with 1-7.[77] The program also consisted of a covert camera system tied to an extensive sensor array on the Syrian-Iraqi border. The battalion intelligence cell made extensive use of pattern analysis using the in-formation from the different collection techniques. All of these programs had a symbiotic effect: Marine and Iraqi foot patrols with enhanced skill sets tailored more toward law enforcement than traditional massed fire conventional op-erations; better intelligence collection and the enhanced situational awareness that resulted from the patrols; and a flexible battalion command element set up both to receive information and to push information down to the lowest levels quickly in support of operations. The de facto flattened organizational hierarchy created with the free flow of information up and down the command would be repeated elsewhere by other units in their COIN operations.

Morten's deployment with 1-7 and the attempt to adapt law enforcement technologies and TTPs to the COIN environment in Iraq were judged to be a great success. In its report to Lockheed-Martin Corporation on the utility of its suite of sensors, 1-7 noted that while not all the technologies worked well, the COPLINK database and supporting sensor suite "vastly [reduced] the time necessary to create a target package from several hours to several minutes," and that the system was extremely useful in counter-IED operations.[84]

The law enforcement TTPs also greatly assisted in tailoring 1-7's patrol tech-niques to the environment. One resulting new TTP assigned specific neighbor-hoods to specific daily patrols. The unit reported that the new TTPs "allowed for them [Baker Company] to develop the 'cop on the beat' mentality, knowing their terrain, and more importantly, knowing the people of the area. The level of familiarity gained with the area and its inhabitants allowed for easier detection of suspicious activity/items/personnel. More importantly, these tactics greatly facilitated the relationship with the local population, providing them with a much greater sense of security and willingness to provide information."[84]

The initial focus on law enforcement techniques and the advice received by Morten eventually evolved into a more formalized training program called Combat Hunter, which became integrated into the predeployment training of all Marine units headed to Iraq as part of the Mojave Viper training sequence administered at the Marine Air Ground Combat Center in Twenty-nine Palms Base, California. Under the program, Marines receive training to develop improved observation skills to better spot anomalies in their environment. In addition to using their own faculties, Marines are being shown how to make better use of imaging devices and other observation technologies to spot insurgents and insurgent activities. The program is part of an attempt to instill an offensive mindset in the battle against insurgents in Iraq.[84]

The collective result of the innovative COIN focus resulted in a steady reduction in violence and attacks during the spring of 2006. Unit statistics tracked a slow but steady reduction in violence in and around Al Qaim from December 2005 to July of 2006. IEDs remained a persistent problem throughout the deployment for 1-7, which focused extensively on the IED supply chain, gradually reducing insurgent attacks during the deployment. In March 2006, 1-7 stepped up recruiting local Iraqis for the ISF. Nearly 400 appeared on March 27, 2006, to join up. According to Marano, "A lot of these guys were insurgents. It wasn't long ago we were shooting at them."[84] The focus on building the ISF occurred simultaneously with the buildup of the local police force that had been started by 3-6 in the fall of 2005. Also building on the local leader engagement efforts mounted by 3-6, 1-7 successfully created a series of new police stations in and around the unit's outposts throughout the area. By the end of the spring, the unit had built a police force totaling 1,400 in the Al Qaim area. After receiving support from the local tribal leadership, new Iraqi police stations were stood up in Husaybah, Ubaydi, Karabila, Sa'dah, and Al Qaim. Marano stationed the police forces near U.S. outposts along with ISF that steadily increased in number throughout 1-7's deployment. Concurrent with the focus on standing up the local police, developing the ISF, and conducting counterinsurgency operations, Marano's unit focused intensively on reconstruction and infrastructure in the towns throughout the area.

The last arrow in 1-7's quiver of LOOs consisted of economic development projects throughout the Al Qaim area. The battalion systematically set about attempting to resurrect critical parts of the area's neglected infrastructure. The unit rebuilt schools, water treatment plants, health clinics, recreation centers, roads, and even soccer fields. Two of the most important of these projects were the construction of two bridges over the Euphrates that had been destroyed during heavy fighting in 2005. The bridges were vital to restoring the local commerce in the Al Qaim region and western Iraq.

By the spring of 2006, the environment in western Iraq had improved dramatically. By this point in the campaign, Colonel Blake Crowe, commander of all the Marines in western Anbar, called the area around Al-Qaim "the model for where they want us to go."[84] Unsurprisingly, the progress made in western Anbar over the period received attention from the senior military leadership. Head of U.S. Forces in Iraq, General George Casey, told a reporter in the spring of 2006: "Look at what Colonel Alford accomplished [in Al Qaim]. He was one of my best battalion commanders. He showed how to turn a city around."[84]

SUMMARY OF TACTICAL ADAPTATION AND INNOVATION BY THE 3-6 AND 1-7

Operations in western Anbar featured a number of critical tactical adaptations that effectively resulted in new organizational best practices for the conduct of counterinsurgency operations in the area. A critical and underlying feature of all these steps was the freedom of action granted by MEF headquarters in Fallujah and the MNF-I in Baghdad to unit commanders. In the cases examined here, neither Alford nor Marano reported significant micromanagement or opposition to their initiatives at higher headquarters. Both units received wide latitude to structure their tactical approaches to the environment.

Both Marine units made significant adaptations to their respective approaches in fighting the counterinsurgency in western Iraq. The evolutionary approach to the environment gathered momentum over the period of 2005–6, which saw fundamental changes to the way the units were used on the battlefield. The approach saw growing awareness of the complexity of the battle space and of the need to look at military operations through the analytical lens of effects-based operations. The process of building new and flexible SOPs to cope with the dynamic environment would prove to be a feature of many of the units fighting the insurgents elsewhere in Anbar.

Almost none of the major TTPs developed by the Marines in western Anbar came specifically from military doctrine—though many were informed by the experiences of the commanding officers and the previous deployments of units in both Iraq and Afghanistan. It is clear that each of the commanding officers sought an optimal solution to the counterinsurgency—a solution framed by previous personal and organizational experiences and perspectives. Both commanders successfully created "learning organizations" that could evolve and adapt relatively quickly in the environment. The learning process first manifested itself with a new method of tactical employment taken by 3-6 in distributing the unit widely throughout the area in combat outposts. These outposts provided the means to patrol on foot on a near-constant basis. The outposts became part of a hub-and-spoke network of outposts and logistics centers used by the units to push their presence down to the local level. Metrics were developed by battalion leadership to encourage local interaction.

Both battalions developed a variety of new procedures to conduct the counterinsurgency, starting with 3-6's move to the concept of combined action platoons with joint, local operations to start the process of building local security. Then 1-7 built on the momentum, first building a census database for people and vehicles. Information gathered during these activities were combined in the METRO program and COPLINK software that added law enforcement training techniques to build new organizational capacities to meet the demands of the environment. Importantly, the application of law enforcement technologies and techniques was possible because senior Marine Corps leaders recognized the need to develop new organizational capacities in the summer of 2005 to fight the insurgents. In this case, organizational innovation became manifested on the battlefield but was supported through a collaborative interagency process. That process drew upon law enforcement expertise that eventually was successfully applied by 1-7 in fighting the insurgent networks along the Iraq-Syrian border.

The census activities created an organizational need for greater information and processing capacities within 1-7, and Marano had the flexibility to build a significantly larger intelligence processing section. Information passed freely throughout the organizations and was effectively used to support decision-making throughout the unit both at headquarters and in the field.

Both battalions clearly grasped the concept of effects-based operations, and each constantly sought to achieve the right balance between kinetic and nonkinetic effects throughout their deployments. Both battalions immediately recognized the need to develop organic intelligence capacities in the forward deployed units. Instead of relying on the formal organizational intelligence structure at the battalion level in which information was pushed down the hierarchy to units, intelligence came to be generated organically from the ground up. Information passed freely up and down the chain of command to all units deployed in the field. Improved intelligence collection led to better situational awareness, which in turn led to better command decision-making on apportioning the mix of kinetic and nonkinetic tools available for the environment. Improved collection manifested itself in increased tips on insurgent presence and operations from the population as the model of building and disseminating intelligence evolved to match the complexities of the operational environment.

The pursuit of local relationships by the units proved crucial to the COIN operations of 3-6 and 1-7. While they may not have created the split in the insurgency, military leaders took full advantage of the splits to successfully enlist the Albu Mahals into the fight against AQI. After the clearing operations that culminated in Steel Curtain, the U.S. tribal outreach activities picked up in speed and intensity to build new political relationships throughout the communities. The relationships developed with the Mahals provided both units with a critical building block in the reconstituting of the local police force in the Al Qaim region and enlisting the local population in the Iraqi Army. The local relationships received an added boost by the civil-military operations focused on reconstruction projects to rebuild local infrastructure.

TF 4-14 CAVALRY GROUP IN RAWAH, WESTERN ANBAR: AUGUST 2005–JULY 2006

While the Marines battled insurgents in Al Qaim and in the towns up and down the Euphrates River in western Iraq in late 2005, the Army's 4th Squadron, 14th (4-14) Cavalry Regiment from the 172nd Stryker Brigade Combat Team, or 172 Stryker Brigade Combat Team (SBCT), took on the insurgents in a piece of northern Anbar that straddled the Euphrates River east of Al Qaim. Its operations centered on the towns of Rawah, Anah, and Riyannah. The unit, commanded by Lieutenant Colonel Mark Freitag, operated in the area sandwiched between the Marine Corps's 1st Battalion, 7th Regiment in Al Qaim and the 3rd Battalion, 3rd Regiment based out of Al Asad Air Base.

Rawah and Anah were predominately Sunni towns that had done well under Saddam. Prior to the U.S. invasion, these prosperous Sunni towns were populated by functionaries and regime loyalists.[84] Both towns had good roads, schools, and water systems. Unlike much of Iraq, there were no persistent electricity outages. Rawah, about 175 miles northwest of Baghdad and 60 miles from the Syrian border, was a town of approximately 20,000, though some estimated that only 5,000 residents were left there when 4-14 arrived. Anah had a population of approximately 30,000. The unit also had responsibility for an area called Ramana—a series of small towns along the northern bank of the Euphrates stretching up to the Syrian border.

In August 2005, 4-14 replaced the 2nd Squadron, 14th Cavalry Regiment of the 1-25 SBCT, which had been ordered to deploy to Rawah from Mosul in July. The 2-14th mounted the first sustained coalition military presence in the town since the invasion. MNF-W gave 4-14 the mission of securing the Iraq-Syrian border and interdicting the flow of insurgents and supplies into Anbar and up toward Mosul. By mid-September 2005, 4-14 had found itself detached from the 172nd SBCT and placed under the operational control of the Marine Corps's 2nd Regimental Combat Team, commanded by Colonel Steve Davis, at Al Asad Air Base. In the fall of 2005, Colonel Davis exercised command over the units conducting counterinsurgency operations in western Anbar Province along the Euphrates River to the Iraq-Syrian border.

Like virtually all U.S. units operating across Iraq, 4-14 functioned as a composite, joint task force—drawing on personnel from across all the military departments and a variety of civilian agencies. Working under the Marines proved to be an adjustment for 4-14, as it did for other Army units in Anbar, because of different vernacular and dissimilar unit reporting requirements required by the Marine headquarters. Like other units, however, 4-14 quickly overcame these difficulties and fashioned a good working relationship with the Marine headquarters staff.[85]

As the insurgency in Anbar gathered strength in 2004 and 2005, concerns at MNF-W grew about the important role that Rawah played as a staging point for supplies and insurgents coming in over the Syrian border. Rawah was also believed to be a way station for insurgents going north to Mosul, and Anah was seen as an important command node for the Anbar insurgency. After the storming of Fallujah in November 2004, U.S. troops periodically swept the area looking for caches and high-value targets. In one well-publicized raid in Rawah in May 2005, U.S. forces captured a key associate of Abu Musab al-Zarqawi, Ghassan Muhammad Amin Husayn al-Rawi, and discovered a car bomb factory housing vehicles, 200 bags of phosphate, machine guns, and ammunition. One Rawah resident told coalition forces during the raid that "Ghassan Amin runs Rawah and nobody does anything without Ghassan Amin's approval."[86] As was the case throughout much of western Iraq during late 2004 and early 2005, however, U.S. forces lacked the numbers to remain in areas after the raids had been conducted. When 2-14 arrived in July 2005, Rawah and Anah were firmly in the grip of an insurgent group called the Jama'at al Tawid al Jihad, or Group for Monotheism and Jihad. This Al Qaeda–affiliated group consisted mostly of local Sunni insurgents, with a few foreign fighters that piloted suicide vehicle attacks. Captain Tom Hart, the 4-14 fire support officer, estimated that 98 percent of the local population in Rawah passively supported the insurgency.[87] In Anah, insurgents had blown up the police station, chased out the police, and killed the chairman of the city council.[88] A campaign of fear and intimidation effectively discouraged the local population from aiding U.S. forces. In a practice that was standard at the time in the province, the insurgents showed particular brutality to any residents trying to join the local police. In July 2005, one unlucky recruit's head was thrown into a banana crate in the Rawah main square as a message to others thinking of joining the police.[89] While the population wasn't necessarily overtly hostile when 4-14 arrived in August, it didn't exactly welcome the new unit with open arms.

The 4-14's parent unit, 172nd SBCT, had no prior experience in conducting counterinsurgency operations and had not been previously deployed to Iraq. The unit was in the process of transitioning from a light infantry unit to one of the Army's new Stryker Brigade Combat Teams. It was fielding its new Stryker vehicles—a 19-ton wheeled vehicle based on the same chassis as the Marine Corps's light armored vehicle—when it was ordered to deploy in Iraq in late 2004. The 172nd SBCT, based in Fort Wainwright, Alaska, represented the third Army infantry brigade to integrate the new Stryker wheeled vehicle. The vehicle and its supporting network-centric technologies constituted the leading edge of the Army's transformation efforts started in 1990s by then Army Chief of Staff General Eric Shinseki to make the Army lighter and more easily deployable around the world. The Stryker brigades represented a centerpiece of the broader Army-wide effort to move its combat organizational structure from division- to brigade-size units. The units incorporated many advanced digital capabilities that gave them the latest technologies for command and control, enhanced situational awareness from sensor feeds, reconnaissance, and networked capabilities that enabled real-time communications between units. Many of the vehicles carried classified computer terminals that enabled intelligence and other information to flow quickly in real time from headquarters down to the tactical level.

The SBCT's digital capability flowed from a suite of electronic systems called the Army Battle Command System, which consisted of a variety of different elements. The backbone was the Force XXI Battle Command, Brigade and Below network, or FBCB2, which forms the principal digital command and control system for all Army units below the size of a brigade. The FBCB2 consists of a variety of hardware and software elements that interconnect platforms through a communications infrastructure called the Tactical Internet, which allows the transmission of encrypted data down to the tactical level for situational awareness, intelligence, and command and control. Another important supporting component of the FBCB2 is the all source analysis system, or ASAS, which automates the processing of various kinds of intelligence (human intelligence, signals intelligence, electronic intelligence, communications intelligence, and measurement and signature intelligence) with an integrated architecture throughout all command echelons.[90] These technical capabilities provided 4-14 with avenues for innovation on the battlefield as will be discussed below.

The 4-14th worked hard in its predeployment training to get its soldiers qualified on these systems—no easy task given the complexity of the various systems and databases.[91] These series of complex systems gave 4-14 the ability to integrate real-time situational information and sensor data into a force level database with simultaneous display and near real-time access for the commander and staff to receive an integrated common operational picture at each echelon. The systems facilitated the flow of voice and data throughout all the tactical echelons of the brigade, providing situational awareness, intelligence, global positioning coordinates, and knowledge of all friendly force locations. The 4-14's communications capacities were augmented during its time in Anbar with TACSAT radios, or tactical satellite radios, which allowed 4-14 to communicate over the wide distances in its area. During its deployment in Anbar, 4-14 scavenged enough of these radios to equip the whole group with the devices, and all patrols out of its bases were required to have them in addition to the organic FBCB2 system.[92]

The 172nd began preparations for its deployment in August 2004 at Fort Wainwright, where deteriorating weather conditions during the fall introduced significant challenges to the training cycle. The unit had not received its full complement of Strykers and had to cycle each company through its training sequence one at a time—handing off vehicles and equipment between each unit entering the training sequence. By November, the unit had constructed a series of new live-fire training ranges and villages to train its soldiers in how to fight in an urban environment. The villages were replete with role playing Iraqis, imams, and local tribal leadership. The 172nd was well aware it was deploying into an active insurgency—a mission for which it had no doctrinal grounding. *FM 3-21.31, The Stryker Brigade Combat Team,* represented the operative doctrine at the time of the deployment—though it played little role as a direct guide in preparing the 172nd for battle in Iraq.[93] The 4-14th performed as the brigade's RSTA, or Reconnaissance, Surveillance and Target Acquisition, and drew also upon *FM 3-20.96, Reconnaissance Squadron (RSTA)* as additional doctrinal guidance in structuring its approach to the battlefield. The 4-14th's overall doctrinal purpose in the 172nd SBCT was to:

> provide accurate and timely information over a large operating area. . . . The cavalry squadron (RSTA) provides a great deal of the information required by the commander and staff to conduct proper planning, direct operations, and visualize the future battlefield. The squadron possesses robust capabilities to successfully meet the varied and unique intelligence, surveillance, and reconnaissance challenges inherent in smaller-scale contingency operations and in major theaters of war. The cavalry squadron (RSTA) has an extensive HUMINT (human-derived intelligence) capability and acts as the eyes and ears of the commander. In addition, RSTA operations allow the commander to shape the battlefield, accepting or initiating combat at the time and place of his choosing.[94]

As was the case with the entire unit, there were no plans to use the 4-14th in its doctrinal role operating across the brigade's area of operations. The 172nd was scheduled to fall in on the battle space of 1/25 SBCT on a unit-for-unit replacement in and around Mosul and Ninewa Province in northern Iraq. The 172nd structured its training and deployment preparations based on extensive information from video conferences with the 1/25 SBCT, classified e-mail, and information transmitted via the Army's growing informal digital network of passing along lessons learned in Iraq counterinsurgency operations via the website managed by the Army Center for Lessons Learned (CALL) at Fort Leavenworth.[95] In addition to the CALL website, the 172nd drew extensively on information on Strykernet—a dedicated website for all Stryker units to pass along after-action reports and other documents dedicated to improving the situational awareness of incoming units. The 4-14 was slated to replace the 2-14 in Tal Afar to the west of Mosul and to act as "land owner"—operating similarly to an infantry battalion but with fewer personnel. Hence, the unit's training prior to deployment focused on standard infantry small unit tasks of patrolling and fire and maneuver.[96] In the spring of 2005, 4-14 detached from the 172nd in Alaska and moved south to Fort Bliss, Texas, to train in cooperation with the U.S. Border Patrol around El Paso. Freitag believed that the experiences of border interdiction working along the U.S.-Mexico border might prove relevant to conditions in Iraq. The wide open spaces of the southwestern United

States were similar in some respects to the terrain he expected to encounter in northern Iraq. He devised a training sequence while at Fort Bliss in which each third of the unit cycled through gunnery training, military operations in urban terrain in an old mining town, and operations in support of the border patrol.[97] After completing its three-month sequence at Fort Bliss, the unit cycled through the Joint Readiness Training Center in Fort Polk, Louisiana, in May 2005 along with the rest of the 172nd SBCT—the final stop for most Army units before deploying to Iraq in August.[98]

After the unit arrived in northern Iraq in the late summer, it deployed into northern Anbar to replace the 2-14 cavalry group as part of the broader effort to stem the flow of insurgents and supplies down the Euphrates River valley to Ramadi and Fallujah. While 4-14 arrived in Rawah with no operational experience in fighting a counterinsurgency, the unit worked hard to prepare itself for the environment in its training workup and availed itself of the Army's extensive informal network that passed along previous experiences of units through e-mail, the Army's Center for Lessons Learned website, and Internet blogs.[99] The unit drew heavily on the prior experiences of 3/2 and 1/25 SBCT deployments in Mosul from February 2004 to October 2005.[100] The lack of doctrinal background in COIN proved no hindrance to the unit; it quickly built a series of COIN competencies as it adapted to the environment around Rawah. As noted by the 4-14 Operations Officer (S-3), Major Doug Merritt: "There was a lot of learning on the fly. It was the fight you get versus the fight you want."[101] Like the Marine units operating in adjacent sectors, the COIN-related practices built by 4-14 were generated organically within the unit and built via a series of complex feedback loops that included all command echelons. As will be detailed below, the tactical intelligence fusion cycle developed by 4-14 included inputs from virtually all parts of the organizational structure—ranging from the soldiers in the field to the intelligence section and unit's senior leadership. The 4-14's process of organic battlefield innovation proceeded in much the same way as the Marine units in adjacent sectors as the unit sought the right balance between kinetic and nonkinetic tools. The process was also undoubtedly shaped by its institutional predispositions as an Army unit and the particular technical capabilities brought to the fight by its RSTA-SBCT structure. Like its parent organization, the 4-14 demonstrated significant learning capacities during its deployment that flowed from an organization-wide philosophy that emphasized cross-functional collaboration and learning.

The 4-14 consisted of 800 troops and sixty Stryker vehicles with additional personnel that took the task force numbers to between 1,200 and 1,500 personnel. The unit's main combat power came from its two cavalry troops and one infantry company. When it deployed into Rawah in August 2005, it partnered with the Iraqi Army's 3rd Battalion, 1st Brigade, 1st Division, or 3/1/1 and the 5th Battalion, 3rd Brigade of the Department of Border Enforcement (DBE) stationed in a small outpost along the Syrian border. The ISF's 3/1/1 was later replaced by a brand new Iraqi battalion (3/2/7) in the fall of 2005. Training the new ISF battalion became a major focus for 4-14 in the late fall and winter of 2006.

Throughout its year fighting in Anbar, 4-14 self-generated a scheme of operations that included commonalities and differences with the Marine units operating in adjacent sectors. Like the Marines, 4-14's mission was relatively straightforward: (1) prepare Iraqi Security Force and the border detachments to assume their own battle space and provide security across the area of operations, or AO; (2) engage the local tribal and city leadership to respect the Rule of Law and to establish a city government structure in Rawah and Anah; (3) disrupt the insurgents' ability to conduct operations and prevent foreign fighter movement from Syria into Iraq; (4) deny insurgent access to the civilian population through information operations and civil-military operations; (5) control the lines of communication through vehicle control points; (6) maintain the initiative through precision targeting of insurgent command and control and their support structure; (7) fight in the insurgent decision cycle; and (8) protect coalition soldiers by improving force protection and the standard of living on COP Rawah, COP North, and COP Anah.[102] As straightforward as these priorities seemed, 4-14's innovation process differed significantly from that of its neighboring Marine units.

The unit conducted operations in what was known as AO Saber—an area of 27,200 square kilometers in western Iraq that stretched north along 68 kilometers of the Iraq-Syrian border. The area was the size of the state of Rhode Island—the largest battalion-size area of operations in western Iraq. Freitag freely described 4-14's operations as "an economy of force mission."[103] The wide open spaces of the area were conducive to the unit's twenty-five Long Range Advanced Scout Surveillance Systems, or LRAS, mounted on the surveillance version of their Strykers. The system provided units with ability to do real-time, long-range optical reconnaissance across Saber's wide open spaces. The unit divided Saber into three operational subsectors: Black Horse, along the Syrian Border; Assassin, north of the Euphrates River; and Apache, south of the Euphrates.

Like the Marine Corps units in the neighboring sectors, 4-14 slowly spread its presence throughout its area in a series of outposts. In late August, 4-14 deployed to Rawah and completed COP Rawah three miles outside the town.[104] As part of its mission of securing approximately seventy miles of the Iraq-Syrian border, 4-14 drew upon help from the Seabees' Naval Mobile Construction Battalion 17 in building Combat Outpost North, or COP North, and improving the road leading from the outpost back to Rawah. COP North served as the 4-14 platform on which to begin standing up the Iraqi border enforcement battalion to seal the Iraq-Syrian border. By the spring of 2006, 4-14 had helped establish a series of small border posts manned by the Iraqis. The border outposts had a measurable impact on reducing the flow of insurgents across the Syrian border, and the outposts throughout the rest of Saber proved decisive in the defeat of the insurgents in the area. By the late spring of 2006, the network of outposts had spread to COP Anah and a smaller outpost in Reyanah in the southeast section of Saber.

While 4-14 worked on securing the Iraq-Syrian border, it confronted a violent insurgency in and around Rawah and Anah that greatly complicated other COIN activities, such as civil-military operations, information operations, and development of the police force.[105] The unit quickly realized the importance of developing a tactical intelligence fusion cycle to better integrate intelligence and operations. The 4-14th had a robust intelligence analysis section, or S-2, that worked to integrate all the different "ints" of the intelligence discipline: MASINT, or measurement and signature intelligence; ELINT, electronic intelligence; COMINT, or communications intelligence; HUMINT, or human-derived intelligence; SIGINT, or signals intelligence; and IMINT, or imagery intelligence. Since the 4-14th functioned as an SBCT RSTA, its intelligence section was larger than a conventional infantry battalion (eight versus six). Prior to its Iraq deployment, the unit also picked up a trained, all source intelligence technician (Chief Warrant Officer Matt Gray) that had significantly more experience than comparable intelligence specialists in a typical infantry unit.[106] According to the 4-14 operations officer, "The ability of the squadron to fuse intel into valuable targeting was phenomenal. The Army assets provided by our brigade gave the squadron a significant advantage [over the Marines], which resulted in our targeting process to be superior."[107] While 4-14 had studied and practiced the integration of intelligence and operations during training, it never developed the integration process until combat. The fusion process received critical support from special operations forces that operated throughout Anbar in coordination with conventionally structured units.

The relationship between intelligence and operations is a lively topic for debate in the Army. The respective arguments can be summarized in two positions: (1) intelligence drives maneuver; and (2) maneuver drives intelligence. The tension between these positions was summarized by the Army's Joint Readiness Training Center in its 2004 newsletter with the statement: "Remember, Intelligence drives maneuver, but the commander drives intelligence."[108] The 4-14's experience demonstrated that neither of these perspectives was correct. The unit discovered that intelligence and maneuver went hand in hand, enabled through its digital network that tied patrolling soldiers to their S-2 and higher intelligence echelons. Early in the Anbar deployment, the unit's intelligence fusion process proved instrumental in the discovery of what at the time was one of the largest discoveries of insurgent arms and supplies in Anbar Province—the so-called Chicken Farm cache in early October 2005. In late September, 4-14 launched Operation Appaloosa in Anah. It had been provided a series of "high value targets," or HVTs, by its intelligence section that were believed to be involved in the insurgency. The operation picked up seven of the ten targeted individuals during the operation. In the course of the interrogations, several of the detainees provided information on additional members of the insurgent network as well as the presence of a large cache of weapons used for insurgent operations located southeast of Anah. While initial searches of the suspected areas proved unsuccessful, information from the interrogations helped vector JSTARS, or Joint Surveillance, Tracking and Surveillance Radar System, coverage of the area. JSTARS is an Air Force aircraft that provides wide area surveillance coverage through a variety of different sensors over the province that was controlled by the MNF-W headquarters. The JSTARS surveillance subsequently picked up indications of activity at night in the area. That information helped direct a 4-14 patrol to a farm southeast of Anah. While the farm appeared empty, one of the enlisted men in the raiding party hotwired a backhoe on the site and started digging in an area just south of the farm that had several odd-looking depressions in the terrain. The patrol soon uncovered a cache of 220 rocket-propelled grenades; 40,000 7.62mm armor-piercing rifle or machine gun rounds; 100 2.75-inch-diameter rockets; 10 mines; 1,000 .50-caliber rifle or machine gun rounds; 68 mortar rounds; 100 shotgun shells; 20 improvised claymore mines; 1,959 artillery projectiles; one rifle; a mortar bipod; four 122mm rocket engines; one mortar tube; 3,000 feet of detonation cord; 37 40-pound bags of red and black explosive powder; and 100 1-ounce primers.[109] The ammunition took three days to destroy.

Continued development and refinement of the intelligence fusion cycle proved its worth throughout the 4-14 deployment in Anbar. The task of intelligence collection got down to the unit level, with information then pushed back to 4-14's S-2 section virtually instantly for analysis and matching against various data sets available to the All Source Analysis System. The fusion of tactical, operational, and strategic-level data sets allowed soldiers to use the group's digital links as intelligence enablers that got coupled with the mobility of the Stryker to cover extremely large areas in the SABER area. The fusion cycle worked both ways: information got pushed up the chain of command almost instantly, and the 4-14 S-2 section could push analyzed SIGINT hits to a platoon on patrol forty-five minutes away from its headquarters to guide the patrol's tactical questioning at that point on the ground by a platoon.

The information allowed units to determine target locations, execute raids, and capture their targets—a process that featured continuous information flow back and forth across the digital domain in near real time from the tip of the spear to the command and intelligence elements. The process was further refined and perfected in the 172nd's deployment in Mosul, as will be detailed in Chapter 5. After assisting in the November 2005 clearing operations in Steel Curtain, 4-14 continued refining its fusion process that steered its own kinetic approach away from clearing operations to swarm tactics and precision raids featuring the Stryker's mobility.[110]

The fusion cycle again demonstrated its value in the disruption of insurgent operations during the fall of 2005 and into 2006. The slow but steady progress of gathering locally generated intelligence and fusing that with national-level databases allowed 4-14 to continue targeting insurgent leaders that led to steady discovery of insurgent arms caches throughout the area. On February 16, 2006, 4-14 picked up a high-value target in Rawah that revealed the general locations of arms caches used by the local insurgent cells. Three days later the unit uncovered what up until that point was the largest arms cache discovered in Anbar.

The fusion process worked well in vectoring the Iraqi border detachments and 4-14 elements to intercept border crossings. JSTARS feeds and imagery intelligence were used repeatedly in the spring of 2006 in a variety of operations to stop the flow of smugglers and insurgents entering Iraq on a variety of routes. In January JSTARS reported on eight to nine crossings per month. By June, the border crossings had been reduced to one.[111]

The refinement in the intelligence fusion cycle perhaps reached its peak in the spring and summer of 2006 in the elimination of an insurgent cell operating

An insurgent cache or artillery shells found by the 4-14 in Anbar province in the fall of 2005.

out of Anah by the 131 troops of Apache Company, 4th Battalion, 23rd Infantry (4-23) commanded by Captain Matthew Albertus.[112] Operations by 4-23 reflected a firm grasp of the intelligence fusion cycle in its four-month operation against an entrenched insurgent cell. Albertus relied primarily on the development of locally derived intelligence, which he integrated with other intelligence sources being fused at COP Rawah to build a comprehensive understanding of the insurgent network. Albertus successfully combined the intelligence fusion cycle with the mobility and data processing capacities of his Strykers that destroyed the insurgent cell with comparatively few force-on-force engagements.

The troops took up residence in COP Anah in late March, about two miles outside the town—the first sustained presence around Anah since the invasion. The establishment of COP Anah was followed by the establishment a month later of a small outpost in the village of Reyanah with eight U.S. and thirty Iraqi soldiers. Critical elements of the intelligence fusion process were put in place immediately. The 4-23 brought a tactical intelligence human intelligence team with it into COP Anah and began receiving volumes of technical intelligence from COP Rawah soon after it opened.[113] These technical sources of information were gradually complemented by a stream of human intelligence being gathered through the 4-23 patrols in and around the town on the insurgent cell there headed by Abu Hamza—a senior AQI operative in western Anbar.

Albertus began parallel efforts in April and May to reintroduce a police force in Anah and managed to recruit seven applicants that were subsequently sent off to Jordan for training. He also began outreach efforts to the city council, which had been cowed into submission by AQI. By June, the insurgent cell was feeling the pressure and mounted a series of unsuccessful attacks on COP Anah using mortars and suicide vehicle bombers. The lack of success of these attacks gradually undermined the insurgents' support in the town. By the end of June, the newly trained policemen returned. The intelligence from several of the new police enabled the human intelligence team to build a wiring diagram of Anah's sixty-person insurgent network. Through the intelligence sourcing, the unit's tactical intelligence team built a comprehensive understanding of the history of network members that had previously worked together, as well as the social re-lationships of the network participants. As described by Albertus, "This is where the targeting process at the company level really starts to come together. We've got a source that's very reliable; a HUMINT team that's executing on a daily basis, gathering information; we've got platoons out there gathering informa-tion on a daily basis; we've got an S-2 shop that we're completely tied in with. Now we've got actionable targets that we're able to [conduct close target recon-

In addition to finding large quantitites of artillery and mortar shells, the 4-14 operating in Anbar routinely uncovered arms caches like those above, comprised of IED triggering devices.

naissance] targets on, conduct these precision raids."[114] In early July, Albertus conducted a series of targeted raids on locations identified from the fusion of signals and human intelligence. The raids detained fourteen of Abu Hamza's top aides—all without firing a shot. The key catch was Wissam Hussein Ali, a senior AQI operative coordinating the movement of insurgent supplies and men across the Syrian border. Abu Hamza was subsequently withdrawn from the area by AQI. The intelligence flow that had started as a trickle in April and May had turned into a waterfall over the course of several months, and by the end of July the Anah cell had been completely disrupted. In the three months of taking down the cell and capturing thirty-two of its members, Company A fired live rounds on only three occasions: engaging two suicide vehicle bombers and when ambushing a roadside bomb cell. The HUMINT team leader summarized the action by stating: "It's been more of a police action than combat."[115]

The 4-14 approach to fighting the insurgency evolved gradually over its deployment in Anbar. Operations in October were dominated by the constitutional referendum in which 4-14 provided local security for the vote in Rawah during which 1,500 residents voted. In December during the parliamentary elections, 3,864 residents of Rawah voted. In November, the unit focused upon dealing with improvised explosive devices (IEDs), conducting cordon and search operations, and supporting Operation Steel Curtain in November. Operation Percheron in the first two weeks of December found the unit and its ISF counterpart conducting cordon and search operations in the Ramana region—the towns along the Euphrates River in the western part of the Saber area of operations. These cordon and search operations disrupted insurgent operations, provided local security for the December 15 elections, built relationships with ISF and border detachments, and continued to generate detainees to feed intelligence into the 4-14 fusion process. Operation Percheron established an ISF/4-14 presence in Ramana, instituting a series of tactical control points throughout the area at key road junctures. The operations uncovered thirteen weapons caches in the area and detained twenty-one suspected insurgents.

By December, after continuing to gain familiarity with the area, Freitag's staff developed an overarching COIN framework for the entire unit that integrated kinetic and nonkinetic effects. The methodology became the basis for 4-14's operations during the remainder of its deployment. The four LOOs— developing the Iraqi security forces, combat operations, civil military operations, and information operations—bore striking similarities to the emphasis in the neighboring Marine sectors. The development of the COIN methodology coincided with the decision in the spring of 2006 to minimize organization-wide squadron operations and instead push operations to company- and platoon-level operations in their various sectors.[116] This allowed local commanders to develop their own battle space by themselves without undue interference from the headquarters in Rawah. As noted by 4-14 Operations Officer Major Doug Merritt: "The biggest success was early on, breaking up the battle space and pushing responsibility down from the squadron commander to the company and troop commanders and letting them develop their own AOs. We did that, backed off in the headquarters and minimized squadron-level operations."[117] Pushing the fight down to the platoon level led to further improvements in the flow of information from the units up the chain of command that improved situational awareness throughout the area of operations. Meritt noted: "Information was bottom fed for the most part, aside from some SIGINT or higher assets we'd tie together."[118]

The four tiers of the 4-14 COIN methodology (ISF training, combat operations, civil-military activities, and information operations) became the basis for the development of an integrated approach to the battlefield as the unit searched for the right mix of kinetic and nonkinetic effects. After focusing on kinetic operations during the fall of 2005, 4-14's emphasis during the spring began to reflect the integration of the other pillars into the unit's operations. Like the Marines in neighboring sectors, Freitag and his staff began reaching out to the local leadership—with mixed results. Relationships with the local tribal and political leaders never developed as fully as they did in other neighboring sectors. Freitag also never built a comprehensive information operations campaign, because of the requirement that all information operations be routed for prior approval through the regimental headquarters.

Other pillars of the evolving COIN strategy began to fall into place during the fall. In November, 4-14's B Company started individual and small unit training programs with the newly arrived Iraqi Army 3/2/7—a brand new battalion with extremely poor skills. During February and March of 2006, 4-14 cycled the Iraqi battalion through a series of training exercises that emphasized weapons handling and safety, reflexive fire techniques, vehicle searches, squad level movement techniques, and developing rules of engagement. On March 6–8, 4-14 conducted weapons training and marksmanship proficiency for 3/2/7, following that with an eight-day course on advanced medical procedures for the battalion's medical platoon.

January 2006 marked the beginning of the "Year of the Police" in Iraq, and

4-14 moved to build up the ISF and Iraqi police capacity throughout its area. TF 4-14 initiated the process through a series of recruiting drives that began in March and went through June. In March, 4-14 launched Operation Lippizan—a three-day recruiting drive in Rawah that began with handbills and broadcasts urging the locals to sign up. The recruits went through a four-station interviewing process. At the first station the recruits were interviewed by the Police Transition Team to make sure they fit the requirements to be an IP. The second station checked their proficiency in reading and writing Arabic. At the third station the recruits were medically screened to ensure they did not have any medical issues. The recruits were then given a physical fitness test to make sure they were able to meet the physical requirements of being an IP. The operation attracted thirty-one recruits that got sent off to training. In early April, four recruits were identified and sent to the senior leadership courses at Baghdad.

To coordinate the unit's efforts, 4-14 created two police training teams, or PTTs, from within the unit supported with vehicles, radios, and other supplies. The PTT established a training regime that included advanced marksmanship, sensitive site exploitation, and combat lifesaving skills. Some of 4-14's senior noncommissioned officers took the lead in creating the training schedule and establishing the facilities for use by the new police. In Operation Brumby, 4-14 partnered with the 3/2/7 Iraqi Army to set up police recruiting drives in and around the towns of Rawah and Anah. The first IP screening took place at the Youth Center in Anah on April 6. Over the next four days, seven recruits completed the screening process and were sent to COP Rawah in preparation for onward movement to the Jordan Police Academy. In Rawah, twelve additional candidates were screened on the same day. The recruits were put through a four-stage interview process designed by the Police Transition Team (PTT). At the first station the recruits were interviewed by the PTT to make sure they fit the requirements to be an IP and check their proficiency in reading and writing Arabic. At the second station the recruits received a medical screening. The third station was a BATTS screening where the candidates were placed into a database and screened against known AIF. The recruits then received a physical fitness test to make sure they could meet the physical requirements of being an IP. The IP screening site closed with a total of nine candidates screened with seven approved. By the middle of June, the first police recruits began returning to the area from their training in Baghdad and Jordan and started standing up the first police force in the area in nearly two years.[119]

The 4-14 experiences in AO Saber featured civil-military operations tailored to fit within the evolving approach on the battlefield that sought to balance kinetic and nonkinetic activities. The unit launched $75,000 worth of construction projects in its area as part of its effort to enhance the area's governmental infrastructure.

The COIN methodology of 4-14 reflected the evolution of the unit's approach to the COIN fight that, during the fall of 2005, started out with cordon and search operations and, as the situation stabilized in Saber, created space for the unit to integrate civil-military operations into its repertoire. The unit worked to help support the redevelopment of local governance in Rawah and Anah. In the spring, it ran a series of civil-military operations programs at various small towns in its sector, distributing radios, blankets, and medical care into local communities. It also launched some small reconstruction projects to help improve local services, focusing on projects such as water treatment and repairs to government buildings.

The experience of 4-14 in Saber reflected the clear evolution of counterinsurgency procedures throughout its one-year deployment in Anbar. Despite its lack of doctrinal grounding in counterinsurgency, the unit drew extensively upon multiple sources of information to structure a training cycle that prepared it for the environment in western Iraq. This process developed iteratively over time until, by the spring of 2006, 4-14 had built an integrated approach to the battlefield that balanced kinetic and nonkinetic effects. The unit immediately demonstrated its proficiency and adaptability in the kinetic portions of the fight. The cordon and search operations in the fall of 2005 demonstrated the unit's conventionally oriented capacities. For example, the unit appeared ready to apply the intelligence fusion cycle quickly upon arrival in its discovery of the chicken farm cache in October 2005. The procedures developed early in the deployment enabled 4-14 to develop an HVT targeting process that unit members believed was superior to its Marine counterparts.

SUMMARY OF 4-14 INNOVATION

The experience of 4-14 reflected both commonalities and differences with the Marine units fighting in its contiguous sectors. Like the Marine units, 4-14 first established a continuous presence in insurgent areas, using its COPs to disrupt insurgent operations and gradually improve local security. Like the Marine units, it also partnered with and helped develop Iraqi military capability as well as Iraqi police units. As was the case in other sectors of Anbar, the local police forces had been destroyed or driven into hiding by AQI's campaign of fear and intimidation.

Working continuously on its intelligence fusion cycle, 4-14 was helped by the SBCT's advanced technologies and its robust intelligence manning structure. The intelligence fusion cycle played a major role in the unit's operations in disrupting insurgent operations through the discovery of caches and the building of the knowledge of the insurgent networks. In Anah, this process reached its peak over a four-month period in which the fusion of all-source intelligence drove unit operations that rolled up the insurgent network in the town with little direct kinetic operations and no collateral damage to the town and its inhabitants. Like Lieutenant Colonel Marano's 1-7 operations in Al Qaim, 4-14 proved adept at orienting its organizational capacities in intelligence generation and analysis to the needs of its operators.

A critical underlying element to the evolution of 4-14's approach over the year was the mindset of the unit leadership that had a number of important characteristics. First, the leadership had no preconceived ideas about how it was supposed to structure its operations to achieve battlefield success. Just as important, there was no "school solution" being forced down either the military or civilian chain of command.

Like the Marine battalions in adjacent sectors, 4-14 demonstrated itself to be a learning organization that constantly searched for an optimal solution to the problems posed by the insurgency in its area. It drew upon disparate sources of information to overcome its lack of historical experience and perspectives in fighting an irregular war. The organizational leadership freely delegated authority and, by necessity because of its small size and large operating area, quickly adopted a scheme of distributed operations not unlike that of its Marine counterparts.

The unit clearly understood that the human terrain constituted the critical center of gravity in the fight. Since it lacked the numbers to establish a continuous presence in the area, it creatively drew upon the technical and operational capacities of the Stryker to effectively contest control over the population with the insurgents. The tactical intelligence fusion cycle employed by 4-14 developed iteratively over the deployment and proved effective in uncovering numerous arms caches and, in the spring of 2006, helped take down the insurgent network in Anah in operations that included little overt applications of force. It is clear that 4-14 grasped the concept of effects based operations and throughout its deployment sought an appropriate mix of kinetic and nonkinetic tools in applying its organizational capacities in the environment. It built new organizational capacities from scratch with the development of its police training teams that flowed from its recognition of the critical role that Iraqi police could play in helping to establish local security.

4 WARTIME INNOVATION IN ANBAR
The Battle for Ramadi, July 2005–March 2007

As Marine and Army units slogged through different phases of the clear, hold, and build approach to COIN in western Anbar, units in and around Ramadi confronted a very difficult environment but nonetheless exhibited the same dialectical process of organically generated innovation as they also executed their version of clear, hold, and build. Much of the halting first steps in the COIN campaign in Ramadi happened under the watch of the 2nd Brigade, 28th Infantry Division brigade combat team, or 2/28, which deployed to Anbar in late July 2005. The unit conducted operations in an immense 18,000-square-mile area that included Ramadi, the area west of Fallujah, east of Hit and extending north to Lake Tharthar and south of Lake Habbaniyah. The unit's area of operations extended from Ramadi to Habbaniyah, about thirty miles to the east, encompassing about 450,000 people living along the Euphrates River. Ramadi, the capital of Anbar, clearly represented the most important city in the area—the largest city between the Syrian, Jordanian, and Saudi borders and Baghdad. Like Al Qaim in western Iraq during 2004 and 2005, Ramadi had become an insurgent haven. During 2005 and 2006 the city arguably became the key battleground between the U.S. military and the insurgents for control over Anbar. Over this period, Ramadi enjoyed the reputation as the most dangerous city in Iraq outside Baghdad.

This chapter covers combat operations by the 2/28 and the 1/1 in Ramadi over the period from July 2005 to March 2007. It opens with a summary of the insurgency in Ramadi before moving on to a discussion of the process of battlefield innovation within the two brigades. The 1/1 section includes two in-depth case studies of battalion-level operations by 1st Battalion, 6th Marines and 1st Battalion, 37th Armored that operated next to each other in Ramadi during the fall and spring of 2006–7. Both battalion-level cases clearly illustrate a process of iterative tactical adaptation that developed into organizational innovation. Operations by these two brigades need to be seen as a continuum on which the wrenching, iterative process of adaptation and innovation by 2/28 set the conditions for the 1/1's successful COIN campaign in the fall of 2006. The iterative process of adaptation and innovation that unfolded between the units when 2/28 was replaced by 1/1 a year later bore a resemblance to the experiences of the two Marine battalions examined in Chapter 3. Like the Marine battalions in western Anbar, the momentum established by the 2/28 in its COIN campaign proved instrumental in creating the necessary conditions for success when the 1/1 took over a year later in the summer of 2006. The commander of the 1/1, Colonel Sean MacFarland, described the twelve-month period of the 2/28's operations as critical to the success of the 1/1 in the fall of 2006. A standard Army way of thinking about a battlefield is that the objective is to "find, fix, flank, and destroy the enemy." As described by MacFarland, the 2/28 performed the "find and fix" portions of the mission, which gave him the opportunity to "flank and destroy" the enemy, as will be described in the second half of this chapter.[1] The COIN campaign of these two units spanning eighteen months together represented a critical turning point in the war that broke the back of AQI and the Sunni insurgency in Anbar by the spring of 2007.

When the 2/28 arrived, the insurgents had fought the U.S. military to a standstill in Ramadi—and some U.S. commanders doubted whether "victory" was achievable in any form. Marine Colonel Steve Davis, a commander of Marine Forces in western Anbar, told a reporter in August 2005: "I don't think of this in terms of winning," adding that he expected the insurgency in Anbar to last for years.[2] In May 2006, one correspondent aptly summarized the situation: "The sheer scale of violence in Ramadi is astounding."[3] The same reporter quoted a Marine officer citing statistics indicating that Ramadi accounted for two-thirds of all the roadside bombs, outright attacks, and exchanges of gunfire in all of Iraq during a recent reporting period.[4] Throughout the 2/28's deployment, the unit experienced forty-two events a day involving gunfire, IEDs, or direct attacks—one of the highest rates of all U.S. forces in Iraq. During its deployment the brigade suffered 1,052 attacks by IEDs, and successfully detonated another 1,083 roadside bombs. When the 2/28's successor unit arrived a year later, it reported on the existence of a system of complex, subsurface IED belts throughout the city.[5]

By the summer of 2005, Ramadi had become a center of insurgent resistance in Anbar in the aftermath of the Fallujah battles in late 2004. In and around the city an array of nationalist groups, criminals, and AQI cells competed and cooperated in the struggle for local power and influence. AQI represented the most dangerous of the insurgent groups because of its brutal tactics and its lack of interest in negotiating with coalition forces. The second most powerful group consisted of Iraqi nationalists, and included a wide array of religious and tribal leaders. This group sought to drive U.S. forces from the city and restore their political and economic power. Nationalist groups were particularly entrenched in Ramadi, which was home to former members of the Ba'ath Party and un-employed Iraqi soldiers who had been thrown out of work when the Coalition Provisional Authority disbanded the Iraqi Army in May 2003. The last problem group for the 2/28 in Ramadi consisted of criminals—who exerted a powerful influence on the area's underground economy that had built up during Saddam's era. While the criminals had no overarching formalized structure, they sold arms to the insurgents and actively intimidated the police and local tribal leaders.[6]

As in western Anbar, opposition to the occupation initially united the di-verse array of insurgent groups and criminals operating in the city. During 2004 and 2005, the lack of troops crippled attempts by U.S. and Iraqi armed forces to exert control over the city's urban neighborhoods. COIN operations by U.S. units in the city mostly consisted of targeted raids mounted out of their base areas. In the spring of 2005, a variety of reports noted that the Marines of E Company, 2nd Marine Division had lost a third of its troops—the highest casualty rate of any unit in Iraq—during its six-month deployment.[7] Sergeant Tom Coffey, a platoon commander for the 2/28 in southern Ramadi, summa-rized the predicament of U.S. forces: "There's no way I can control this area with the men I have," said Coffey. "The reports are that the insurgents are using these southern control points because they're open. We can't keep them closed because I don't have the manpower."[8]

Large sections of the city had been largely abandoned by U.S. troops, giving the insurgents de facto control over many neighborhoods. Public beheadings by insurgents were widely reported in the summer of 2005, and in one particu-larly gruesome incident children were reported to be playing soccer with the head of a decapitated Iraqi Shiite militia member.[9] Insurgents had blown up all but one of Ramadi's police stations in the winter of 2004–5, and the Iraqi police and National Guard in the city had effectively disbanded. To make mat-ters worse, in the spring of 2005 the Iraqi national government in Baghdad sent Shiites to police Ramadi—a city that was nearly 100 percent Sunni.[10] Needless to say, most of the police remained barricaded inside their stations.

In early 2005, coalition troops mounted a series of conventionally oriented clearing operations, but the lack of troops made it impossible to keep a sustained presence in the city.[11] Iraqi Army Colonel Ali Hassan voiced the frustration of many when he stated, "We just go out, lose people, and come back. The insurgents are moving freely everywhere. We need a big operation. We need control."[12] The troop shortage became so acute that one Marine unit acknowledged stationing cardboard dummies with camouflage shirts along highway observation posts.[13] The casualties suffered by the Marines in Ramadi by IED attacks on their high-mobility multipurpose wheeled vehicles, or HMMWVs, became a cause célèbre in the U.S. Congress to speed up deliveries of more heavily armored versions of the vehicles.[14]

The 2/28 deployed into Anbar in July and August of 2005, relieving the 2/2 Infantry Division. The composite unit consisted of four battalions from the Pennsylvania National Guard, the 1-172 Armor Battalion from Vermont, the 2-222 Field Artillery Battalion from Utah, the 231 Military Intelligence Company from Kentucky, the A/138 Signal Company from Indiana, the A/1-167 Armored Cavalry Troop from Nebraska, and the 779 Maintenance Squadron from Tennessee. Other task force members included the 3rd Battalion, 8th Marine Regiment (which replaced 1st Battalion, 5th Marine Regiment in September 2005), and the 1st Battalion, 506th Infantry Regiment (from the 101st Air Assault Division), which replaced the 2nd Battalion, 69th Armored Regiment in January 2006).

The unit faced significant built-in hurdles as it deployed into Iraq—circumstances that might have militated against the innovation process. At the time of the 2/28's deployment, the Army was only a year into its plan to "transform" its force structure by moving from larger and heavier division-size units to a lighter and more flexible brigade that boasted greater organic support capacities. The 2/28 deployed as a "legacy" unit largely structured and equipped to fight a campaign-style conventional war. In its case, the primary combat power of the 2/28 came from its M-1 tanks and Bradley Fighting Vehicles—hardly a force structure suited to the demands of the urban COIN environment that it would confront in Ramadi. The brigade's core consisted of National Guard elements that could not be expected to display the same combat competencies as their active-duty counterparts.

Other hurdles stood in the 2/28's path. As a legacy unit, the 2/28 arrived in Iraq expecting to be sourced in its area of operations for critical logistical requirements, such as heavy equipment transporters, trucks, and tractor trailers to move its troops and equipment. For an armored brigade, battlefield mobility depends on robust transportation support. Doctrinally, logistical support should have come from an Army main support battalion, consisting of a transportation company with three platoons (light, medium, and heavy). These three platoons would have provided fifty to sixty 5-ton cargo trucks, tractor/trailers, and, most important, heavy equipment transporters (HETs)—the only Army tactical transportation asset that can move M1 tanks, Bradley Fighting Vehicles, and Paladin tracked artillery. Upon arriving in Ramadi, the 2/28 discovered that it would have to rely on one Marine heavy equipment transporter platoon with only four HETs that supported operations throughout Anbar. As an expeditionary light infantry force with a ship-to-shore logistical support structure, the Marines were simply not organized or equipped to support an Army armored brigade. As the 2/28 logistics officer, Major Mark Pike, commented: "The lack of a major support battalion in our area of operations coupled with virtually no support from the Marine Corps meant we were on an island logistically."[15] Eventually, the 2/28 consolidated its logistical operations at Taqqadum Air Base, stocking 5,000 lines of stock numbered parts managed by the 228th Forward Support Battalion. The 228th had to build a wall around its logistical hub to stop logistics-starved neighboring Marine units from stealing parts. The unit's adaptation to its logistical shortfalls would constitute one of the most significant parts of the innovation process during its deployment.[16]

The brigade deployed into Iraq with no prior experience operating together outside the training workup, and it had no prior experience in conducting counterinsurgency operations on an organizationwide basis. Five months of training at Camp Shelby, Mississippi, and the National Training Center at Fort Irwin, California, focused almost exclusively on conventional military operations that emphasized fire and maneuver exercises designed to bring firepower to bear on the enemy.[17] As noted in the unit after-action report: "The training was maneuver oriented and focused primarily on survival on the battlefield of Iraq."[18] Upon arriving in Iraq, the 2/28 discovered that much of its training was irrelevant in Ramadi.[19] Over the course of its deployment, the 2/28 reoriented itself into an organization that embraced effects-based operations in a complex environment—although limitations in its capacities prevented the unit from fully executing effective operations across the spectrum of combat operations.

Upon its arrival in Anbar in July 2005, MNF-W's command guidance to the 2/28 was to "neutralize the insurgency and develop the Iraqi Security Forces in order to create a secure and stable environment for the Iraqi people."[20] The

2/28 commanding officer, Colonel John Gronski, initially established a series organizationwide tasks to achieve this objective: (1) protect the force; (2) defeat insurgent leaders; (3) reduce insurgent weapon systems; (4) destroy or detain insurgent forces; (5) increase public support for military operations; (6) train and integrate Iraqi Security Forces; (7) treat the Iraqi civilians with dignity and respect; and (8) conduct aggressive combat patrols (mounted and dismounted) and employ observation posts. These tasks represented Gronski's commander's intent for units in structuring their battlefield operations. He continuously revised this intent through the 2/28's deployment in recognition of his evolving understanding of the complex environment and the need to rebalance the lethal and nonlethal tools at the unit's disposal. While the 2/28 did not fully achieve the objectives given to it upon arrival, the unit clearly played an instrumental role in setting the conditions for the success of the units that followed.

The brigade's deployment scheme sought to surround the insurgent bastion in Ramadi, restrict the insurgents' movement, and provide security along the main roads supplying forces in western Iraq. Manpower shortages represented an important limiting factor in the 2/28's building the diverse array of operational capacities needed to fully prosecute a successful COIN campaign. Many of the 2/28's fixed locations were located on the roads—major supply routes, or MSR, Michigan and Mobile. This was for a good reason—the roads represented the main supply routes to all units operating in western Anbar, and they were frequent targets for IED attacks. Requirements for base security as well as providing convoy security along the main roads drained the combat power of the brigade and reduced its ability to provide a continuous presence in the contested city. The unit constantly searched for work-around solutions to generate additional combat power. Longer shifts were employed on enduring tasks that made possible the temporary generation of combat power in the elections during the fall of 2005, but the lack of manpower proved to be a systemic problem throughout the deployment. Providing base security at Camp Blue Diamond, Camp Ramadi, and Camp Taqqadum airfield and the Al Asad airfield represented a huge drain on the 2/28's available manpower to mount sustained patrols throughout contested areas in the province's urban and rural areas. Gronski estimated that inherited tasks associated with base security and protecting the roads connecting his base areas absorbed 80 percent of the 2/28's combat power.[21] The unit had deployed into theater with less combat power than its predecessor, the 2/2 Brigade Combat Team, which had two additional battalion headquarters and four additional maneuver companies. Gronski estimated that the 2/28's enduring tasks limited the ability of the unit to provide the continuous presence needed throughout the city.[22] Some parts of the city were rarely patrolled at all because of manpower shortages. Most of the 2/28 remained in outposts outside the city center, with the exception of the embattled 3-8 Marines, which occupied the government center and a few other facilities in downtown Ramadi. Establishing a continuous presence in Ramadi's insurgent-controlled neighborhoods proved impossible for the 2/28. The 2/28's successor, the 1/1, arrived in the summer of 2006 with two additional maneuver battalions and a reduction in the battle space assigned to the brigade.

In addition to limited combat power, the unit struggled throughout its deployment to overcome a shortage of transportation vehicles of all kinds: the unit lacked its own organic transportation equipment. Because it was a legacy organization, the logistics for the unit were supposed to be "service provided," but the Army never provided the main support battalion to provide the brigade with equipment. Sometimes the unit had to wait a month to receive heavy equipment transporter (HET) support—a critical capability for the brigade, particularly its armored battalion.[23] Heavy equipment transporters were the only equipment capable of moving battle-damaged vehicles from the battalion areas of operations to the repair and cannibalization depot at Camp Taqqadum. During its time in Iraq, IED attacks destroyed 94 of the 2/28's vehicles: 8 M1A1 Abrams tanks, 19 M2A2 Bradley Fighting Vehicles, and 45 M114 and M1151 up-armored HMMWVs.[24] Removing destroyed equipment to base areas for repair and cannibalization represented a major challenge throughout the deployment.

The unit worked hard to overcome these limitations, devising its own transportation section—an ad hoc unit consisting of twenty-five soldiers split between Taqqadum Air Base and Camp Ramadi. The unit built its own transportation security detachment to protect convoys on Topeka's dangerous roads and established a quick reaction force to move to attack sites quickly to retrieve damaged or destroyed vehicles. These organizational changes resulted from individual initiative in the unit to meet the difficult logistical challenges of the environment. To counter persistent IED attacks on the main roads, the unit built procedures to mount resupply operations at night in blackout conditions using night vision goggles. Since the insurgents lacked infrared night vision equipment, their attacks proved less effective during these operations. In the fall of 2005, the brigade's logistics support elements overcame these obstacles to erect 1,000 concrete barriers in Ramadi for the October referendum and the

December elections. In the spring of 2006, the unit constructed six new Iraqi police stations and company-size outposts for the ISF in central Ramadi. None of the organizational changes or tactical adaptations introduced by the 2/28's logistics elements were covered under existing doctrinal SOPs. As noted by the brigade's logistics officer, Major Mark Pike: "Doctrine is only a guide. The operational environment ultimately dictates mission requirements. In combat, leaders must be flexible and willing to break with doctrine to ensure mission success." [25]

The task of securing MSR Mobile fell to the 2/28—one of the two largest roads (along with MSR Michigan) running from east to west through Anbar. The six-lane highway received heavy use to keep the Iraqi and U.S. military bases resupplied throughout the province all the way to the Syrian border. Needless to say, the highway also received heavy use by the local population and the insurgents. Insurgent attacks using IEDs and gunmen mounting ambushes constituted a constant headache and source of casualties for the 2/28 during its deployment. The unit also had no experience in joint operations with the Marine Corps and lacked experience in working with a higher Marine headquarters, which had control over the MNF-W area of operations. Midway through the 2/28's deployment, the unit was given responsibility for providing security of forward operating base Blue Diamond, the former headquarters of the 2nd Marine Division adjacent to Camp Ramadi. Last, but not least, the 2/28 had to provide manpower for four military transition teams (or MiTT teams), two of which were not in Topeka, to train the ISF. Over the course of its deployment, two additional ISF brigades deployed into the area for partnering operations. All of these myriad requirements reduced the tactical flexibility of the 2/28.

The 2/28 faced a complex battlefield and challenging physical terrain. Ramadi was a densely populated urban environment intersected by the Euphrates River and various canals that divided the city and provided numerous ingress and egress routes for insurgents and their supplies. Insurgents mounted approximately three to five IED attacks each day. The unit successfully found and detonated another 1,100 IEDs during its deployment.[26] It also faced constant sniper fire, mortar attacks, and RPG ambushes. The unit averaged forty-two "significant activities" per day in the form of IED attacks, complex insurgent attacks, sniper fire, and attacks via indirect fire like mortars and rockets.[27] Major Brad Tippett, the operations officer for the 3-8 Marines, which patrolled central Ramadi, summarized the general rule of operating in the city: "You can't just walk down the street for a period of time and not expect to get shot at."[28] The operational tempo of the brigade remained extremely high throughout the deployment.[29] During the winter of 2005–6, the brigade mounted a series of "cordon and knock" operations throughout the sector, turning up numerous arms caches of insurgent weapons and equipment. On January 16, one operation discovered eleven arms caches that took two days to unearth. Nearly two tons of ordnance materials were blown up by the unit's explosive ordnance disposal team.[30] A series of operations over the next several weeks uncovered a continuous stream of arms caches in and around the city. During *Operation Wadi Aljundi* in late January, Marines of the 22nd Marine Expeditionary unit found 4,300 artillery and mortar rounds, rockets, and mines, 267 kilograms (590 pounds) of explosive powder, 10,000 rounds of various types of ammunition (ranging from small-arms to tank main gun rounds), 300 blasting caps, approximately 100 feet of detonation cord, and several working machine guns and mortar systems.[31]

While the 2/28 faced an adversary shooting at it every day, it also became quickly apparent that kinetic tools could play only one part—albeit a very important part—in applying combat power in that environment. The brigade slowly transitioned from a unit trained for a conventional battlefield to one working in a "full spectrum" environment. This required a change in the mindset of the entire unit. General Gronski described the intellectual evolution in his and the unit's approach as follows:

> I will admit, due to the violent nature of the insurgency, it was a challenge to de-escalate. Let me explain this further; we were keeping in touch with 2/2 ID when we were still at Camp Shelby via the secure internet protocol router network (SIPRNET) and we saw that things in that particular area of operation were very kinetic. So, we were going in with the mindset that we were going to have to maintain that level of operations tempo (OPTEMPO) and the training that we were getting at Camp Shelby was more oriented around kinetic operations rather than non-kinetic, as I already mentioned to you. And, by the way, no knock on 2/2 ID; but they were not doing that much with leader engagement before we got there just because of the way things had been evolving there. It was not that they didn't want to. There just weren't that many opportunities for them to engage the tribal leaders. So, when we got there, a level of tribal leader engagement was just beginning and I'm sure if 2/2 ID had stayed there longer that they would have evolved into more robust leader engagement. But, it was just the nature of the timing and evolution. So, and I think I told you this in the mission statement that we had, our mission statement

that was given to us by 2d MARDIV was to neutralize the insurgency, which really put the onus and focus on killing and capturing insurgents. But, as we continued to conduct operations there, we came to realize that we had to transition more to securing the population."[32]

The evolution in the 2/28's approach on the battlefield in the apportioning of its resources between the kinetic and nonkinetic tools gathered momentum throughout the summer and fall of 2005. The brigade immediately recognized the importance of building local relationships, which were virtually nonexistent when the unit arrived. Gronski gradually reoriented his commander's intent priorities to reflect the need for nonkinetic tools. One of his initial changes featured a focused command emphasis on the importance of "first do no harm" as a governing philosophy.[33] This first order principle constituted a significant departure from the initial commander's intent upon arriving in Ramadi. As noted by Gronski, "When we first got to Iraq, we thought it was necessary to dominate our area of operations at the physical level and over the course of time realized that dominating at the moral level would be more decisive. That meant adjusting our approach to do our best at de-escalating situations, rather than escalating."[34]

In July and August 2005, the 2/28 initiated a plan of local leader engagement to try to draw the local tribal sheikhs into a dialogue on how to improve local security. Working with the governor of Anbar who lived in Ramadi, Maamoun Sami Rashid al-Awani, Gronski and his staff struggled to set up a weekly meeting with the sheiks in central Ramadi. The local tribal leadership in and around Ramadi had been disrupted by war—much of the leadership had either been killed or had fled the country and resided in Jordan. This had created a vacuum that AQI had exploited in entrenching itself in Ramadi and the surrounding villages. During the first meeting in midsummer, tribal leaders complained bitterly about the checkpoints set up around the city and the disruptions caused to the residents. The reality was that citizens in Ramadi could spend hours in traffic jams caused by the roadblocks. The local sheikhs also objected to random searches of houses and what they regarded as petty harassment by the Iraqi Security Forces.[35] During the meetings the sheikhs expressed strong opposition to the coalition presence and urged the United States to leave— quickly.[36] Gronski and his staff developed two information operations themes out of these meetings: (1) that the U.S. presence would be reduced when the violence subsided; and (2) that the United States would make every effort to limit collateral damage and the deaths of innocent civilians. Gronski noted that "many of the Sheiks that showed up at the government center once a week and that we engaged with were local insurgents. They had some level of control over these local insurgents and they could have cared less about Islamic law type government forming in Anbar Province, like AQI wanted. What these nationalists wanted, what these local insurgents wanted, was simply the American force to leave the city so that they could start to get back to some semblance of normalcy."[37]

Following the weekly meetings, the 2/28 gradually changed its procedures to address the sheikhs' concerns and the atmosphere in local interactions started improving. Checkpoint procedures changed so that the units conducted only random searches, improving the flow of traffic into and out of the city. The unit also abandoned the practice of random house searches in targeted neighborhoods and instead searched houses based only on intelligence gathered from local Iraqis. Another outcome from the meetings was that Gronski and his staff realized that its indirect fire on insurgent positions was having a negative effect on the local populace. The brigade had a platoon of M109A5 Paladin howitzers at Camp Ramadi and another in Camp Habbaniyah that it used for "terrain denial" and counterfire in response to incoming mortar and rocket attacks. By the end of 2005, the 2/28 had greatly reduced both counterbattery and terrain denial fires by its artillery. Instead, the unit moved to more targeted indirect fire missions that used specific tactical intelligence on insurgent positions—intelligence that gradually improved over the year. During heavy fighting in April 2006, the 2/28 used the guided multiple-launch rocket system, which could deliver rounds from forty miles away at Camp Fallujah into an area fifteen by fifteen feet.[38]

During the engagement meetings, Gronski and his staff pressed the local leadership to generate local recruits for the police force, emphasizing that the U.S. presence would decline as Iraqis took responsibility for local security. Throughout the fall of 2005, the 2/28 sought to establish a system of local security to support the December 2005 parliamentary elections.

The contest of wills between the 2/28 and the insurgents ricocheted back and forth in December 2005 as the unit prepared for the parliamentary elections. In an attempt to disrupt the elections, a hooded group of 300 insurgents seized control of the city center on December 1 and distributed leaflets stating that the city had been taken over by Al Qaeda.[39] Undeterred, the 2/28 kept pressing ahead with its program of local leader engagement, with some limited success. On December 9, angry local citizens turned over the so-called Butcher of Ramadi, a senior AQI operative named Amir Khalaf Fanus, providing an indication of local splits among insurgent groups.[40] Progress continued in the nonkinetic sphere in the fall during the run-up to the December 15 elections in which 60 percent of eligible voters participated—a significant increase from the 2 percent of the population that voted in the January 2005 elections. The emphasis on building local relationships and reconstituting the internal police continued to gain momentum. At a widely publicized recruiting event held at the glass factory in Ramadi, hundreds of local residents appeared to join the police. The unit believed that the high turnout represented a turning point with the local leadership, which by this time had clearly decided to support the 2/28's efforts to reconstitute the police force.[41]

While the 2/28 gradually built relationships with the local leadership over the fall of 2005, AQI struck back with a vengeance in early 2006. While approximately 1,000 Iraqis stood in line to sign up for the police outside the Ramadi glass and ceramic factory, a suicide bomber attacked the site, killing 70 and wounding hundreds of the potential recruits. Also killed was Lieutenant Colonel Michael McLaughlin, leader of the 2/28's local leader engagement programs, who had been instrumental in convincing local leaders to support the recruiting drive.[42] The recruiting continued during that day and through the next week, and 200 recruits were later shipped out for Iraqi police training.[43] By the end of February 2006, the 2/28 had screened and identified 1,586 recruits, and 379 had been shipped off for training. Following the successful recruiting efforts, the 2/28 re-established the Iraqi Police Provincial Headquarters in Ramadi and built two additional police stations in the vicinity of Habbaniyah, located halfway between Ramadi and Fallujah.[44]

The glass factory attack and the halting steps toward reconstituting the local police represented the beginning of the deterioration in the relationship between AQI and local leaders.[45] In late January, an unattributed report appeared in the London-based newspaper *Al Hayat,* asserting that "Tribal Popular Committees" had stopped operations against U.S. forces and turned on AQI. Other Sunni organizations in Ramadi, however, reported that they were engaged in warfare against the Iraqi government and AQI.[46] Sunni nationalist insurgent groups—the 1920 Brigades, the Anuman Brigade, and the Islamic Mujahidin Army, were also reported to have formed a body known as the Advisory Council to combat AQI. During the spring of 2006 AQI launched a brutal and extensive murder and intimidation campaign to prevent reconstitution of the local police. On January 16, 2006, AQI assassinated Sheik Nasser al-Mukhlif,

the leader of the Albu Fahad tribe and a former professor of physics at Anbar University—one of the most powerful and influential tribal leaders in Ramadi.[47] Mukhlif had strongly condemned the glass factory attacks and had met
with Iraqi Prime Minister Al Jafari and U.S. Ambassador Zalmay Kahalilzad the
day before his murder. The Albu Fahad had a long history in Ramadi dating
back hundreds of years. It was one of the main subtribes of the Dulaym tribal
confederation—the main Sunni tribal group in Anbar. Like many of the Sunni
tribal groups, the Albu Fahad, while not ardent supporters of Saddam, opposed
the coalition occupation and were strong Iraqi nationalists. While initially supportive of AQI, Mukhlif and the tribe grew disaffected with AQI during late
2005 and participated in meetings with the 2/28 to establish local security for
the parliamentary elections.[48] His death had a particularly chilling effect on the
willingness of the local tribal leadership to cooperate with the 2/28, although
in retrospect the killing of such an important tribal leader represented another
important step down the road that led to the deterioration of relations between
Sunni nationalists and AQI.

AQI also destroyed cell phone towers throughout the Ramadi area, causing a
disruption in the communications between sheikhs, government officials, and
U.S. military units. AQI's murder and intimidation campaign slowed the momentum of the 2/28's local engagement efforts in early 2006, and local leaders
eventually stopped coming to the Provincial Government Center to meet with
Colonel Gronski and his staff.[49] However, many of those who already had seats
for police training classes did show up and ship to training. Through the early
months of 2006, hundreds of Iraqis who had been processed did ship to police
training. AQI then began to murder local Iraqi police once they had returned
from training and begun to work at local police stations. The battle with AQI
continued through the spring of 2006. Anti-AQI local militias began appearing
in March and April. One militia participant, a welder named Ahmed Abu Ilaf,
seemed to capture the mood of the period in stating: "We are a group of the
Anbar people who want to get rid of Zarqawi . . . because this is the only way to
make the Americans withdraw from Ramadi or Iraq in general."[50] One of the
important militia leaders was said to be Ahmed Ftaikhan, a former intelligence
officer in Saddam's disbanded army.

Despite growing opposition, AQI unquestionably remained in control of the
city. One Sunni sheik who declined to be quoted by name aptly summarized the
dilemma for the local tribal leadership: "We hope to get rid of al-Qaeda, which
is a huge burden on the city. Unfortunately, Zarqawi's fist is stronger than the

Americans. . . . [In Ramadi] Zarqawi is the one who is in control. He kills anyone who goes in and out of the U.S. base. We have stopped meetings with the
Americans, because, frankly speaking, we have lost confidence in the U.S. side,
as they can't protect us."[51] Another sheikh, Bashir Abdul Qadir al-Kubaisi of the
Kubaisat tribe in Ramadi, expressed similar views, noting: "Today, there is no
tribal sheikh or a citizen who dares to go to the city hall or the U.S. base, because Zarqawi issued a statement ordering his men to kill anyone seen leaving
the base or city hall."[52]

As the police began to reconstitute itself, the brigade established a cordon
of operating outposts within the city. As the ISF stood up additional units, the
brigade slowly spread out into outposts surrounding the contested neighborhoods. The brigade eventually established eleven combat outposts between Ramadi and Habbaniyah. The outposts in Ramadi would form the cordon from
which its successor unit, the 1st Division, 1st Brigade (1/1), would then assault
the contested city in the summer and fall of 2006. While the ISF and Iraqi police were located in and around these outposts, neither organization had yet
emerged as an effective instrument in improving local security.[53]

During 2005–6, General Casey sought to stand up the ISF as quickly as possible to take over responsibility for fighting the insurgents. The 2/28 encountered numerous hurdles as it struggled with the dual missions of fighting the
insurgents and standing up the Iraqi Army. When the 2/28 arrived in July 2005,
there had been one Iraqi Army unit task organized to its predecessor unit, the
2/2. Throughout its year in Iraq, the 2/28 eventually partnered with three Iraqi
Army brigades and an Iraqi Special Commando Police Brigade. Although the
unit gladly received these additional troops, the 2/28 quickly discovered that the
Iraqi Army units had limited combat capability and no organic logistics capacity. The Iraqi Defense Ministry contracted much of the support requirements
for its army. As the 2/28 discovered, these arrangements were a disaster, since
much of the contracted support never materialized or, if it did, was totally inad-
equate. It meant that the Iraqi Army effectively had no dedicated internal logistics support, and its units received little if any basic sustainment needs for food
and water. Iraqi units were delivered to the field and left on their own. During
April 2006, for example, the eastern Ramadi Ministry of Defense contractor
provided only four truckloads of food to sustain 1,200 Iraqi Army troops. The
remaining food convoys either never arrived or arrived with rotten food that
had to be thrown out.[54]

Lacking an organic support capacity meant the Iraqi forces had no trucks to move themselves and their supplies. As noted in the unit's after action report: "The IA basically had an entire division in the 2/28 BCT [area of operations] with no transportation company to move their commodities."[55] The result was the logistical requirements to support three new Iraqi brigades fell to the already stretched 2/28 logistics infrastructure. To support Iraqi Army troop movements, the 2/28 support battalion up-armored the troop/cargo areas of its five-ton cargo trucks using ballistic armor plating to protect the Iraqi troops from small arms fire. The Iraqi troops finally received their own up-armored vehicles from the Iraqi Defense Ministry in April 2006.[56] Gronski characterized the 2/28 attitude to this unanticipated mission:

> We had to provide the logistical support to these Iraqi units, because if we did not, nobody else would. I understood the MNC-I and Division Commander's intent was to get the Iraqi Army more involved in the fight and for my BCT to mentor, coach, and train the Iraqi Army so they could get more involved and take on more and more responsibilities for themselves. So, in preparing to deploy to Iraq, we really were not aware of the role we were to have in providing logistical support to the IA. It simply became an operational reality.[57]

The 2/28 gradually redeployed out of its main forward operating bases over the course of its deployment, establishing combat outposts in and around central Ramadi, along the main roads, and near the provincial headquarters. These outposts were jointly manned by U.S. and Iraqi troops. The unit also established four rebuilt Iraqi police stations during its deployment.

During the spring of 2006, a change in the brigade's mindset and COIN-oriented procedures further developed as the organization broadened its approach to integrate lethal and nonlethal tools on the battlefield. The unit launched an array of civil affairs projects as part of the "do no harm" philosophy that came to govern the activities of the 2/28. The brigade worked extensively with Marines from the 5th, 6th, and 3rd Civil Affairs Groups to bring millions of dollars to Anbar Province to start reconstruction projects focused on sewage control, clean water, electricity, educational assistance, and basic sanitation infrastructure.[58] These projects included the following:

- $2 million in medical supplies and equipment to 22 hospitals and clinics.
- 150 transformers at a cost of $800,000, improving the average availability of electricity from 8 hours to 12 hours per day.
- School supplies for 31 schools with 15,000 students at a cost of $305,000.
- Generators for the Ramadi General Hospital and the Women's and Children's Hospital that provided electricity 24 hours a day, 7 days a week.

JULY 2005–MARCH 2007   109

- Paid $900,000 in claims brought by Iraqis whose property had been damaged or destroyed by U.S. forces.
- The Provincial Reconstruction team in Ramadi was established.[59]

SUMMARY OF WARTIME INNOVATION BY THE 2/28

This unit arrived in Iraq in the summer of 2005 organized, trained, and equipped for a conventionally oriented battlefield—not for the COIN environment (even a very violent one) in and around Ramadi. The unit quickly realized that the skills practiced before its arrival would be of limited use in Ramadi. The 2/28 made numerous tactical adaptations in the field that flowed from a collective shift in the mindset of the brigade as it steadily gained an understanding of the environment. The unit built a complex mix of new organizational capacities during its deployment that did not exist prior to its arrival to meet the demands of the environment in Ramadi. The combination of the changed organizational mindset and the new organizational capacities make the 2/28 experience a textbook case of organically generated wartime innovation.

Initially, the brigade focused on neutralizing the insurgency and trying to build up the ISF in accordance with the mission priorities handed down from the Marine Expeditionary Force, or MEF, headquarters. To be sure, the 2/28 continued aggressive actions against the insurgents throughout its deployment, killing and wounding an estimated 1,750 insurgents. Gradually, and despite its systemic limitations, the 2/28 BCT shifted its focus to protecting the population and evolved toward the philosophy of "first do no harm" in its COIN operations. The 2/28 leadership worked hard to communicate this intent to small unit leaders and troops at all levels during battlefield circulation. The intent was consistently emphasized as documented in the fragmentary orders, or FRAGOs, and other communications from the brigade staff sent throughout the unit. Other steps taken to "de-escalate" on the battlefield included efforts to integrate the growing ISF forces into its operations in the spring of 2006. By March and April of 2006, the 2/28 started mounting combined and dismounted patrols with the Iraqi Army. Lastly, the 2/28 suspended most counterfire and terrain denial missions to minimize collateral damage to the local population.

Some of the most significant innovation occurred in the herculean tasks of the 228th support battalion to overcome its systematic limitations in logistics support. The unit created new organizations from scratch to provide security for its logistics convoys and developed procedures to keep its forward operating bases (FOBs) supplied at night to avoid IED attacks. The brigade developed work-around procedures to keep logistics support flowing to the combat elements despite the lack of expected logistics support that never materialized from the Army. Operating in the irregular warfare environment, the 2/28's logisticians effectively became additional combat elements in their convoys and vehicle rescue operations.

Eventually, the brigade established eleven combat outposts outside the established main forward operating bases, which made possible joint Iraqi-U.S. patrols in the contested areas. A number of police stations were created and manned by Iraqi police returning from training academies throughout Iraq. As a result of this success, insurgents began a murder and intimidation campaign that eventually had a destructive backlash in the fall of 2006. The challenge of executing the mission to protect the population during the 2/28's deployment was due primarily to the limited number of troops available to conduct operations in an area that was not only geographically large but also densely populated.

WARTIME INNOVATION OF 1/1 IN RAMADI, 2006–7

The 1st Brigade Combat Team, 1st Armored Division "Ready First" combat team, or the 1/1, replaced the 2/28 in Ramadi in June 2006. During the 1/1's deployment, the struggle with insurgents reached its climax in Ramadi. The fight progressed week-by-week, block-by-block, through the city's neighborhoods as the 1/1 re-established control over the city. The 1/1 campaign in Ramadi will go down as a textbook example of successful COIN operations that its commanding officer, Army Colonel Sean MacFarland, later referred to as a "three dimensional game of chess."[60] The deployment of the 1/1 into Ramadi came before the surge increased the overall numbers of U.S. troops in Iraq by approximately 30,000 during the first six months of 2007. It also came as the Defense Department reported that insurgent violence throughout Iraq had reached its highest levels in nearly two years.[61]

The progress made by the 1/1 in Ramadi in the fall of 2006 built on the steps taken by 2/28 in what could be called the "setting the conditions" phase of the battle. Like the 2/28, the 1/1 cycled through a variety of tactics, techniques, and procedures (TTPs) to find a combination that worked on the battlefield. That process saw organizational adaptation evolve into innovation as the organization juggled and then eventually arrived at the right balance between lethal and nonlethal tools.[62] In the case of both the 2/28 and the 1/1, each unit moved through iterative phases in the process of tactical adaptation that, at its end, had fundamentally changed the way the units applied their kinetic and nonkinetic tools on the battlefield.

A legacy armored brigade based in Freiburg and Giessen, Germany, the 1/1's organization normally consisted of two armor battalions, a mechanized infantry battalion, a headquarters company, and a brigade reconnaissance troop. Six months before its deployment, the unit received its direct support field artillery, engineer, and forward support battalions. Prior to the deployment, the armored portion of the brigade was lightened as two tank companies and two field artillery batteries were transformed into "motorized" formations. These predeployment modifications to unit organizations were not uncommon in Iraq as the U.S. ground force sought to better match its cold-war organizational structure to the demands of the Iraqi COIN environment. As will be detailed in Chapter 5, the 172nd Stryker Brigade turned its dedicated field artillery battalion into a maneuver element to provide additional combat power for the stretched brigade. An additional two tank companies in 1/1 served as "dual purpose" formations, trained for motorized and tank operations. The brigade's mechanized infantry retained all their Bradley Fighting Vehicles and also trained on motorized tasks.

The brigade deployed with a total of fifteen maneuver-capable companies. This organization provided two tank companies, two "dual-purpose" companies, four motorized companies, four mechanized infantry companies, the Brigade Reconnaissance Troop, and three combat engineer companies. Upon arrival in Ramadi in June, the 1/1 integrated the 1st Battalion, the 6th Marine Regiment (1-6) out of Camp Lejeune and the 1st Battalion, 9th Army Regiment out of Fort Carson, Colorado, as well as the 1st Battalion, 506th Infantry; the 1st Battalion, the 6th Infantry Regiment; and the 1st Battalion, 35th Armored Regiment. In the late summer of 2006, a series of routine unit rotations occurred; the 1-6 Marines relieved the 3-8 Marines; the 1-9 Infantry relieved the 1-506 Infantry; the 2-37 Armored relieved the 1-6 Infantry; and the 1-77 Armored relieved the 1-35 Armored Regiment. The 1/1 unit structure reflected the widespread use of task-organized combat teams that fought the Iraq war. These teams integrated disparate elements from a variety of sources into a single combat unit. In this case, the 1/1 added the 1-6 Marine Battalion from Camp Lejeune and the Army's 1-9 from Fort Carson, Colorado. The brigade also had a mechanized infantry company attached from the 2nd Brigade, 2nd Division.

The 1/1 boasted important advantages over the 2/28 when it deployed into

Ramadi in June 2006. First, much of the brigade had prior experience operating in Iraq in 2003–4 during the Shia rebellion, and its German-based noncommissioned officer corps had spent significant time in the Balkans in the 1990s policing the Dayton accords.[63] Importantly, the brigade also spent four months in Tal Afar in western Ninewa Province from January to May 2006 where it got acclimated to the counterinsurgency environment following the 3rd Armored Cavalry Regiment's COIN operations in the city. The experiences in Tal Afar in executing the clear, hold, and build approach to COIN proved instrumental in structuring the 1/1's approach to operations in Ramadi.[64] When the 1/1 deployed into Ramadi in June 2006, MNF-I and MEF headquarters reduced the area of operations in Topeka by taking away responsibility for Habbaniyah from the 1/1. Lastly, MEF headquarters gave the 1/1 two additional maneuver battalions to add further to the unit's usable combat power. These steps combined to give the 1/1 greater flexibility in structuring its operations in Ramadi.[65]

The four months spent in Tal Afar proved to be a particularly important phase of the 1/1's deployment that helped prepare it for operations in Ramadi. The brigade arrived in Tal Afar in January 2006, relieving the 3rd Armored Cavalry Regiment that conducted a much publicized COIN campaign in the city that had been masterminded by Army Colonel H. R. McMaster. After clearing operations through the city, Colonel McMaster dispersed the regiment into platoon and company-size outposts in the fall of 2005. While overall security inside Tal Afar dramatically improved after operations in late 2005, concentrations of insurgent resistance remained in the city.[66] The 1/1 deployment in the spring of 2006 saw its units spread widely throughout Ninewa Province, ranging from the wide-open spaces along the Syrian-Iraqi border to the urban areas of Tal Afar. During the 1/1's deployment in Tal Afar, the unit focused extensively on building local relationships and mounting civil military operations to restore order in the city. The unit built on the momentum in the area generated by the 3rd ACR, developing and refining various TTPs that would be used in Ramadi several months later, such as operating out of combat outposts, local leader engagement and community relations, and civil-military operations, or CMO.

MacFarland received broad guidance from MEF headquarters when his unit deployed into Ramadi to relieve the 2/28. As recalled by MacFarland, he was told to "fix Ramadi" and not destroy it, as had happened in the pitched battles to wrest control of Fallujah from insurgents in November of 2004 that had largely destroyed the city.[67] When the 1/1 arrived in Ramadi in June, the local population believed that another Fallujah-type assault to retake the city was imminent.[68] MacFarland's staff developed a plan to retake the city, but sought to avoid destroying it in the process. The unit planned to spread the brigade out slowly throughout the city in jointly manned Iraqi and U.S. combat outposts to take on the insurgents directly in the areas where they were strongest. Within a month after arriving in Ramadi, the 1/1 began dispersing out of the main forward operating bases at Camp Ramadi, Camp Corregidor, and Blue Diamond.[69]

MacFarland later referred to the 1/1 campaign developed by his staff as similar to the "island hopping" campaign employed by the Marines in the Pacific during World War II: "With new outposts established in an ever-tightening circle around the inner city, we wrested control of areas away from the insurgents. As areas became manageable, we handed them over to newly trained Iraqi police forces (whom we kept a watchful eye on), and used the relieved forces elsewhere to continue tightening the noose."[70] The operation would first complete the isolation of the insurgents in the city, deny them the use of key infrastructure, and secure the major lines of communication across the city.[71] The brigade's campaign minimized the use of close air support, and tank and artillery fire in an effort to limit collateral damage that would alienate the local population. The battle in Ramadi would be fought on the U.S. side primarily by company commanders and their rifle squads in tandem with special operations forces.[72]

The unit had actively developed critical SOPs that it would use during the Ramadi campaign—the building of combat outposts.[73] The experience of the 1/1 with COPs was deemed so significant that the unit recommended that the Army integrate TTPs for COP design and use into formal doctrine.[74] By the end of the 1/1's deployment, MNF-I headquarters would release guidance to all units in Iraq urging the adoption of the COP planning and construction SOP developed by two of the 1/1's units: the 1st Battalion, 37th Armored Regiment "Bandits" and the 16th Engineer Battalion.[75] As will be shown in the 1-37 case study, site selection and COP construction proceeded on a systematic basis during the unit's push into the contested neighborhoods of south-central Ramadi. To man the COPs, MacFarland increased available manpower for combat operations by reducing the personnel performing mission route security and by removing many of the static posts along the road network in and around Ramadi that had been established by the 2/28.[76]

MacFarland sought and received the authority from his higher headquarters at the MEF in Camp Fallujah and MNF-I in Baghdad to design his own campaign plan. As was the case in the western Anbar operations, higher headquarters freely delegated authority down to its executing units and made little attempt to micromanage the battle from afar, despite the political pressure that would follow from the casualties incurred in the campaign's initial phase. Mac-Farland commented to one journalist: "You name it, I tried it. . . . I had a lot of flexibility, so I ran with it."[77] The fight for Ramadi would involve the simultaneous application of lethal and nonlethal tools. MacFarland freely delegated responsibility to his battalion commanders for the initial kinetic "kick in the door" phase of the campaign,[78] but he and his battalion commanders would be intimately involved in helping to build local relationships with tribal leadership in the fight against AQI to consolidate the gains after the clearing operations. When MacFarland arrived in Ramadi, he built on the 2/28's aggressive efforts to rebuild a local police force and worked to enlist local tribal leadership to split off the Sunni nationalist groups from the insurgency in the fight against AQI. The spring of 2006 had seen AQI aggressively striking back at the 2/28, killing at least six tribal leaders and other locals it suspected of cooperating with coalition forces. When the 1/1 arrived in Ramadi in July, the unit found a Ramadi Police Force that was virtually nonexistent, despite the efforts of the 2/28 throughout the spring. The police claimed to have 420 active police officers out of 3,386 authorized, although only about 140 of these officers ever showed up to work, with fewer than a hundred present for duty on a daily basis.[79]

When the 1/1 arrived in Ramadi, much of the established local tribal leadership had either been killed or had fled to Jordan. Anbar's democratically elected governor, Maamoun Sami Rashid al Awani, exercised little authority outside his sand-bagged compound in central Ramadi guarded by the Marines. The deputy governor had been assassinated during the fall of 2005. One school of thought at MNF-I headquarters argued for conducting the local liaison through the leadership in Jordan, which claimed to exercise influence over the tribes still in Ramadi.[80] MacFarland argued that it made more sense to co-opt and empower the tribal leadership on the ground by offering them jobs in the local police force that would remain in their own neighborhoods and, simultaneously, a hand in desperately needed reconstruction projects.[81] As was the case in Al Qaim, western Anbar, U.S. commanders adopted a lenient attitude toward the tribes' smuggling operations—so long as those operations didn't involve weapons and money that could be used against Coalition forces. The MEF headquarters voiced two objections to this plan: (1) the official U.S. approach emphasized backing the national government in Baghdad and the establishment of local institutions through elections. Re-arming the traditional power elite ran counter to this approach; and (2) it had questions about the backgrounds of the local tribal leadership that was involved in what it regarded as criminal and smuggling networks that also undermined the government in Baghdad.[82] Just as important, reaching out to the local leadership meant engaging insurgent resistance figures that were responsible for the deaths of U.S. soldiers and Marines.[83] MacFarland won the argument with the MEF staff.[84]

Tragic events played a role in the situation. On August 21, AQI murdered a local tribal leader, Albu Ali Jasim, mutilating his body and hiding it from his family—thereby denying the family a proper burial. The murder sparked outrage by members of the Jasim tribe.[85] The assassination coincided with an assault of 100 to 200 AQI fighters on a newly built Iraqi police station in the Jazirah area of western Ramadi near Camp Blue Diamond. The attack featured an explosive-laden dump truck detonated on the doorstep of the police station, directing channels of flames over the station's walls, spreading throughout the compound. Unlike previous attacks, however, this time the Iraqi police stood and fought and refused to be driven from their base. The Iraqis asked for and received assistance from the 1/1, which responded to the attack with reinforcements, medical attention for the burn victims, and air cover.[86] Within hours of the attack, the Iraqi police had resumed their patrols. Several weeks later, Colonel MacFarland and Lieutenant Colonel Tony Deane, commander of 1st Battalion, 35th Armored Regiment, called on a local sheikh, Abdul Sattar Al Rishawi, only to find twenty to thirty tribal leaders stuffed into his compound. The Americans had stumbled into the beginnings of the Anbar awakening that would prove critical in their battle with AQI in and around the city.

The Al Rishawis had crossed swords with AQI during 2006 in response to AQI's disruptions of the Rishawis' smuggling operations on the Baghdad-Amman highway, which had been an important source of revenue for the Rishawi tribe for many years. Sattar's father and two of his brothers had been killed by AQI in these clashes.[87] The meeting represented the beginnings of coordinated, armed tribal resistance to AQI by former soldiers in Saddam's army. The local sheikhs first called themselves the Jazeera Council in Ramadi—a group that expanded by September and then called itself the Sahawah Al Anbar, or the Awakening in Anbar. On September 17, twenty-five of Anbar's thirty-one tribes announced a broad agreement to unite against AQI.[88] This group subsequently became the focus of the 1/1's local engagement, with Sattar emerging as the leader of the anti-AQI tribal coalition. Sattar's group came to be called the Anbar Salvation Council. MacFarland and his staff immediately took steps to help provide security for the sheikhs, authorizing the establishment of neighborhood watches consisting of internal tribal militias that the 1/1 called "provincial Iraqi police." The 1/1 provided the groups with uniforms and authorized them to carry weapons within their defined areas.[89] From June through December 2006, nearly 4,000 local residents joined Ramadi's police force, with 90 percent of this number coming from tribes supporting the awakening.[90] The unit's successful local engagement program owed much to Captain Travis Patriquin, an Arabic-speaking former Special Forces soldier assigned to serve as the brigade's local engagements officer. Patriquin was later tragically killed by an IED in December 2006.

While MacFarland refused Sattar's offer to deal directly with nationalist insurgent groups like the 1920s Revolutionary Brigade, he indicated a willingness to "live and let live." The 1920s Revolutionary Brigade was a prominent Sunni-nationalist insurgent group, made up largely of former Baathist military officers.[91] MacFarland rationalized his stance as follows: "My view was that every saint had a past and every sinner has a future."[92] The Sunni nationalist insurgents went after AQI in the fall of 2006, with Fridays being a preferred day for operations, since AQI cells were typically in local mosques for prayers on Fridays.[93] On November 25, AQI responded to the east of Ramadi with a coordinated attack on the Albu Soda tribe, which had decided to join the awakening group. The 1/1 quickly responded with close air support and by the next day had moved elements of the 1st Battalion, 9th Infantry Regiment in to help defend the tribe's area.[94] The 1-9 commanding officer, Lieutenant Colonel Chuck Ferry, quickly helped augment security for the Albu Soda after the attack. The successful response to the AQI attack provided additional momentum to the 1/1's efforts to build local relationships. By the end of 2006, the local engagement initiative had significantly increased local support for the coalition. Support provided by the tribal leadership for local police proved extremely successful in improving security on the outskirts of the city. Tribal cooperation expanded dramatically over the six-month period following the 1/1's arrival.

For the purposes of this analysis, the experiences of the 1st Battalion, 37th Armored Regiment (1-37) and the 1st Battalion, 6th Marine Regiment (1-6) will highlight the process of tactical adaptation and innovation during the battle. These units were stationed in contiguous sectors of Ramadi: the 1-37 in the south-central section and the 1-6 at the very center of the city. The two units highlighted in this chapter, the 1-37 and the 1-6, operated in the epicenter of the fight in central Ramadi.

THE 1-37 IN SOUTH-CENTRAL RAMADI

Aggressive local engagement initiatives and police recruiting efforts proceeded simultaneously with sustained conventional military operations in the
city that began in July 2006. The fight in Ramadi was extremely violent, particularly in its initial stages. Like the 2/28, the 1/1 deployed into Ramadi as an
armored regiment with equipment (M1A1 tanks and Bradley Fighting Vehicles)
not traditionally thought of as relevant to successful COIN operations. The
1-37, however, found its armored vehicles extremely useful in its operations in
Ramadi. When the unit made contact with insurgents, it used its Bradley vehicles to maneuver troops with precise, direct fire support that could quickly
finish insurgent forces in fixed locations. The vehicles also proved instrumental
in securing the lines of communication and resupply between the COPs. As
noted by the 1-37 commanding officer, Lieutenant Colonel V. J. Tedesco: "A tank
cannon or a Bradley TOW missile are very precise weapons in an urban fight.
My tanks could kill AQI in a specific room and leave civilians in another room
of the small house shaken but unhurt. In short, tanks and Bradleys gave us an
advantage in the direct fire fight within the city that was a critical enabler to all
our operations, from installing COPs to census patrols."[95]

Only two weeks after arriving in Ramadi, the 1-37 started construction of
COPs to help cut off insurgent ingress and egress routes for south-central Ramadi—neighborhoods that had been off limits for coalition forces.[96] The unit
had started developing an expertise in COP construction when it rebuilt COP
Remagen in late May 2006 after it had been destroyed by a vehicle-borne improvised explosive device (VBIED). Lessons from this experience got applied
early in the campaign with the construction of three initial COPS—Iron, Spear,
and Falcon.[97] Insurgents responded to the COPs with platoon-size attacks on
the outposts that the 1-37 repulsed with heavy losses that crippled the insurgents' ability to launch future large-scale assaults. The 1-37 campaign gradually
pushed the insurgents to the western and northern parts of the city.

Tedesco established three main priorities for the unit. First, he wanted to
seize the physical terrain in order to gain access to the population and disrupt insurgent operations. Establishing the combat outposts would provide
the 1-37 with the ability to establish a constant presence through patrols in
the contested neighborhoods. Building COPs would provide the unit with the
means to begin seizing the physical terrain from the insurgents. The battalion
would also need to seize and control the lines of communications to sustain
the outposts and make possible communications between them. His logisti-

1-37's planning meeting for the operation to establish combat outpost Falcon in the fall of 2006.

cians would need access to the COPS to keep them resupplied. Second, he planned to expand his unit's control over the terrain through clearing operations and aggressive area ambushes of insurgents. The control over the terrain supported through census operations would move through each block, compiling a database on neighborhoods, residents, and their vehicles. Third, Tedesco sought to build capacities in the ISF so it could finish the fight against the insurgents.[98] Tedesco's priorities recognized that the city's population represented the critical objective for the battalion's operations. He developed his own plan of how the unit could best apply its conventionally oriented capabilities and training into Ramadi's COIN environment in ways that were consistent with MacFarland's plan.

The 1-37 executed its operations from June 2006 through February 2007. The unit's plan saw each sector within their section of the city bitten off in successive chunks through the establishment of COPs from July through December, starting with the establishment of COPs Iron, Spear, and Falcon in June. The 1-37 plan reflected the island-hopping approach sought by MacFarland. Each of the COPs provided bases from which to start patrols and provide the continu-

Tanks from the 1-37 on the move near COP Grant in Ramadi in the fall of 2006.

ous presence, as envisioned by MacFarland's plan, to wrest the neighborhoods from insurgent control.[99] During the battles surrounding the construction of COP Grant in late August and early September 2006, 1-37 mounted Operation Vicksburg to establish the COPs. MacFarland commented that "Vicksburg also cut the Confederacy in half, and that's what we're doing right now is cutting the enemy's safe haven in half."[100]

Seizing the physical terrain became the means for the 1-37 to address the critical component of the battle—securing the population. During nine months of operations, the 1-37 built six COPs and ten long-duration observation posts and secured the streets connecting these sites.[101] The unit conducted an estimated 3,200 combat patrols and mounted 275 company-level operations, killing an estimated 480 insurgents.[102]

Over the course of its nine months in Ramadi, the unit continued to refine and develop its procedures on COP construction that coherently synchronized all the necessary tasks throughout the battalion. By the end of its deployment, the 1-37 could construct a COP in less than twenty-four hours. The procedures developed by the 1-37 and other units in the 1/1 to build COPs were sent by the brigade to General Petraeus after he arrived in the spring of 2007 and later became the basis for the "COP in the Box" routines that got distributed throughout U.S. units in Iraq.[103] The so-called COP Package consisted of 100 cement barriers, 100 sheets of plywood, 200 two-by-four beams, 40 four-by-four beams, eight air conditioners, 100 strands of concertina wire, a generator, wiring, fluorescent lights, and sand bags. The planning process involved virtually all members of the task force in developing criteria for site selection, ensuring that the site design could defeat a complex insurgent attack using IEDs, establishing a transportation plan to move the materials to the site, supervising the offloading of the materials, and the actual site construction.

While COP construction proved a critical component in 1-37's COIN operations, a host of new procedures helped the unit establish and maintain control over its ever-widening swath of territory in the city. While the COPs were being built, the unit concurrently developed a census plan to improve its situational awareness of the neighborhoods into which they were moving.

Tedesco's staff developed the "census loop" to demonstrate the linkages between the census activities and the unit's patrol activities through insurgent-controlled neighborhoods. Data gathered in the census would support patrolling activities, which in turn helped develop local human intelligence networks. The census patrols helped 1-37 peel back the complex layers of the social environment in their neighborhoods throughout south-central Ramadi. The idea of compiling a census started with one of the unit's company commanders, Captain Greg Pavlichko.[104] Pavlichko's Company C deployed to the area of Ramadi around COP Spear at the outset of the campaign. After standing up COP Spear, Pavlichko sent patrols out to knock on doors in the neighborhoods, taking pictures of the inhabitants and then linking the pictures to PowerPoint files with overhead pictures of the houses he had entered. In so doing, his unit slowly built an ad hoc database of the neighborhood near COP Spear. The utility of the data-gathering activity became apparent after an IED attack in Ramadi killed an Abrams tank gunner, Sergeant Mark R. Vecchione, on July 18. In trying to track down the IED cell that had executed the attack, the battalion intelligence section had a source that provided names of cell members. Pavlichko's database not only contained the pictures of the cell members by name but also identified the exact location of their residences. Within twenty-four hours of the meeting, the 1-37 had mounted an operation and detained eleven of the twelve members of the attack cell with a minimum use of force.[105]

As the value of the initiative became obvious, Tedesco and his staff quickly spread the procedures for gathering census data throughout the battalion.[106] As a first step, the unit refined Ramadi's street and house numbering system, which it distributed to all unit members to give everyone a common baseline understanding of the area. The unit created questionnaires to collect information, identified a Microsoft database to store and manage the information, and built new TTPs for the patrols that would conduct the census. The "census patrols," as they were called, consisted of fifteen to thirty soldiers. Each patrol tried to cover eight to ten houses per mission, spending between ten and thirty minutes in each home.

The 1-37 staff developed a standardized, bilingual census questionnaire to be filled out either by the patrol leader's interpreter or the local residents. A completed questionnaire provided the patrol sector, building number, date visited, full name (including tribal affiliation), date of birth, and occupation and location of work for each military age male in the household. It also listed the number of women and children living in the house along with the religion of the household, whether the house was owned, rented, or if the residents were squatters. The form included the serial number for the household AK-47, and whether or not the house had power and water available. The census questionnaire also collected the license plate number and description of any vehicle owned by the family. Upon completion, the census patrol photographed all military age males in the household with the subjects holding up their identification card and a placard with their name and house number.[107]

Tedesco and his staff realized that the census patrols represented far more than typical reconnaissance operations, which conventionally oriented Army training and doctrine viewed as a tool to prepare the battlefield for larger kinetic operations. In Ramadi, the 1-37 reversed this order, using larger scale cordon and searches as shaping operations for the census-reconnaissance patrols that would follow later.[108] The SOP for the unit typically focused on: (1) planning and establishing the COP; (2) ensuring route security so each outpost could be kept resupplied; (3) clearing operations after the COP had been stood up to clear IEDs and find weapons caches; and (4) census patrols to follow after the clearing operations to consolidate the position and gradually work its way into the human terrain of the area—the real target of the brigade's campaign.

The unit came to grasp that the census data and information potentially could contribute more to the long-term success of its operations than kinetically oriented cordon and search operations. Eventually, the 1-37 developed the right balance between these tools as demanded by the environment. Like the Marines in western Anbar, the census patrols in Ramadi increased the face-to-face contact between the U.S. forces, the ISF, and local communities and began to generate organically driven intelligence on insurgent cells and weapons caches. The census also provided a structured way for local residents to file claims for any damage that might have occurred during the cordon operations. Patrol leaders provided a claims card to the family and instructed them to deliver the claim to one of the battalion's three Civil-Military Operations Centers for processing.[109]

As the patrols started collecting data, two final tools were developed. Tedesco's staff developed a Microsoft Excel spreadsheet to compile the questionnaire data; one worksheet listed information about the house and a second worksheet compiled information specific to each military age male. The database refined Pavlichko's initial product built with Microsoft PowerPoint. A hyperlinked presentation allowed one to click on a patrol sector, then a building, to show the pictures and names of all the military age males, vehicles, or any additional pictures of importance (a suspicious hole in the wall, the observation from the rooftop, and so forth). Each company team was augmented by an intelligence analyst to help properly compile the census products. Each company then briefed progress in filling out their census databases at the weekly battalion-level targeting meeting to ensure compliance and completion.[110]

In conjunction with the census patrols, the 1-37 developed a "small acts of kindness" initiative. Realizing the frightening effect a nocturnal visit by fifteen heavily armed and armored foreign soldiers had on the residents of a home, each patrol carried an assortment of small toys, candy, and several two-pound packages of sugar. Patrol leaders discovered that these gifts helped reduce the tension of census visits and helped generate exchanges that increased their understanding of local dynamics. Patrols found that the bags of sugar—a scarce commodity in Ramadi—proved particularly effective in generating positive feedback from the home's residents.[111]

From the outset of 1-37's campaign in central Ramadi, Tedesco and his staff identified the population of their sector as the decisive terrain—as opposed to any particular geographical feature. The census patrols provided the battalion with a critical tool to perform area reconnaissance of the human terrain. While the patrols started out as instruments to collect intelligence data to support counterinsurgency operations, they eventually also became vehicles to conduct civil-military operations, information operations, and the development of human intelligence networks. The census patrols evolved into the battalion's main instrument of fighting the counterinsurgency. By the end of its deployment, the 1-37 had censused 80 percent of the buildings in south-central Ramadi.

SUMMARY OF 1/37 INNOVATION

It is worth repeating that the 1-37 deployed into Ramadi as an armored battalion—a legacy unit organized and equipped for conventionally oriented fire and maneuver missions. The unit demonstrated significant adaptive flexibility and built what can only be described as sophisticated and systems-oriented COIN capacities in executing its part of MacFarland's campaign to retake Ramadi. While the Army is particularly noted for a rigid command hierarchy and a campaign-style approach to warfare, this unit clearly demonstrated its capacity for learning and searched for optimal solutions, accepted disparate sources of information, and constantly sought to build its understanding of the operational environment. As demonstrated in the building of the census program and supporting series of COIN-related procedures that followed, initiative bubbled its way to the top of the organization and then back down again in the form of routinized procedures. This organizational characteristic allowed the 1-37 to develop capacities and organizational structures that produced outputs that met the requirements of the complex environment.

As was the case in the other units discussed in this book, the unit realized the central role played by intelligence in building a successful COIN campaign. Development of census databases proved instrumental in prosecuting counterinsurgency operations against high-value targets. The unit clearly grasped that the population represented the critical terrain in the campaign, which required the discriminate use of force. The use of intelligence in a tactical fusion cycle that drove high-value targeting raids helped minimize collateral damage. The city was not destroyed in the process.

COP construction techniques developed into a repeatable SOP as part of the execution of MacFarland's campaign plan. The 1-37 developed and refined its plans for COP construction, increasing its control over the physical terrain so it could seize the critical terrain—the people.

1ST BATTALION, 6TH MARINES IN RAMADI, SEPTEMBER 2006–MARCH 2007

The 1st Battalion, 6th Marine Regiment, or 1-6, arrived in Ramadi in September of 2006 and took over responsibility for clearing central Ramadi, the sector just to the north of the 1-37's area. The 1-6 inherited the sector from the 3rd Battalion, 8th Marine Regiment, commanded by Lieutenant Colonel Steven Neary, which was based in Hurricane Point. Neary's battalion had established three outposts in the area of operations—the government center, another at the Iraqi veterans affairs building called observation post VA, and a third observation post known as Hawk, close to the government center.[112]

In many ways, the 1-6's overall approach reflected the unit's successful past

COIN experiences. The battalion's commanding officer, Lieutenant Colonel William Jurney, wanted to embed his Marines with their partnered host-nation units, rather than driving to see them periodically from military megabases.[113] The command mindset embraced the uncertainty and complexity of the environment and recognized that organizational capacities had to be tailored in ways that reflected those complexities. As noted by Marine Lieutenant Colonel Todd Desgrosseilliers, commanding officer of the 3rd Marine Battalion, 2nd Marine Regiment stationed at Habbaniyah in 2006: "The more unorthodox and unconventional we are, the more successful we're going to be."[114] Jurney shared this mindset. The building block of the 1-6's approach would be the relationships between Marine units and their Iraqi counterparts. Jurney demanded that the Marine and Iraqi units share the same comforts and hardships, all the while increasing the level of trust between them. The units subsequently built a web of mutual respect between the officers of the 1-6 and the political and tribal leadership they engaged. The strategy would lean heavily on civil-military operations and information operations while aggressively building the capability of their partnered ISF units.[115]

As Jurney and his staff confronted the environment in Ramadi during their predeployment site survey in the summer of 2006, they saw nothing that they had not encountered before either during their previous experience in Iraq or, in Jurney's case, during his fifteen years of prior experience in places like Liberia, Haiti, and Kosovo.[116] The unit had deployed into Fallujah in February 2005 in the aftermath of the pitched battle for the city in November 2004, and hence had extensive experience in Iraq and in building organizational SOPs to deal with the environment. Jurney developed LOOs for Ramadi that were identical to the ones he had used in the spring of 2005 in Fallujah: (1) neutralize anti-Iraqi elements and criminal threats to improve security and stability; (2) train, employ, and operate in coordination with partnered Iraqi Army and police; and (3) conduct and support civil-military operations and information operations to develop the confidence and trust of the Iraqi people in their elected officials and the ISF. All three of these LOOs were to be conducted simultaneously.[117]

As battalion commander, Jurney specifically sought to build an organization that could seamlessly and quickly transition between the three LOOs in applying the tools at their disposal that matched the challenge of the environment.[118] As the executive officer of the 1-6, Major Daniel Zappa commented: "It's a combination of improvised explosive devices, quick gun battles in the streets, and then handing out school supplies to the kids 20 minutes later."[119]

Jurney took pains to emphasize the complex nature of the task facing his organization in achieving the right balance between lethal and nonlethal operations. Jurney emphasized that each phase of his plan to retake the sector had to have one civil-military project in process at all times, which, in turn, should be synchronized with information operations. Jurney emphasized to the unit: "Do not forget we want to neutralize [the insurgents], we can 'neutralize' or at least make them less effective through kinetic and nonkinetic means . . . by doing those things which separate the [insurgents] from the people—we are having a neutralizing effect. CMO, IO, and how our Marines treat the people and conduct themselves professionally can do more to neutralize the insurgency than anything else we do."[120] The battalion's 120-day campaign would strive concurrently to apply a complex mix of kinetic and nonkinetic effects each day. The synchronization of these effects depended above all on individual initiative supported by the battalion leadership.[121]

While preparing for the deployment at Camp Lejeune, Jurney's staff kept abreast of MacFarland's campaign to retake Ramadi from the insurgents.[122] The day before the unit assumed responsibility for its sector, Jurney's staff briefed MacFarland on their plans to seize control of central Ramadi. Jurney's staff developed a time-benchmarked plan by week to disperse the battalion throughout its sector in jointly manned outposts with Iraqi police and military units. The environment throughout their sector was extremely violent, with a mix of insurgent activity that consisted of sniper attacks, coordinated insurgent unit attacks, VBIEDs, IED attacks along the main supply routes, and indirect-fire mortar attacks. Insurgents exercised control over central Ramadi and had driven off all but a few of the Iraqi police. The Iraqi Army remained a nonfactor and rarely ventured outside its base in western Ramadi. At the outset of 1-6's operations, only two police stations remained open, located on the periphery of the sector. The few police that remained did little active patrolling. As recalled by Jurney, there was virtually no police presence in the central section of Ramadi, except for a contingent of provincial police stationed at the government center to provide security for Anbar Governor Mamoun.

Jurney's plan to retake his sector of Ramadi consisted of four one-month blocks. Block 1 consisted of the four-week period from September 23 through October 20, with each successive block identifying tasks by the week to complete what Jurney characterized as the "Complete Gated Community" in central Ramadi.[123] The concept of the "gated community" simply meant that the 1-6 could construct a series of interlocking physical and human "gates" throughout the sector to drive the insurgents from their havens and construct an environment to ensure that they couldn't easily re-establish themselves in the same kind of strength that was present in the fall of 2006. The gated community plan layered together several different steps: (1) vehicle checkpoints and barriers to channel traffic through certain areas; (2) the construction of jointly manned security stations that would push a 24-hour, 7-day (24/7) patrol presence in their respective sector; (3) census patrols throughout the neighborhoods to build situational awareness of the neighborhood inhabitants; and (4) the concurrent application of civil-military operations and information operations throughout the sector.[124] The plan was to conduct a kind of "island hopping" campaign through the sector via the security stations.[125]

The campaign began in late September 2006 when the 1-6 seized what became known as intersection 295 just in front of the government center in central Ramadi. The government center, which had been a sand-bagged, shell-pocked outpost up until that point, had been subjected to frequent insurgent attacks throughout the year.[126] The facility housed the offices of Anbar Governor Maamoun Sami Rashid al-Awani and a handful of employees who lived inside the building during the week. Insurgents had made thirty-one attempts on al-Awani's life in the months before the 1-6's arrival.[127] After seizing the intersection, the battalion spread out from the government center, providing security so that rubble could be cleared from around the center that had provided cover for snipers. The rubble removal by the Army's 16th Engineer Battalion and the Marines' 2nd Combat Engineer Battalion would be the start of a pattern in the 1-6's sector in which the unit sought to drive out the insurgents and, concurrently, clean up the environment using Iraqi laborers employed through CMO contracts.[128]

After stabilizing the area around the government center, Jurney gradually sought to expand the battalion's control over the sector by creating a series of what he called "security stations" jointly manned by ISF (police and army) and Marines. The security stations would provide the basis for the battalion to wrest control over the physical terrain from the insurgents so the critical terrain of the fight could be addressed—the people.[129] The security stations would be used to re-establish government control and restore some semblance of normalcy to the neighborhoods. While Colonel MacFarland successfully rebuilt the police force in outlying neighborhoods of Ramadi in August and September, the 1-6 had to recruit and build a local police force from scratch in its sector. The battalion established its first security station in October, a three-story building called 17th St. Station, directly north of the government center in a neighborhood known as Jumaiyah. The pitched battle to establish this station lasted nearly a week. As the battle for the 17th St. Station concluded, Anbar Governor al Awani provided Jurney with a list of 125 volunteers for the police drawn from his own Abu Alwani tribe, which lived in the 1-6's sector.[130] The volunteers represented the first of the tribal "flips" in the 1-6's area as a result of negotiations with Anbar's governor and Sheikh Sattar, who had thrown his allegiance to the 1/1 several weeks earlier. The first volunteers—drawn from the neighborhoods—represented a victory for the 1-6. The insurgents immediately began a campaign of fear and intimidation against those that had volunteered for the police, mounting their own information operations and attacks against them.[131]

Several weeks later, these police—many of whom had prior backgrounds in Saddam's Army—were ready to start patrols from the Warrar station, which was initially commanded by the impressive Lieutenant Colonel Salaam al-Dalaimi, who was later assassinated by AQI. Over the next three months, the 1-6 moved systematically through its sector establishing eleven security stations manned by locally recruited and trained Iraqi police.[132] By January 2007, the number of Iraqi police in Ramadi had steadily increased to an estimated 4,000 deployed throughout the city.[133] In the spring of 2007, an influential leader in the city, Sheikh Jasim Swidawi, also threw his support behind the police recruiting efforts, which greatly increased the recruiting pool.[134] By February 2007, the 1/1 had also introduced emergency response units (ERUs)—or tribal militias—to further augment the police in Ramadi. The ERUs were considered provisional police until the members of the units went to formal police training.[135]

The stand up of the police force, however, represented only one component in the security LOO. Like other battalion commanders, Jurney wanted Iraqi units to assume greater responsibility in his sector as quickly as possible. Jurney colocated his Marines with the ISF and stopped the previous practice of rotating out entire Iraqi Army companies every month for leave, permitting only platoons to rotate. Jurney also had formed a close relationship with the head of the Military Training Team, or MiTT, training the ISF unit in his area. Major Joe Jones had previously served as executive officer of the 1-6 during the unit's prior deployment in Fallujah. While the MiTT team did not technically report to Jurney (it technically reported to MNF-W), the prior relationship proved vitally important to the integration of the ISF into the 1-6's operations.[136] Jones and Jurney closely coordinated to reduce Iraqi Army unit turnover in the combat areas, building their core competencies.[137] The ISF competencies became advanced enough so that the 1-6 turned over independent operations in western Ramadi to the 2nd Battalion, 1st Brigade, 7th Iraqi Army division on January 22, 2007.[138] All the security stations in the 1-6's sector eventually housed Marines, Iraqi police, and Iraqi Army units.

Knowing this effort was critical, the battalion created augmentation teams of Marines taken from each company to augment police stations and substations as they were built throughout Ramadi.[139] This combined presence ensured the long-term success of these stations. The battalion ensured that brigade-level support was available to the security stations, including information, surveillance, and reconnaissance (or ISR), communications, and intelligence. The battalion worked hard to synchronize security station operations with the 1/1's activities.[140]

When the 1-6 departed in the summer of 2007, it had built four police stations, eight substations, and fifty-five district police neighborhood watch observation posts. During Operation Okinawa in March 2007, the Iraqi police (with considerable 1-6 support) spearheaded a ten-hour operation to clear north-central Ramadi from west to east, resulting in several weapons caches being found and the apprehension of forty-five suspected insurgents. More important, Iraqi civilians responded positively to the operation, reporting insurgent activity to the police as they cleared neighborhoods.[141]

Engagement with the local leadership proved critical to the 1-6's operations. As the 1-6's area of operations included the government center, the battalion staff met regularly with Governor al-Awani as well as with the mayor of Ramadi, Latif Obaid Ayadah, who arrived on the job in January 2007. The battalion executive officer, Major Dan Zappa, met several times per week with the mayor as well as Sheikh Sittar and with other tribal and political figures.[142] Neighborhood leaders also were engaged daily by captains, lieutenants, and sergeants. Many of these interactions in the neighborhoods took place as a result of census patrols in which the joint Iraqi-Marine units went door to door gathering information on neighborhood inhabitants.[143] Information from the patrols populated a database maintained at the local security stations.[144]

The 1-6 experience in Ramadi is a classic case of a unit mastering battlefield competencies in its COIN operations in which prior experience, common sense, and adaptation all factored into the process of organizational innovation. Most U.S. units deploying to Iraq in the first couple of years after the invasion had no prior experience working CMO, and there was no doctrine on how it should be integrated with other battlefield tools.[145] Yet the 1-6 clearly regarded CMO efforts as important as any other enduring task in its sector, and CMO routinely took center stage in the battalion's overall effort.[146] There was no ambiguity in the minds of the commander's subordinates as to whether CMO was a priority—they needed only to review Jurney's stated commander's intent: "I want at least ONE focused CMO project [per every four-week block] in your AO to support your nonkinetic effects . . . you will be actually executing at least one and planning/coordinating the next." Jurney emphasized to the unit that they should expect to start working CMO immediately upon arriving in the sector, which "might be school supplies/backpacks . . . we might also start working a 'scrap metal' type clean up project as it helps our force [protection] to get all the burned out vehicles off the side streets and certainly starts making the city look like its time to get back to normal."[147] He anticipated the need to distribute "heat/blankets, generators, electricity, water, etc., with cold and rain coming." The battalion relied heavily on input of local residents to prioritize which CMO projects should go first, letting each neighborhood define its own requirements. Jurney specifically called for "bottom up input and initiative based on your population needs . . . you have to know the area and the people. Look for those 'gaps' where CMO/IO can gain you a tactical advantage."[148] This statement indicated that CMO represented a critical organizational priority because of the impact it could have on separating the insurgents from their base of support.

To synchronize the lethal and nonlethal activities, the battalion established a "Non Kinetic Effects Working Group," headed by its executive officer, Major Dan Zappa, to work on integrating CMO and IO with the other activities in the sector.[149] That the executive officer was placed in charge of the group is noteworthy for two reasons. Zappa had no prior experience or formal training in that area, but he and several staff officers nonetheless melded together a powerful informal organizational structure composed of a nine-man civil affairs detachment headed by Colonel Scott Kish with several other personnel working on psychological operations, or PSYOPS. Major Tiley Nunnick and the battalion's interpreter worked closely with Zappa on the information operations side to mold a successful IO program in the sector. By placing Zappa in charge of the group, Jurney signaled to the rest of the organization that the working group's initiatives would receive priority and not be sidelined in favor of kinetic operations.

The leadership at the 1-6 expected CMO to be conducted at the lowest level possible, which was consistent with the intent of higher headquarters. When

Colonel MacFarland called for Commander's Emergency Response Program (CERP) payments to be given out at the company level, the commander of the 1-6 called for squads to be directly involved in generating CMO projects. By pushing CMO to the lowest possible levels, squad-level Marines worked directly at the street level in the city blocks.

While the small units were improving Ramadi's neighborhoods, the commander and executive officer worked to provide a structure to further engage local political leadership. In March 2007, Jurney and Zappa convened the first meeting of the western Ramadi District Council, which was composed of several of Ramadi's prominent sheikhs and business leader and other interested citizenry.[150] These meetings facilitated the airing of grievances, spurred competition for various contracts, and resulted in the dismantling of IEDs by members seeking to improve security in their area of the district. District members also attended meetings of the mayor's city council.[151] The initiative became a template used throughout the area for U.S. forces working with local groups. In June 2007, commanders in Fallujah adopted Jurney's ideas of establishing district councils and using a system of neighborhood watches to supplement the police force's efforts to involve the citizenry in improving local security.[152]

In executing operations consistent with the commander's intent, the 1-6 initiated scores of CMO projects across its area of operations, including paving roads, improving schools, rubble removal, food drops, water and sewage repair, re-establishing bus service, trash removal, providing medicines, and creating youth sports programs. Whenever possible, Iraqis did the work under the estimated $9.2 million in reconstruction contracts. As the battalion orchestrated the placing of contracts to reconstruct the city's destroyed infrastructure, the nonkinetic effects group in parallel developed a sectorwide plan to utilize Iraqi day labor to clean up the city. Needless to say, there was no shortage of labor in Ramadi given widespread unemployment in the city. Clean-up operations began in earnest in March 2007.[153] The relationships that the 1-6 painstakingly built with Ramadi's local leadership paid off as the CMO projects gained momentum. Ramadi's sheikhs were only too happy to increase their own influence by farming out lucrative contracts, and the amounts of money involved generated excitement and competition for future ones.

While it worked on CMO, the nonkinetic effects working group assiduously worked on information operations—a neglected portion of the battalion's operations in a domain that had been ceded to the area's insurgents. As noted by the group's head, Major Dan Zappa: "We were getting our clocks cleaned in the information domain."[154] Jurney's focus on the nonkinetic portions of its operations forced the battalion to rethink the role that IO and information management could play in prying the population away from the insurgents. The battalion was reluctant (despite considerable pressure) to provide public affairs officers with stories on incidents within its battle space that might serve the insurgents' cause. For example, the 1-6 rarely agreed to generate press reports on insurgent sniper attacks, attacks on the Ramadi government center, friendly casualties, and the like. However it actively provided public affairs with stories on its progress with the Iraqi police or CMO projects. This also applied to visiting reporters, who were placed strategically by the battalion where they would see the things that were likely to keep them "on message."[155] The second IO method (much to the chagrin of the brigade psychological operations officer) was to generate and disseminate their own IO messages.[156] This was done via handbills and loudspeakers, which became commonplace throughout their sector. The nonkinetic effects cell developed the idea all on its own. The group carefully crafted messages that would then be broadcast from the loudspeaker system of police stations all over the city for about fifteen minutes per day.[157] The broadcasts were composed of popular music, news from the *BBC* and *Al Jazeera,* and, most important, messages from local officials about developments in the neighborhoods.[158] The positioning of the loudspeakers allowed them to cover most of the sector with their messages. Very often the broadcaster would be a tribal leader, politician, or policeman that was working closely with the battalion. While the battalion had not realized it, the loudspeaker system of disseminating information to the populace had been commonplace in Saddam's era in Ramadi and became an important element in the battalion's attempt to create a sense of normalcy in the neighborhoods.[159] The system became a preferred venue for local leaders to distribute information to the local communities in the 1-6's sector.[160] The battalion's PSYOPS team soon developed a lively business, working actively with local officials, coaching them on presentation style, and helping to craft messages. The facility also recorded these messages, transferred them to CDs, and passed them out at the vehicle checkpoints throughout the sector.[161] The information operation campaign was regarded by the unit's leadership as a critical part of its COIN strategy in the sector.

SUMMARY OF 1-6 INNOVATION

The COIN campaign of the 1-6 saw the unit develop competencies across the full spectrum of capacities, ranging from high-intensity, conventionally oriented warfare all the way to tailoring an information operation campaign that featured messages delivered via loudspeakers throughout its sector. In between, the 1-6 simultaneously pursued civil-military operations, stood up jointly manned security stations, developed the Iraqi Army to such an extent that it conducted independent operations, and built local political relationships that helped further isolate the population from the insurgents. The 1-6 campaign in Ramadi has to be regarded as a textbook COIN campaign in which the organization clearly built capacities over the course of the campaign tailored to the unique demands of the environment. The battalion organizational structure underwent many changes over the course of the deployment to accommodate the need for additional organizational capacities. As Jurney had predicted, the nonkinetic effects working group repeatedly proved its worth in the sector, tailoring an innovative IO campaign and integrating CMO into the organization's daily operations.

CONCLUSION

By March 2007, the security environment in Ramadi had improved dramatically. Insurgents no longer had free rein in the city. Data compiled by the 1/1 documents the reduction in violence over the period from July 2006 through January 2007. Over the period, monthly direct fire attacks by the insurgents had been cut by two-thirds, and the number of IED attacks had been cut in half. By the spring of 2007, the ability of the insurgents to conduct combined, coordinated assaults had dwindled. While the IED attacks persisted, their effects had been reduced significantly on the battlefield. As the attack trends decreased, finds of insurgent arms caches increased significantly through the joint efforts of the Iraqi police and military.

The reduction in insurgent violence was accompanied by a parallel increase in the reintroduction of the Iraqi police force and the buildup in the Iraqi Army. From April 2006 through January 2007, the 1/1 and 2/28 recruited 3,000 new members of the police force. In early 2007, nearly 1,500 of these police were present for duty on a continuous basis. The brigade simultaneously worked hard to integrate CMO into its operations, steadily building in more projects as the security situation grew more manageable. After wresting the Ramadi General Hospital from insurgent control in the summer of 2006, the brigade quickly returned it to operational status, providing power and medical supplies.

The 2/28 and 1/1 COIN campaigns in Ramadi did not win the war in Iraq, but it is clear that the retaking of the city broke the back of AQI in Anbar. To be sure, some criticized the re-empowerment of tribal leadership under the guise of the so-called Awakening, and it is clear that the support of tribal leadership was critical to the success of the COIN campaign. Managing these delicate relationships, however, was no easy task. The efforts of soldiers and Marines like Sean MacFarland, William Jurney, Vincent Tedesco, Travis Patriquin, Dan Zappa, and Greg Pavlichko spoke to organizations that recognized and developed talent long before it appeared on the battlefields of Iraq. The building of organizational capacities in the Ramadi campaign—as in the western Iraq campaigns—demonstrated the ability of the organizations to learn and seek optimal solutions. The Ramadi campaign was so successful it became the model for COIN operations elsewhere in Iraq as the surge of American forces in 2007 began to bear fruit in reducing insurgent violence. As he exited Iraq when the 1/1's deployment ended, Colonel MacFarland was asked whether he had read the new COIN doctrine that was promulgated in December 2006. "I said no," he recalled, "but they told me I didn't really need to read [it] since I had already done much of what the document said I was supposed to do."[162]

5 WARTIME INNOVATION IN NINEWA PROVINCE

COIN Operations in Mosul and Northern Iraq, September 2005–July 2006

The 172nd Stryker Brigade Combat Team, or 172nd SBCT, deployed into northern Iraq from August 2005 through July 2006, when the brigade was unexpectedly extended and redeployed to Baghdad to quell violence in the city. The 172nd, commanded by Colonel Michael Shields, consisted of approximately 4,400 personnel—one of the first Army infantry units to convert to the new combat brigade structure under the transformation process initiated by then Army Chief of Staff General Eric Shinseki in the late 1990s. A centerpiece of the 172nd SBCT and of all Stryker units was its eight-wheeled Stryker vehicle, designed to provide the brigade with combat power, mobility, and flexibility to operate across the spectrum of combat operations. The 172nd received 300 new Stryker wheeled vehicles several months before deployment.

The Stryker brigades represented leading-edge Army "transformational" units as the service gradually reorients its force structure away from divisions to smaller, modular brigades. The units are designed to be more deployable on short notice, more mobile on the battlefield, and possess more organically supported capabilities than their legacy force counterparts. As detailed in Chapter 3's summary of the 4-14 Cavalry troop COIN operations in Anbar Province, the units drew upon an integrated digital and satellite-based communications infrastructure designed to support network-centric operations. At the time of the 172nd deployment, Stryker doctrine and training remained in their infancy relative to other Army legacy units. While advertised as a unit capable of full-spectrum operations, many of the Stryker doctrinal manuals written in the last five years reflected the belief that the Stryker units and their vehicles would operate in a fire and maneuver conventionally oriented operational environment.

The 172nd represented one of the very first Army infantry units to convert to the new combat brigade structure. The 172nd and it sister Stryker brigades will eventually constitute the Army's dominant unit organizational structure. A recent iteration of this plan—called the Grow the Army plan announced in December 2007—calls for the Army to increase the active-duty component from 42 brigade combat teams and 75 modular support brigades to 48 brigade combat teams and 83 modular support brigades by 2013.[1] The 172nd SBCT constituted a leading edge unit in another respect—it represented one of the first units to utilize the Army's "unit manning system" that kept personnel in a dedicated unit for thirty-six months instead of rotating individual unit members according to their career plans. The objective of the plan is to stabilize the manning of combat units. The unit manning system helped immeasurably in building unit cohesion and a cross-trained workforce for the Iraq deployment.[2]

This chapter details the wartime innovation process of the unit and its task force components while conducting COIN operations in northern Iraq in Ninewa Province prior to the unit's movement to Baghdad. The chapter opens with a description of the unit's unique characteristics as an Army "transformational" unit. These characteristics provided some important enablers to the process of adaptation and innovation that will be covered later in the chapter. Following this, the chapter will summarize the evolution of the insurgency in northern Iraq, which is important as a framing narrative to the description of tactical operations by the 172nd. The chapter will then cover the brigade-level approach to its COIN campaign, and then proceed to a more in-depth coverage of operations by several units: the 2nd Battalion, 1st Infantry Regiment, or 2-1, which operated in the northeastern section of Mosul, and Company C from 1st Battalion, 17th Regiment operating in southwestern Mosul. The operations of 4th Battalion 11th Field Artillery Regiment in southern Ninewa will also be covered. Both the 2-1 and 1-17 operated in dense urban terrain, while the 4-11 operated in a more rural environment in the southwestern reaches of Ninewa. The case studies will chronicle the evolution of tactical adaptation into organizational innovation as the brigade oriented its COIN operations to the demands of the environment. The unit showed extraordinary organizational flexibility in structuring its approach on the battlefield—an approach in part enabled by the brigade's advanced digital backbone and by the tactical capabilities provided by the unit's Stryker wheeled vehicles.

The 172nd arrived in northern Iraq in August 2005 and completed its handover from the 1st Brigade, 25th Infantry Division, or 1/25 SBCT, in September. The 172nd represented the third consecutive Stryker brigade that had been deployed into northern Iraq, following the 3rd Brigade, 2nd Infantry Division Stryker Brigade, or 3/2 SBCT (January–October 2004) and the 1/25 SBCT (October 2004–August 2005). The 172nd was relieved by the 3rd Brigade, 2nd Infantry Division in August 2006—also a Stryker Brigade. By the end of its deployment in northern Iraq in July 2006, the 172nd exercised primary war fighting responsibility over a vast area of nearly 19,000 square miles and 3.85 million people.

The two main urban centers in northern Iraq were Mosul and Tal Afar. Of these two cities, Mosul represented the main focus of effort for the 172nd. Mosul is the third largest city in Iraq with an estimated population of 1.8 million, located approximately 250 miles north of Baghdad. Regarded as the "Pearl of the North," Mosul had for centuries served as a vital regional trading center linking what are today Turkey, Iran, Syria, and Central Asia. The city has a centuries-old history as a cultural, ethnic, and religious melting pot. In modern Iraq, Mosul sits astride an ethnic dividing line of sorts. To the north and east of the city all the way to the Iranian and Turkish border, Kurds constitute the major ethnic group. To the West, the population is primarily Sunni Arab, with Turkoman, Yezidi, and other ethnic groups. Mosul had served as an important staging area for Baghdad's armies in quelling repeated Kurdish uprisings in Iraq during the second half of the twentieth century.[3] After 1996, backed by U.S. security guarantees, the Patriotic Union of Kurdistan and the Kurdish Democratic Party administered Kurdish areas of northern Iraq without interference from Baghdad. The two major ethnic groups in Mosul are Sunni Arabs (60 percent) and Kurds (30 percent), with significant Turkoman, Christian, Assyrian, and Armenian minorities. The city is intersected by the Tigris River, which also served as a boundary to ethnic cleavages in the city, with significant Kurdish neighborhoods on the eastern side of the river and Sunni Arab neighborhoods on the western bank. While these populations had commingled and lived together for centuries, the aftermath of the invasion and the emergence of the insurgency in Mosul and the surrounding areas fueled tensions between these groups—particularly between the Sunni and Kurdish populations. The Sunni-Arab portion of the city's population believed that the Kurds sought to control the city and integrate it into the Kurdish-administered areas that lay to the east of the city. Clashes between Sunni militias and Kurds erupted in the days following the surrender of the city in April 2003.[4] During Saddam's reign, he purposefully resettled Sunni Arabs in the oil-rich area and expelled indigenous Kurds. After the start of the invasion, many transplanted Arab villagers hastily evacuated for fear of reprisals from the advancing Kurdish militias.[5]

Like its predecessor units in the north, the 172nd administratively fell under Multi-National Division-North, located 150 miles south of Mosul at Forward Operating Base Speicher, located outside the city of Tikrit. It reported directly to Task Force Freedom based on FOB Courage in Mosul, which had been used by Saddam as his VIP presidential residence. The 2.2-square-kilometer site had several palaces and was used by U.S. forces to host visiting dignitaries. In November 2005, the 101st Airborne Division assumed responsibility for MND-North, and in late December assumed responsibility for MND-Northwest, which included the 172nd area of operations in northern Iraq. Task Force Freedom was subsequently renamed Task Force Band of Brothers. The 172nd deployed its main combat elements principally around the province's urban centers in Mosul and Tal Afar: two of the brigade's battalions (the 1st Battalion, 17th Infantry Regiment and 2nd Battalion, 1st Infantry Regiment) were deployed into different sections of Mosul, while the 4th Battalion, 23rd Regiment deployed near Tal Afar, and the 4th Battalion, 11th Field Artillery operated in areas directly to the south of Mosul. The brigade support battalion, or BSB, operated out of the main operating base called FOB Marez in southern Mosul. In April 2005, the combat strength of U.S. forces received a big boost when the 3rd Armored Cavalry Regiment and its 4,000 troops were deployed to Tal Afar to wrest control of the city from insurgent groups and deal with sectarian Sunni-Shia tensions. The 3rd ACR, then commanded by Colonel H. R. McMaster, went on to conduct a much publicized COIN campaign in the city over the next nine months.[6] The 3rd ACR operated independently from the 172nd.

Like other combat formations in Iraq during the war, the 172nd operated as a task force, integrating a variety of different units under its leadership. These units included the 3rd Air Support Squadron, the 709th and the 165th Military Police Battalions, the 2nd Battalion, 37th Armored Cavalry Regiment deployed near Tal Afar, the 1st Battalion 101st Aviation Regiment, the 1st Battalion 10th Aviation Regiment, the 401st and 403rd Civil Affairs Battalions, and the Military Training Teams, or MiTTs, deployed throughout the province. Also part of the effort was the 1st Battalion, 5th Special Forces group, which, like the MiTTs, provided training to Iraqi Army and police units. The complex series of organizations was never formally tied together by any single administrative action, but there was a general understanding in most units throughout the province that they all supported the primary owner of the battle space in northern Iraq—the 172nd SBCT. As recalled by the 172nd Operations Officer, Lieutenant Colonel Mitch Rambin, "Where there was no formal command and control directed, it was 'handshakecon' and relationship building, especially with SOF [special operations forces] in zone."[7]

The brigade itself was distributed in up to twenty-five different locations in the province, while the 900-odd soldiers of the 4-14 Cavalry group (nearly one-quarter of the brigade end-strength) deployed to Rawah in Anbar Province and served under the 2nd Marine Division, which exercised overall command there. Like units elsewhere in Iraq, the brigade employed a hub-and-spoke network approach to its basing infrastructure that linked forward operating bases, or FOBs (usually battalion headquarters), with a number of different combat outposts, or COPs, manned by anywhere from 100 to 250 troops. Most FOBs were larger areas with permanent structures built to support soldiers on a long-term basis, while COPs typically were temporary locations used to conduct operations. The distribution of U.S. forces in a hub-and-spoke network of bases played an important role in the turnaround in the Anbar COIN campaign in 2005–6. In northern Iraq (as in Anbar), the networked approach helped push the brigade presence into contested areas in such places as Mosul and Tal Afar and provided the means to establish a presence near the Iraq-Syrian border to disrupt insurgent supply lines. The dispersal of the unit over such a wide area ran the risk of diluting the brigade's limited combat power and created serious logistical challenges for the brigade's support battalion, or BSB, headquartered at FOB Marez in southern Mosul. The brigade's hub-and-spoke network of bases in Ninewa consisted of the following elements: the 4-23 and its task force elements operated from FOB Sykes located five miles south of Tal Afar and forty miles east of the Syrian border. The main base at Sykes supported three COPs at Tal Afar, COP Rabiah, and COP Sinjar.

- The 2-1 operated out of FOB Marez in southern Mosul. Its network of operating bases included FOB Courage, COP Maqloub, COP IMN (the local TV station), COP Al Kindi, FOB Resolve, and COP Fortitude, all of which were spread throughout eastern Mosul and housed Iraqi troops, MiTTs, and battalion personnel.
- The 1-17 infantry operated from FOB Marez and supported four COPs: Gator, Eagle, Apache, and Aggies. Gator and Eagle were manned by Iraqi soldiers with MiTT team support and brigade company-elements. In these

cases, the 1-17 provided a Stryker platoon for security while the logisticians moved fuel to the sites, both ten minutes from FOB Marez. COP Aggies, a training site used by both the U.S. and Iraqi armies, was home to 30 U.S. soldiers and 400 Iraqi soldiers.

- 4-11 field artillery operated from FOB Q-West and supported three COPs: Mahkmur, Jaguar North, and Tallabath. An embedded logistics support element with the 4-11 traveled to each of these sites with organic security.

- TF 4-14 CAV was based at COP Rawah and supported COP North and COP Anah. This site had the largest FAST (80 BSB soldiers), as it was more than 120 miles from the rest of the brigade. While TF 4-14 CAV was part of the 172nd SBCT, the unit had been administratively assigned to the 2nd Marine Division. Operations of the 4-14 at Rawah (and later at COP Anah) required support from 80 BSB soldiers, including 27 mechanics that worked on the 130 vehicles, 16 cooks that prepared two meals a day for 900 soldiers, 5 water purification specialists that produced 5,000 gallons of water a day for showers and laundry, and 24 medics, nurses, and doctors that ran a daily sick call and care for the entire COP.

- The brigade headquarters operated out of FOB Marez, colocated with the airfield in southern Mosul. The brigade headquarters was fully equipped to handle the Strykers' digital and satellite communications processing requirements. The headquarters also incorporated advanced signals intelligence equipment and a Remotely Operated Video Enhanced Receiver, or ROVER, that enabled ground units to view aerial images in real time on their laptop computers.

Like other Stryker brigades, the 172nd could reach outside the brigade to higher-echelon military and civilian organizations while simultaneously ensuring that its own constituent elements remained connected to each other and to the information assets available in the brigade. These capabilities were technologically enabled by something called the SBCT network. The brigade's network consisted of five subnetworks: the wide-area network, a network connecting the brigades' tactical operations centers, a tactical encrypted internet, the command net radio network, and the global broadcast system. In addition to these subnets, various components of the SBCT used specialized communications equipment to reach back to national-level intelligence organizations and transmit imagery from unmanned aerial vehicles. As will be detailed in this case study, the 172nd used this network to its fullest—flattening the organizational structure that brought national-level intelligence and imagery support down to the tactical level. Each of the brigade's subnetworks helped connect organizational elements with one another and with non-SBCT entities.

The preceding background illustrates several unique factors that make examination of 172nd SBCT COIN operations particularly relevant to this study. First, while the Stryker brigades were clearly designed for conventionally oriented fire and maneuver operations, their first wartime deployments to Iraq occurred in a COIN contingency. Like the preceding SBCTs, the 172nd deployed into an operational environment at an extremely early stage of the Stryker Brigade's fielding plan in the Army—before the establishment of an extensive doctrine and training base. Second, the COIN environment in northern Iraq consisted of both urban and rural settings, requiring different competencies and different operational schemes executed by units separated by significant physical distances. As noted above, the 172nd Brigade Support Battalion performed the herculean task of keeping these units continuously supplied in ways that had never been envisioned in Stryker doctrine. Third, the technical capabilities of the Stryker brigade and its concept of network-centric operations represented another unique feature of the 172nd deployment in Mosul, making it an interesting case to examine the impact of these technologies on the process of wartime innovation. These technologies functioned as "enablers" for wartime SBCT innovation across the full spectrum of combat operations. The 172nd COIN operations in Mosul provide an opportunity to analyze the impact played by these technologies on wartime operations. As will be detailed in this case study, it is clear that the 172nd SBCT wartime operations reflected the innovative use of its technical capabilities by a well-trained, extremely adaptive force that produced a variety of new organizational competencies on the battlefield over the course of the deployment. Last, the 172nd deployment into Iraq occurred at an extremely early phase in the history of the unit, which had only recently converted to the new brigade structure and which had received its full complement of Strykers only several months prior to deployment. The unit thus perhaps had less of an established institutional identity than other units in the Army. Moreover, like its sister Stryker Brigades that had deployed before it, the unit leadership realized that its performance would be closely watched by senior Army leadership, and that there would be significant operational and doctrinal implications from the unit's performance.

THE INSURGENCY IN NORTHERN IRAQ

At the outset of the war, the Iraqi 5th Corps and its 30,000 troops defended Mosul, although press reports indicated that some 120,000 Iraqi troops were deployed across a 250-mile front in the Mosul-Kirkuk area. The United States had intended to move troops into northern Iraq through Turkey in the spring of 2003 as part of the invasion—a plan subsequently thwarted when the Turkish Parliament denied the U.S. request to transit through Turkey. The United States subsequently opened the so-called northern front in March 2003 soon after the invasion of the south began when Special Forces were airlifted into Sulaimaniya in northern Iraq. Operating with Kurdish Peshmerga militia, these Special Forces advanced on Mosul and Kirkuk aided by air strikes on Iraqi Army positions. On April 11, 2003, the Iraqi 5th Corps surrendered to Kurdish forces. The next day American Special Forces and the Kurds entered the city unopposed. Most of the Iraqi soldiers simply discarded their uniforms and went home. As had been the case in Baghdad, looters quickly went to work, raiding banks and the Mosul Museum, stealing among other things, a two-thousand-year-old statue of King Saqnatroq II—a long-forgotten Iraqi monarch. Looters found the University of Mosul to be a lucrative hunting ground. The university computer center had its computers ripped from their sockets, and cars were seen packed with office furniture and scientific equipment exiting the campus in the days following the surrender of the city.[8] The first U.S. conventional military units arriving in the city on April 14 were met with protests and gunfire after Marines tried to raise a U.S. flag over the governor's office in downtown Mosul. Ten Iraqis were killed in the confused melee surrounding the incident—an inauspicious beginning to the U.S. occupation. By the end of April, elements of the 101st Airborne had finally arrived in Kirkuk and Mosul.

The 101st Airborne Division, commanded by General David Petraeus, administered northern Iraq through January 2004. The 101st was structured as a legacy Army unit consisting of three combat brigades, two aviation brigades, one artillery brigade, three engineering battalions, and an attached military police battalion. The unit boasted an end strength of approximately 17,000 soldiers and its additional task force members added another 2,000 personnel to the unit. The city's population exhibited a mixed reaction to the arrival of the occupation force. While Kurds living primarily in eastern Mosul enthusiastically welcomed the Americans, Sunni-Baathist Iraqis in western neighborhoods appeared more apprehensive. Mosul had a large, established Sunni-Baathist population that served as home to as many as 100,000 Iraqi Army personnel and 1,000 retired generals and other high-ranking officers. One city resident presciently commented to a journalist immediately following the occupation of the city: "The Baath, the Special Republican Guards, the Fedayeen, they are sitting at home, waiting."[9] The first reported attacks on U.S. troops came in late April, when positions on the western bank of the river came under sustained machine gun and small arms fire. Four insurgents were reported killed in the encounter.[10]

The 101st Airborne hit the ground running and worked hard to defuse local tensions, enlisting former Iraqi Army leaders in engagement activities and even held a special election in early May to appoint a twenty-four-member town council to take over administrative duties in Mosul. It established a police academy to rebuild a local police force as well as an employment office for former Iraqi military personnel. In June, however, clashes broke out in the city center between U.S. units and unemployed Iraqi soldiers in a sign of what was to come. Ambushes of American convoys south of Mosul were reported in early July by insurgents armed with RPGs and Kalashnikov assault rifles.[11] Despite these episodic attacks, however, some saw northern Iraq as the exception to an otherwise badly bungled postinvasion period in the rest of the country. Cross-border trade between the north and Turkey was quickly re-established, and local Iraqis had been installed in many governmental posts. Nearly $17 million in reconstruction funds were disbursed by the 101st in the first several months of its deployment in northern Iraq, further contributing to the stabilization effort.[12]

Whatever successes the 101st experienced, however, the unit could not not stem the inexorable increase in violence that steadily grew in Mosul as it did elsewhere in the country for the remainder of 2003. In September, insurgents killed Sana Toma Suleiman, deputy director of the oil products department in Ninewa Province for the North Oil Company, as he got into his car to go to work. In October, the head of an Iraqi military training center was killed. Other attacks also came against Kurdish political party offices in Mosul. Insurgents mounted the first reported IED attacks on U.S. convoys in November 2003.[13] That fall, insurgents unveiled the same brutal tactics used elsewhere in Iraq: the targeted assassination and intimidation of Iraqis cooperating with the occupation. Interpreters helping the United States and journalists believed to be providing favorable coverage became particularly favored targets. As many as fifty interpreters were killed by insurgents through the spring of 2006.[14] In early November 2003, gunmen assassinated the president of the Mosul Mag-

istrate Court, Judge Isma'il Yusuf, and seriosuly wounded the director of the
Mosul Northern Oil Company, Muhammad Zebari. Insurgents also beheaded
the dean of the Mosul law school. In a sign of their growing capabilities, in late
November insurgents shot down two Black Hawk helicopters operating over
Mosul, killing seventeen U.S. soldiers.[15] The first suicide bombings occurred as
the 101st prepared to depart in early 2004. In January, insurgents attacked the
101st base near the city of Tal Afar with a suicide attack, injuring sixty soldiers
in the attack.[16] In early February, as the 3/2 Stryker brigade took over from the
101st, a suicide bomber smashed through a protective barrier at an Iraqi police
station in Mosul, killing nine and injuring forty-five.[17] The pattern of attacks
continued throughout the rest of the year, with attacks against U.S. forces and
any Iraqis deemed to be aiding in the occupation. The drastic reduction of
U.S. forces from 19,000 to approximately 5,000 in 2004 provided the insurgency
with breathing space to consolidate, organize, and mount increasingly deadly
operations.

During late 2003, the outlines of several insurgent organizational structures
emerged in and around Mosul that would remain through the 172nd deployment (and remain so as of this writing). In interviews with journalists, the 101st
Division's Chief Intelligence Officer, Lieutenant Colonel Daryl Reyes, identified several groups operating throughout the area. Baathists had created at
least two insurgent groups: al-Rifah ("Prosperity"), composed of high-ranking military officers, and a second, called, al-Awdah ("The Return"), consisting
of former Baath Party members.[18] Islamist militant groups had also organized
themselves. One, called Mohammed's Army, had been detected in the city, and
an offshoot of the Muslim Brotherhood had been found in a poor suburb of
Mosul called Hamman al Alil.[19] A Muslim preacher who had been jailed by Saddam for sedition told a journalist that Islamists in Hamman al Alil were stir-
ring anti-American sentiment: "The longer it takes to bring Iraq to its feet, the
harder it will be" for the United States, he said. "It is those who lost jobs who are
conducting operations against the Americans. Mosul is like a little Baghdad."[20]
One of the most vicious groups that appeared in late 2003 was the group Ansar
al-Islam (also called Ansar al-Sunna, or AAS), which had long been operating
in the remote regions of northeastern Iraq. The 101st detected efforts by Ansar
to establish command and control units in the city in late 2003.[21] AAS would
later achieve notoriety by claiming credit for two gruesome attacks in Mosul: a
December 2004 suicide bombing attack in the mess hall of the U.S. base at FOB
Marez, killing twenty-two and wounding seventy-two; and the beheading of

twelve Nepalese contract workers in August 2004. Ansar triumphantly posted gruesome videos of the killings of the Nepalese workers on a website along with a statement that the Nepalese were "fighting the Muslims and serving the Jews and Christians" and "believing in Buddha as their God."[22] The involvement of Islamist groups in the insurgency also reflected itself in increased attacks on Christian churches and those of other denominations in the city. In another tactic practiced elsewhere in Iraq, an Islamic fundamentalist group called the Islamic Council of Mosul distributed "Brides for Jihad" letters from mosques in the Sunni sections in the western part of the city urging women to marry foreign-born jihadists—and demanded that names of marriageable women be placed on a list and provided to the council.[23]

Violence in Mosul reached a climax in November 2004 as U.S. troops carried out the assuault on Fallujah in Anbar Province. On November 11, an estimated 500 to 1,000 insurgents stormed police stations in Mosul and laid seige to Kurdish political offices, effectively ending the police presence throughout much of the city. U.S. officials were stunned by the scale of the attacks. Some observors asserted that many of the police had joined with the insurgents. Indeed, as many as 3,200 of the 4,000 police in Mosul effectively left their posts in the attacks. Militants looted and emptied at least six police stations of arms, and trucks full of armed insurgents had free rein in the city for several days.[24] Kurdish Peshmerga militias fought running gunbattles with the insurgents on the bridges over the Tigris River to keep them out of the Kurdish neighborhoods in eastern Mosul. U.S. troops from the 1/25 SBCT and Iraqi Army commandos fought pitched battles with insurgent groups numbering as high as fifty fighters—killing many insurgents in these encounters. By November 17, U.S. forces and Kurdish Peshmerga militia units had pushed back into the seized areas. In late November, Kurdish forces arrested Mosul's former police chief, Muhammad Kheiri Barhawi, on suspicions of collaborating with the insurgents. Kurdish militia apprehended Barhawi with $600,000 in cash in the trunk of his car.[25] In the aftermath of the attacks, it became apparent that groups affiliated with Abu Musab al Zarqawi had arrived in Mosul. Some press reports indicated that Zarqawi himself had arrived in the city to escape the U.S. offensive in Fallujah. In the weeks following the fighting, bound and gagged bodies that clearly had been executed began appearing in public places—a favored tactic of Zarqawi's groups. Websites affiliated with Zarqawi began publicly taking credit for the gruesome executions and beheadings in and around the city in late 2004.[26]

After the battles of Fallujah and the resultant "Awakening Movement" in Anbar Province, many Sunni fighters turned to Mosul as a new base of operations.[27] An estimated 500 to 700 of Zarqawi's fighters gravitated to Mosul in late 2004. The evolution of the insurgency in Mosul over the period in some ways mirrored the trends elsewhere, as Sunni Islamist extremists and Baathists initially united over their opposition to the occupation. Their objectives diverged after this, although in Mosul the tactical alliance between the groups endured. In late 2004, Ansar al Sunna had emerged as a dominant jihadist group in Mosul. The main leader Mohammed Sharkawa was said to direct several hundred insurgents. Sharkawa favored the creation of a Taliban-like state in northern Iraq that reflected his Salafist beliefs. Sharkawa was finally captured by U.S. forces in July 2005.[28] The other side of the insurgency in Mosul was overwhelmingly secular and composed of former Baathists. Both groups took advantage of the steady stream of cash that arrived from Syria to pay for operations.[29] In late 2004, these insurgent groups mounted complex, coordinated, unit-size attacks against U.S. forces.[30] By early 2005, Ansar al-Sunna was reported to be increasing its influence in the city, gradually overshadowing the Baathist groups involved in the insurgency.[31] Other reports indicated that former Baathists had established a command apparatus in Syria to direct a growing number of cells in Mosul and Tal Afar.[32] In some cases local families were divided—with different members of the same family joining different insurgent groups.[33] Unlike the case in Anbar, however, relationships between the Baathist and Islamist insurgent groups did not break apart as they had in late 2006 during the battle for Ramadi, although some U.S. commanders reported Baathist disaffection with the Islamist/Zarqawi/Ansar Al-Sunna elements in early 2005.[34] Still, there were few public reports indicating confrontations between these groups like those that had unfolded in Anbar Province in 2006. The character of the insurgency in Mosul changed in the spring of 2005, with U.S. forces seeing many more foreign fighters from such places as Algeria, Libya, Yemen, and Saudi Arabia. These fighters were less well trained than the Baathists and the foreign fighters that initially had appeared on the battlefield in late 2003 and 2004.[35] Suicide vehicle and suicide bomber attacks became the preferred insurgent attack in the late spring and summer of 2005.

Mosul's location near the Syrian border and its traditional role in smuggling and trade clearly represented one reason why the city became a favored location. The terrain represented another attractive feature. Mosul's urban landscape and the topography around the city provided a rich environment for the insurgents. The urban environment featured an extremely dense population and a warren of winding streets and ancient buildings The area around Mosul contains many forests and groves as well as marsh lands on both sides of the Tigris. These features provided plenty of cover to hide training areas and insurgent compounds. The size alone allowed space for the various insurgent groups to act independently of each other, in cooperation with each other, or in direct confrontation with each other, depending on the conditions of the region and the overall political landscape.[36] Insurgents mounted a series of vicious suicide attacks in early 2005 against Shiite mosques in Mosul, suggesting Sunni Islamist groups sought to stoke sectarian violence there as they had elsewhere in Iraq.[37]

Like everywhere else in Iraq, U.S.efforts to control the violence and provide local security clearly were hampered by the lack of troops. The sheer size of the area greatly complicated COIN efforts by U.S. and Iraqi forces after the departure of the 101st in January 2004 and its replacement by the 3rd Brigade, 2nd Infantry Division, or 3/2 Stryker Brigade—a force one-third the size of the 101st. Insurgents clearly exploited the reduction in U.S. troop stength—exacerbated by the 3/2's deployment to several operations outside the province during its deployment. In late 2003, insurgents mounted an average of 15 to 20 attacks per week on U.S. forces. Insurgent violence steadily increased in early 2004 following the departure of the 101st. In early 2004, the average number of attacks doubled, and reached 150 per week by the end of 2004.[38] In January 2005, U.S. commanders lamented the lack of troops in northern Iraq that had hamstrung their ability to control the insurgency.[39] During late 2004, U.S. troop strength nearly doubled in northern Iraq to approximately 11,000 as the United States struggled to scrape forces together to provide security for the January 2005 elections. The environment throughout the 1/25 area of operations was extremely violent as the unit struggled to restore order. The summer of 2005 saw other vicious attacks. In late June, a series of four coordinated suicide bomber attacks over sixteen hours left thirty-eight dead.[40] At the end of July, another suicide bomber killed twenty-five potential army recruits at an enlistment station.[41]

Over 2005, however, the 1/25 unquestionably made enormous strides in its COIN operations and worked hard to reintroduce the Iraqi police force and train the Iraqi Army.[42] By mid-2005, elements of the 1st Iraqi Army Division actively patrolled the center of Mosul. When the 1/25 arrived in September 2004, the unit received 300 mortar attacks a month. By the time it departed, these attacks had been reduced to an average of 6 a month.[43] Nearly 9,000 Iraqi police had been brought back, and the number of intelligence tips called in by the local population had risen from 40 to 400 per month.[44] In September 2005, U.S. military commanders reported that they had disrupted 80 percent of the Al Qaeda network in northern Iraq.[45] Levels of violence had peaked in 2004 with nearly 20 per day and dropped steadily in 2005 to between 7 to 9 attacks per day when the 172nd arrived in August.

PREDEPLOYMENT TRAINING

The 172nd realized it was deploying into a complex political environment and a persistent, violent insurgency. It maintained a situational awareness of events in Mosul and northern Iraq through routine secure video teleconferences with the 1/25 SBCT and the numerous intelligence products available on the Defense Department–wide Secure Internet Protocol Router, or SIPRnet. The unit tailored its training using lessons learned from the 1/25 to build predeployment COIN capacities for which there was no formal SBCT doctrinal preparation. The brigade leadership fully grasped that it could not necessarily rely on existing Stryker doctrine to provide it with guidance on how to fight the battles that awaited the brigade in northern Iraq.[46] Like many wartime commanders before him, Shields grasped the obvious: "You've got to fight the fight you got, not the one you wanted and you know maybe in a future fight doctrine catches up with you."[47] The brigade leadership consciously sought out expertise and background that would help prepare the organization for the coming fight. Battalion commanders encouraged professional reading programs for their unit leaders all the way down to the squad level to promote a general familiarity with COIN theory and practice. Books and articles by authors such as David Galula, John Nagl, and David Kilcullen were shared throughout the brigade, and extensive information on lessons learned in Iraq was gleaned from the Army's Center for Lessons Learned, or CALL, website. The CALL website and its supporting component called Strykernet came to represent an alternative to established doctrine as units from the war posted voluminous after-action reports detailing their experiences and listing SOPs that worked on the battlefield. Just as important, units preparing to deploy to Iraq voraciously consumed the CALL products to get ready for their deployment—the 172nd clearly was no exception to this rule. In addition to educating his organization about COIN, Shields sought to build a mindset throughout the organization that he characterized as "a warrior ethos with the mindset that we're the hunters not the hunted."[48]

The unit constructed a predeployment training program that emphasized five critical skills sets for all members of the unit—ranging from the cooks and supply clerks all the way up to the senior leadership: marksmanship, medical training, small unit battle tactics, physical fitness training, and digital communications competencies.[49] Having an organization with such a systemwide training base helped stretch the combat power of the brigade over the wide areas of northern Iraq. During the deployment, cooks became rifleman and prison guards, artillerymen became infantrymen and civil affairs officers, fire support officers managed information operations, and mechanics protected their own convoys from insurgent attacks. To further squeeze combat power from the organization, the brigade instituted organizational changes to de-emphasize those conventional warfare capacities that wouldn't be needed in northern Iraq. In recognition that large-caliber, long-range artillery would not be of much use in the COIN campaign, the brigade's 4-11th Field Artillery battalion converted itself to an infantry-type maneuver battalion while simultaneously maintaining its core artillery skill sets. Each Stryker brigade has its own indigenous artillery battalion with a complement of M198 155mm howitzers and mortars mounted inside the Stryker vehicles. The 4-11th changed its training program to build maneuver competencies and developed a whole new series of unit TTPs for use around Mosul. The battalion subsequently deployed into an area south of Mosul, conducting successful COIN operations in a 5,000-square-mile-area, partnering with an Iraqi brigade and twenty-one police stations.

The brigade consciously embraced the concept of distributed operations, which leveraged the Stryker's mobility and digital communications capabilities. During predeployment training, Shields established a junior leader development program to build decision-making skills and empower the platoon and squad leaders that would be directly engaged with the enemy, using the varieties of different competencies they would need on the battlefield. The brigade conducted numerous and varied mission-related exercises designed to strengthen the decision-making skills of its junior leaders in a variety of combat and noncombat-related areas. Outreach classes were conducted with the unit's local municipality organizations in Fairbanks, Alaska, where the unit received classes on trash removal, power generation, sewer maintenance, and other municipal-type services.[50] The unit worked with the Fairbanks police to receive training classes in crime scene exploitation and evidentiary procedures. These outreach classes included classroom lectures from the Defense Language Institute on Iraqi culture and basic communications skills.[51] At the tactical level, the brigade knew that it would be conducting dismounted patrols on a 24/7 basis to generate local contact and tailored its TTPs prior to deployment accordingly. The brigade also realized that it would be conducting extensive partnering and training relationships with the Iraqi police and Army and worked hard to be ready to assume these partnerships. The scale of these relationships, however, was not anticipated—but the unit systematically reoriented its capacities in early 2006 to assume the additional burdens associated with training more than 15,000 Iraqi soldiers. All these preparations sought to produce an adaptive organization and a flexible workforce capable of handling decision-making that reflected the demands of full-spectrum operations. As noted by Colonel Shields: "The squad leader and above need to read, need to be experts on counterinsurgency theory cause you've got soldiers and leaders everyday that are making tactical decisions with strategic consequences."[52]

Upon its arrival in September 2005, the 172nd mission was stated as: "172nd SBCT builds capable ISF and conducts counterinsurgency operations to neutralize AIF [anti-Iraq forces] in order to transition the security lead for defeating the insurgency to the ISF and the Nineveh government."[53] Like many units deploying to Iraq in this period, the 172nd initially arrived ready to defeat the insurgents and then gradually reoriented its organizational mindset to embrace the range of kinetic and nonkinetic effects it sought to bring to the environment. By November, the 172nd mission statement had been expanded to include: partner and build Iraqi Security Force capability—both Iraqi Police and Iraqi Army; progressively transition battle space to the 2nd Iraqi Army; neutralize AIF leadership; provide perception of security in the populace; deny enemy freedom of movement/sanctuary; secure the national and provincial and electoral process; develop, execute spheres of influence engagement; protect the force; treat all Iraqi people with dignity and respect.[54] The brigade established a series of LOOs to address security, training the ISF, civil-military operations, and governance. The expansion in the unit's campaign plan reflected the unit's ability to adapt in the environment and build new organizational competencies that addressed the complexities of the battle space. The unit sought to create a series of end-states that reflected its mission priorities:

1. The 2nd Iraqi Army Division has assumed battle space and is capable of conducting independent COIN operations;

2. Anti-Iraq Forces, or AIF, leadership is unable to exercise effective control of the insurgency within Mosul and the broader area of operations;
3. The population has a perception of physical security and provides security forces with information from local sources;
4. The Iraqi police function within the rule of law and are effective in providing law and order in urban areas;
5. Conditions are set for a more limited coalition troop presence;
6. Coalition forces are in a tactical over-watch to support Iraqi Security Forces (police and army) with key enablers, such as command, control, computers, communications, intelligence, and combat support when necessary;
7. The provincial leadership in Nineveh is perceived as legitimate and responsive to public needs, providing hope of a better quality of life for the people;
8. Popular support for the insurgency has eroded, the duly elected leadership enjoys public consent and is able to exercise both security control and enforce the rule of law;
9. Government systems are transparent and accountable.[55]

When the brigade arrived, it focused primarily on neutralizing the insurgency to create favorable conditions for voting in the national referendum in October 2005 and the national elections in December. Only 11 percent of eligible voters had participated in the January 2005 elections. That number increased to

These citizens of Mosul voted with their feet in showing up for the voting on the October constitutional referendum in October 2005.

56 percent in the October referendum and 61 percent in the December national elections. This represented an increase from 200,000 in January 2005 to more than 800,000 in the December 2005 elections. Insurgents mounted no successful attacks that significantly disrupted the December elections. As the brigade saw steadily improving security and increased the readiness of the ISF, the percentage of kinetic operations significantly shifted to a ratio of 80 percent nonkinetic, 20 percent kinetic. As the security environment became less violent, the brigade systematically shifted to building up the capacities of the ISF.[56]

172ND TF PARTNERING ACTIVITIES

In late October 2005, Shields changed the number-one priority from neutralizing the insurgency to increasing the readiness of the ISF—police and Army and border police. This represented an enormous task on a scale that had not been contemplated prior to the deployment. The brigade partnered with the 2nd Iraqi Army Division totaling 11,000 troops and the 3rd Iraqi Army Division of about 7,000 troops. These units were divided into seven brigades, twenty-two battalions, and three emergency response battalions. The police force in the province totaled approximately 18,000, with 8,000 in Mosul and 2,000 in Tal Afar. The police force was divided between 17 different districts and 114 different police stations. Much progress had been made by the 1/25 SBCT in reconstituting the police force after the insurgents took over Mosul in November 2004. Numerous new police stations had been built, and destroyed stations were rebuilt during its deployment. The 172nd built on the momentum of the 1/25 in rebuilding the police during 2005. The brigade's partnering arrangements were executed through the "coalition company," which partnered with an Iraqi Army battalion, a police district, and their corresponding MiTT or Special Forces unit. As was the case in much of Iraq in 2005 and 2006, while there were vast numbers of Iraqi troops identified on briefing slides passed around offices in Washington, DC, their combat capacities were at best limited, or, in most cases, nonexistent. The troops lacked equipment and training and suffered from the previous experiences in an Iraqi Army that featured centralized control, no junior leadership development, and a noncommissioned officer corps that had no background or experience in small unit leadership and tactics. Many Iraqi units had never fired their weapons—if they had any weapons at all. While there were a few competent units in northern Iraq, composed mostly of Kurdish troops, most of the Iraqi Army in the north during this period existed in name only. Many had poor or absentee senior leadership that evinced more interest in taking a paycheck and going on leave than in training and conducting dangerous COIN operations. The training effort in northern Iraq to stand up an Army and police force from scratch fell to the 172nd, a collection of eleven-man Military Transition Teams, or MiTTs, and Special Forces trainers from the 1st Battalion, 5th Special Forces Group that had arrived in Iraq in May 2005.[57]

While the police were on the road to recovering from their collapse in Mosul in November 2004, the 172nd needed to increase the numbers of available trained police that were graduating from the police academies in Mosul and Amman, Jordan. The throughput from these academies simply did not meet the demand. To solve the problem, the 172nd helped create a training and education infrastructure to build and maintain core competencies in both the police and the Army. The brigade leadership decided on these specific steps on its own initiative after arriving in theater.[58] The 172nd and its task force participants designed a comprehensive program to address the deficiencies in Army and police forces. Each unit of the brigade actively participated in the partnering efforts. A centerpiece of the program was the Northern Iraqi Regional Training Center at Hamam al Alil—a facility that housed the Army training course and an Iraqi Police Basic Skills Academy.[59] The 4th Battalion, 23rd Regiment and a team from the Multi-National Security Transition Command-Iraq, or MNSTC-I, helped stand up the center in Hamam al Alil in southern Mosul. The two Iraqi Army divisions enthusiastically supported the idea and immediately sent students to the multifaceted training program that delivered a junior office development course and a noncommissioned officer academy. The NCO academy put Iraqi NCOs through courses in squad leaders' tactics, platoon sergeant responsibilities, and combat medical training. The brigade's 4th Battalion, 11th Field Artillery Regiment played an instrumental role in establishing the center's police training facility along with the 709th Military Police Battalion. The province's police director, General Wathiq, strongly supported the idea and worked with both units to develop the program of instruction. Under the plan, Iraqi police received (1) firearms training with the host battalion (the 4-11th) at a firing range; (2) law and order training from the 709th; and (3) proper search and patrol procedures. After the first three months of operation, the police training curriculum was turned over to trained Iraqi policemen. The 1-17th set up a course to "train the trainers" with a basic and advanced marksmanship academy at FOB Marez in the south of Mosul. These trainers then went back to their Iraqi Army units to administer the course. The brigade's 2-1 infantry administered a training center at Al Kindi, located to the north of Mosul. It stood up two advisory teams that cycled through platoons from the 4th Iraqi Army Brigade to train in maintenance, logistics, driver training, and small unit battle drills.

The 172nd leveraged these ongoing courses with the training program conducted by the 1st Battalion, 5th Special Forces Group (Airborne), which had arrived in northern Iraq several months prior. The 1-5 executed what became known as the "BATT" mission (Battalion Augmentation Training Team) in Ninewa from May 2005 to January 2006. The 1-5, commanded by Colonel Mark Mitchell, provided Special Forces Operational Detachments Alpha ("SFODA," or A Teams) to train battalions of the 2nd and 3rd Iraqi Army Divisions. The battalion initially deployed to northern Iraq when it became apparent that the 1/25 could not provide personnel to cover the training requirement. The arrival of the 1-5 in northern Iraq, as part of the "Special Forces Surge" in mid-2005, came after significant interagency debate, but the dire situation in the north eventually convinced the military leadership to invigorate the attempt to build ISF capacities.[60] The deployment of the 1-5 required a substantial increase (nearly 40 percent) in the total special forces footprint in Iraq and a 300 percent increase (five SFODAs to twenty SFODAs) in the Special Forces presence in northern Iraq. The deployment of Special Forces was deemed necessary because the U.S. Army MiTT program was still in its infancy and the existing transition teams with the Iraqi Army were unable to handle the massive training requirements of 18,000 Iraqi Army personnel in northern Iraq. The Special Forces deployment provided the targeted Iraqi Army units with dedicated, properly resourced trainers whose Special Forces background and training had prepared them for the mission. By contrast, the Army's MiTT program had not yet gathered internal momentum and did not draw from an established professional cadre that had long experience in the training of foreign militaries. In fact, at that stage of the war, many Army officers viewed assignment to a MiTT team in Iraq as a career limiting assignment. The SFODAs lived, trained, and operated alongside the Iraqi Army on a continuous basis in ways that helped take advantage of the Special Forces unique capabilities. One of the Special Forces' core competencies was development of foreign internal defense, or FID. While the unit's orders directed that it conduct training at the company level, the 1-5 mounted a much more aggressive program that included training IA commanders and staffs, especially S-2 and S-3; they assisted with organizing, training, and equipping local Iraqi police forces; and established professional development courses for Iraqi officers and NCOs, all as part of a comprehensive and unique Special Forces approach to FID that sought to build sustainable core competencies tailored to existing Iraqi capabilities. The Special Forces soldiers became mentors and friends to IA soldiers; advisors to U.S. commanders at all levels on COIN and Middle Eastern culture; force integrators for combined operations; and a highly regarded source for unbiased and unadulterated assessments of the situation on the ground.[61] These efforts further leveraged the 172nd training program throughout the province.

The SFODAs helped feed reliable and timely intelligence to the brigade task force members. The language, cultural skills, and advanced capabilities of Special Forces soldiers provided exceptional access to Iraqis from all walks of life. The intelligence developed from the Special Forces was routinely and directly shared with the conventional forces at all levels and vice versa. Both the conventional forces and Special Forces participated in the joint targeting process at all levels of command. The HUMINT networks developed by the Special Forces helped provide a detailed picture of many insurgent activities beyond the borders of northern Iraq. This resulted in the extreme disruption of multiple insurgent cells and networks and a reduction in their operational capabilities.[62]

In just eight months, twenty SFODAs and the 172nd training programs, organized under four advanced operational bases, radically transformed nearly one-fifth of the Iraqi Army—twenty Iraqi Army battalions representing the combat power of two full Iraqi Divisions—from a disorganized, marginally trained, ill-equipped and poorly led rabble into functioning and effective military organizations—units with the training, equipment, and leadership necessary to execute their essential missions in a difficult counterinsurgency fight.[63]

While the 172nd realized it would be partnering with Iraqi Army and Police units, it did not realize the scale of the effort that would be required. Soon after its arrival in theater, the unit realigned its approach to place these partnership activities at the center of its COIN campaign. As noted by Shields, "We knew we'd partner with the ISF, but partnering and really taking on advising, training, increasing the readiness was not something we spent any resources on in the train up. We just embraced it as an organization and everybody bought in and understood." When the brigade arrived in August 2005, none of the Iraqi Army units had transitioned to assuming the lead in combined operations. Only 1,500 Iraqi police had been put through a training program. By August 2006, fourteen Iraqi Army battalions and two Army brigades had assumed the

lead for COIN operations in the province—reaching a "level 2" readiness proficiency—meaning that they were capable of platoon-level actions in the field.
That did not mean they could conduct independent operations, but their capabilities had increased significantly.[64] Setting aside the issue of actual combat
capabilities, most Iraqi Army units throughout the country lacked a logistics
system to support sustained operations. The Iraqi government had contracted
out much of its Army's logistics requirements, which meant that logistical support appeared sporadically or not at all.[65] Over the same period, 9,540 Iraqi
policemen had graduated from the training academies. Twenty police stations
had been rebuilt and twelve remodeled over the course of the deployment.

INTELLIGENCE

The brigade made organizational changes to its intelligence support structure before it arrived in northern Iraq and made still more changes after it
arrived in theater to address shortfalls once operations had commenced. The
relationships and procedures surrounding the collection, dissemination, and
analysis of all source intelligence at Task Force Freedom, the Joint Special Operations Task Force, the 172nd SBCT TF, as well as its predecessor the 1/25 SBCT
should serve as models for the possibilities that can arise when organizational
barriers come down and information flows horizontally throughout organizations involved in the fight. A series of seamless relationships were built between
a wide variety of U.S. government agencies and various operating components
(both conventional forces and Special Forces) that enabled Stryker units in
northern Iraq during the period to feed all source intelligence into an integrated
planning and operations cycle that drove daily operations. The 172nd greatly
benefited from a series of "best practices" that had been built during the 1/25's
deployment that had flattened the organizational architecture for intelligence
supporting units and built extraordinary inter- and intra-agency coordination
in organizational communities known in peacetime for behaving in just the
opposite way. In northern Iraq, many traditional procedures that stove-piped
the usual hierarchical-vertical flow of intelligence information disappeared in
support of the war fighter. In this theater of the Iraq COIN campaign, at least,
it is clear that task-organized groups of technical and substantive experts from
different agencies freely cooperated in their support for tactical operations, leveraging an already well-trained, adaptive military force into becoming even
more proficient on the battlefield. While these relationships were based on
trust and cooperation between professionals, the information flow to the tacti-

cal units was helped immeasurably by the Stryker's digital and satellite communications backbone, which provided commanders with the bandwidth and
encryption capabilities to pass information freely throughout the network—a
network that in this case stretched all the way back to a wide variety of agencies headquartered in the United States. The flattened intelligence architecture
served as an instrumental component in the 172nd's embrace of distributed
operations that drove authority down to the company and squad level. Robert
Kaplan described the phenomenon as it had developed during the 1/25 deployment, but he could just as well have described the phenomenon in the 172nd as
will be illustrated later in this chapter:

> Autonomy is further encouraged by the flat "intelligence architecture" of the Stryker
> brigades. Information now comes to captains less and less from battalion headquar-
> ters, and more and more from other junior officers in other battalions, via informal
> e-mail networks, as well as directly from Iraqi units. The lieutenant colonel who
> commands an infantry battalion, and the major who is the captain's executive officer,
> do not always have to be consulted. Given the results, the commanding officers like
> it that way. One evening in March of 2005, a captain acting on a tip from an Iraqi
> source—and seeking no permission from above—carried out six raids in Mosul over
> a few hours, netting 14 out of 20 members of an insurgent cell, plus large numbers of
> weapons and several vehicles. In August, a tip that the insurgent leader Abu Zubayr
> was planning to assassinate a local police chief led a company captain to develop a
> plan to trap Abu Zubayr by using the tipster as bait. The captain had Abu Zubayr's
> movements tracked by means of an unmanned surveillance plane. Abu Zubayr was
> cornered and killed, along with two other key area insurgents.[66]

In northern Iraq, as elsewhere in the country, a wide variety of intelligence
agencies and their personnel supported military forces: the National Security
Agency (NSA) deployed communications specialists and equipment directly
with field operating units; career professionals from the Central Intelligence
Agency (CIA) developed HUMINT source networks that proved extremely robust particularly early in the 172nd deployment; the National Image and Map-
ping Agency (NIMA) helped provide detailed overhead imagery to all units
to create common situational awareness of complex urban environments; the
National Ground Intelligence Center (NGIC) deployed teams of analysts and
helped gather and analyze information on insurgent networks; the U.S. Army
Intelligence and Security Command (INSCOM) deployed teams to help in the
collection and analysis process. Each of these national-level agencies and others, such as the Defense Intelligence Agency (DIA), supported deployed forces

and vice versa. During the 172nd deployment, these agencies worked seamlessly in informal task groups to directly support military operations.

The organizational changes made by the 1/25, the 172nd, and special operations forces operating in the area observed three main principles: (1) the cross-organization and cross-echelon integration of intelligence sharing in the field and integration of national-level collection capacities; (2) the evolution of procedures where "need to share" overrode "need to know"; this philosophy encouraged the horizontal integration of collection, analysis, and operations; and (3) the lowering of the threshold of what constituted "actionable" intelligence to enable rapid action in the field.[67] Task Force Freedom ensured the continuity of these best practices when the 172nd arrived in September 2005, and the brigade embraced the established procedures and relationships that had been established by its predecessor. For its part, Task Force Freedom facilitated the process by obtaining the necessary equipment to gain access to national-level intelligence and stood up its own mini joint interagency task force, or JIATF, which gave its members access to many different elements in the vast U.S. intelligence community.[68] Members from the agencies in northern Iraq worked with the JIATF to support operations in the field, effectively constituting a national-level organization working in direct support of tactical operations.[69] One of the products developed by the JIATF was a provincewide joint targeting list that got shared with all operational components throughout the province. The effort was facilitated by the development of a series of new intelligence databases employed throughout Iraq that greatly assisted in creating common situational awareness in the intelligence sections of units deployed in the field. The list proved extremely useful in the 172nd information operations campaign, as will be detailed later.

The 172nd fully recognized the importance of Tactical HUMINT Teams, or THTs, before it deployed and took additional steps to build its THT expertise upon arriving in Iraq. When the 4-14 Cavalry got stripped from the brigade as it deployed into Iraq, the unit's THTs got redistributed throughout the brigade's other battalions to boost their THT capacities. In return, the 4-14 received additional infantry components to allow it to do cordon and search operations and establish flash control points on the road network around Rawah.[70] It became clear early in the 172nd's deployment that its tactical HUMINT teams, or THTs, at the battalion level lacked the experience to build local source networks and to gather relevant information during detainee questioning. These deficiencies were not unique to the 172nd—they plagued most units at the beginning of their deployment cycles before personnel gained experience and built expertise. The 172nd leadership recognized this systemic problem and formed a nondoctrinal working group to address the issue. The brigade subsequently beefed up its THT expertise by reaching out to the Joint Special Operations Task Force at Task Force Freedom that had vast experience in building and managing HUMINT networks.[71] The Special Forces personnel helped the 172nd's THTs get up to speed, and intelligence collection from detainee questioning and HUMINT sources greatly increased in the first several months of the deployment. In addition to help from Special Forces, the brigade plussed up their battalion THTs and designed new interrogation strategies based on inputs from a variety of sources. Early in the deployment, the brigade drew upon and successfully leveraged the capacities of resident CIA personnel that had vast experience in building HUMINT networks.[72] The use of so-called OGAs, or other government agencies, proved instrumental in helping the brigade begin developing the local source networks that would prove critical to its COIN campaign. Later in the process, Iraqi Army and Iraqi police were brought into the THT process to help guide detainee interrogations. The partnering efforts enabled through the brigade working group dramatically improved the 172nd's intelligence collection effort and, as will be detailed in the 2-1 section of this chapter, drove successful COIN operations.

The philosophy of "need to share" drove the brigade's approach to intelligence no matter from which source. To assist in the free movement of information between organizations, the brigade dispensed with the bureaucratic requirement that all information be passed through the headquarters and down to its units. Instead, information could be transmitted from collectors in different agencies directly to units either in the field or preparing for their patrols. There is no question that the transmission of highly classified information directly to operating units was facilitated by the Stryker's digital and satellite communications network, which allowed encrypted information to get passed directly to patrolling units. It also was facilitated by the attitudes of the collectors, which technically could have classified the information in compartments that would have prevented the information from being transmitted over the Stryker's digital backbone. The willingness of these agencies to allow the 172nd to disseminate the information widely and quickly proved its worth time and again in successful tactical operations executed by empowered junior leaders. The brigade's encrypted communications network proved instrumental in placing the intelligence analytical unit directly in support of patrolling forces, and it proved its worth in many quick-turnaround operations for both the 1/25 and the 172nd, when squad leaders could quickly cross-reference local tips with established intelligence databases that led to cache finds as well as high-value target raids that netted sought-after insurgent cell leaders.[73] This phase of the war also saw the creation of a new series of databases that helped battalion and brigade staffs to correlate all-source intelligence quickly. Other, simpler steps helped immeasurably. Various company commanders purchased phones in the local economy supported with prepaid phone cards.[74] These cell phones proved to be extremely useful to the brigade's company commanders, who passed their numbers freely around the local communities in which they worked. Soon, tips from the locals began arriving over these cell phones and passed up into the intelligence network collection and analysis apparatus.[75] Each battalion sector subsequently built vast "walls" that diagrammed the insurgent cell structure throughout the area using link-nodal analysis. Units such as the 172nd developed extraordinarily detailed and coherent understandings of their insurgent adversaries through the fusion of various national-level organizational capacities with their own developing skills at tactical collection and analysis.

The brigade successfully lowered the threshold of what constituted "actionable" intelligence. As relationships between the SBCT and the various supporting agencies matured, the brigade leadership encouraged government agencies operating outside the formal SBCT structure to pass their tips directly to operating units. Higher headquarters at Task Force Freedom strongly supported this approach and encouraged the 172nd to mount local operations on virtually all credible local tips.[76] The aggressive approach taken by Task Force Freedom and supported by the brigade had a self-fulfilling cycle as aggressive local operations drew upon an intelligence organizational structure that fused national, operational, and tactical levels in a continuously reinforcing cycle. As noted by Shields, "You can have a centralized intelligence architecture, but you'll lose agility and so we had a phenomenal team in Mosul where we flattened our intelligence architecture, which played into our concept of distributed operations that was based on our junior leader development program."[77]

LOGISTICS

Combat logistics in Ninewa proved to be a challenge that required a departure from doctrinal practice, which in conventionally oriented fire and maneuver scenarios featured combat support on a linear battlefield with clear delineations between friendly and nonfriendly forces. In Ninewa, there was no forward line of troops to divide the battlefield and thereby guide logistical operations using traditional doctrinal practice. The 172nd fought as a distributed unit over extremely wide distances that militated against centrally controlled logistical operations used in conventional warfare. To support the operations of its widely distributed elements in four larger FOBs and seventeen smaller COPs, the BSB and its 600 personnel adapted and innovated as it built support capacities to keep the brigade task force's combat elements in the field. The large distances between its combat unit customers represented just the first of several hurdles facing the BSB. The BSB found itself supporting a far larger force than just the 172nd, also providing varied levels of support to related task force elements as well as Iraqi Army and police units that had little sustained logistical support in place over the period. The BSB, commanded by Lieutenant Colonel Bill Keyes, operated from FOB Marez in Mosul and provided forward support to as many as 10,500 task force personnel in Ninewa and Anbar Provinces—more than twice the number of people in the brigade. The numbers involved, however, told only part of the story. The soldiers receiving brigade-level support were organized into eleven differently configured battalion task forces and eleven separate companies, all of which had different numbers of personnel and required different types and levels of support. For example, the 172nd 4-11 Field Artillery battalion, which had been almost completely reorganized in the predeployment training to function as a maneuver battalion, performed few indirect fire missions, operating in the area south of Mosul, a relatively quiet area. It relied mostly on HMMWVs for its tactical mobility. By contrast, the two maneuver battalions operating in and around Mosul (the 2-1 and 1-17) were in daily contact with insurgents and depended on the Stryker to move around the battlefield. The 4-23 operated in Tal Afar and along the Iraq-Syrian border, which constituted its own unique environment. Last, but not least, the 4-11 cavalry group operated nearly 120 miles to the south in Anbar in Rawah and could count on little if any support from the neighboring Marine Corps units. Eventually, nearly 1,000 personnel operated out of the main operating base at Rawah, requiring herculean efforts by the BSB in weekly eighteen-hour convoys to keep the base resupplied. Beyond the unique support requirements and dispersed locations for each of these complex task forces, each unit worked with multiple Iraqi Army battalions and Iraqi police stations. In total, the brigade partnered with twenty-one Iraqi Army battalions, thirty police stations, and two Iraqi commando units.

During the deployment to Mosul, Keyes realized that he would have to drastically change and streamline his battalion's organizational structure to support the brigade's concept of distributed operations and the additional support requirements created by the 172nd's task force members and ISF partners. The BSB normally consisted of a headquarters and headquarters company (HHC), a distribution company, a maintenance company, and a medical company. Keyes realized that he needed a more fluid and cross-functional organization—a conclusion that had also been reached by his predecessor, the 1/25.[78] Both units broke the proverbial mold in devising creative solutions to the logistical problems confronting them in northern Iraq. During the 1990s, the Army's approach to combat support featured "just-in-time" logistics, which sought to avoid warehousing large stocks of materiel at or near the front lines. Instead, "just-in-time" combat logistics sought to deliver support as the maneuver units needed it for operations. This approach would be impossible to execute for the 172nd because of the distances between the brigade's units, the lack of vehicles to move the equipment, and manpower shortages in the BSB to move such precise amounts of equipment on short notice. Keyes needed to design a flexible and adaptive stockpiling system that could enable the brigade's concept of distributed operations across a range of different scenarios that reflected the diverse tasks being performed by different units in the brigade.

Given the fluid nature of the environment in northern Iraq and the disparate logistical requirements of his units, Keyes reached back to Army doctrine from the 1980s to help solve his problem. During the 1980s as the Army reoriented its doctrine toward the Airland Battle and deep strike maneuver, it created logistical support organizations called forward area support teams, or FAST, that embedded with the maneuver elements. Keyes adopted the same idea for the 172nd, effectively splitting the BSB into a series of cross-functional FAST teams that he sent directly to the dispersed battalions in Ninewa. The unit's predecessor, the 1/25, had employed a similar idea, labeling the groups as logistical support teams. The composition of each FAST team varied from one unit to another based on the location and requirements of the unit it supported. The FAST teams effectively extended the BSB's logistics capability forward to each battalion to facilitate support.[79]

The forward deployed FAST teams served as the BSB's eyes and ears with their maneuver customers, providing a continuous stream of data for the BSB's planning and support operations administered out of FOB Marez. The FAST teams operated under the tactical control of the maneuver battalions and participated in all the battalion targeting and operational cycles. Out of this constant interaction with the battalion executive officers and targeting staffs, the teams developed a detailed understanding of the unit's support requirements. Using the brigade's digital communications system, the teams fed all their information into the BSB headquarters element at FOB Marez. The headquarters element compiled all the inputs from the teams and created an overarching brigade support plan based on a system of flexible, adaptive planning that matched unit support requirements with available support. Keyes and the BSB staff tried to anticipate the unexpected that could change their support requirements by war-gaming different support scenarios throughout the deployment. These war game exercises built a database for a range of different support scenarios that kept the support staff sharp and the BSB prepared to react to unanticipated events.[80]

Manpower shortages were a constant headache for the BSB—a casualty of breaking up the battalion into forward-deployed embedded teams. The unit simply lacked the manpower to deliver the complicated support needs throughout the province. The BSB addressed this by developing creative work solutions that moved the organization "outside the doctrinal box," as characterized by Keyes.[81] Instead of using precious infantry combat power to provide convoy security, the BSB took responsibility for providing its own security teams. All members of the battalion were viewed as combat riflemen and were required to stay current on their combat and medical skills during the deployment. Using the detailed knowledge gained by participating with the customer targeting cycles, the BSB headquarters element leveraged the use of its customer operations with its ongoing support requirements between the FOBs and COPs throughout their areas. In other words, the BSB sought to shoehorn ongoing logistical requirements into maneuver battalion operations. When patrols were operating between the hub-and-spoke network, the FAST teams used their own manpower to help move water, food, and supplies along with the patrols. As was the case with other elements in the brigade, manpower shortages and the emphasis on distributed operations pushed authority down the organizational structure. Keyes placed senior enlisted personnel in charge of convoy security and other critical tasks that would normally have been delegated to officers.

The BSB developed new procedures to push support out to the bases via combat logistics patrols, or CLPs, which varied based on the number of personnel, the amount of fuel used, the amount of food rations, the distance, and the insurgent presence. With continuous inputs from the FAST teams, the BSB

delivered support via combat logistics patrols, CH-47 helicopters, UH-60 helicopters, air drops by C-130 aircraft, and the C-23 Sherpa air freight aircraft
that could land on short runways.[82] To perform the numerous and continuous combat logistics patrols, the BSB took on the task of providing its own
convoy security, training cooks, clerks, and noncommissioned officers in the
task of convoy security. As was the case throughout the 172nd, the BSB personnel received combat-related training and were required to stay current on
their marksmanship and combat medical training.[83] The flexibility of the BSB
workforce extended to other areas. Before deploying to Iraq, the unit realized
that managing detainees could become a significant brigade task. The unit
reached out to the Fairbanks Alaska Police Department before its deployment
and received specialized training from the police in handling and transporting
convicts. The BSB cooks took on the missions of detainee operations, which
involved receiving Iraqi detainees arriving on C-130s from Baghdad and transporting them to the central jail in Mosul.[84]

All the CLPs to each COP were coordinated in daily BSB logistical synchronization meetings at FOB Marez. All logistics functions of the brigade were
planned and coordinated by the 172nd Support Operations Section within the
BSB. The support operations officer, an extension of the brigade staff and the
section itself, was considered brigade special staff. The section consisted of
maintenance, supply, mortuary affairs, food service, medical, and transportation personnel. The section was the center for all logistics issues and coordinated and supervised all execution of logistics missions. The section tasked and
oversaw any support mission for the brigade.[85]

The SBCT concept called for brigade maintenance supported by 240 mechanics all under command and control of the BSB. These mechanics administered maintenance on all the brigade's wheeled vehicles, engineer equipment,
weapon systems, and electrical communication equipment. The wheeled mechanics in the SBCT fell under a two-tier maintenance program that made it
responsible for all vehicle repairs from the operator level to the repair and replacement of major assemblies such as engines and transmissions. Because of
the advanced technology of the SBCT, the brigade relied heavily on contracted
civilians. These civilian maintainers conducted technical inspections, ordering
of all the parts required and the completion of repair on all contractor supported systems. Most of the 180 civilian contractors began working with the
SBCT in Alaska and deployed with the unit to Mosul.[86]

Civilian contractors made immeasurable contributions in the efforts to keep the brigade deployed in the field. Indeed it is fair to say that the 172nd's combat readiness could not have been kept at such high levels without the use of civilian contractors. Keyes estimated that the use of contractors represented a 50 percent increase in logistical support available to the brigade. He estimated that sixty contractors provided the same degree of support as ninety soldiers, because of all the different tasks required of soldiers, such as force protection, physical fitness training, and other tasks. By contrast, the Stryker support contractors could dedicate all their time to the support of the unit's complex machinery. These contractors added a kind of invisible layer of organizational complexity to the brigade in that they appeared on no formal organizational chart or no unit briefing slides. Yet the specialized technical competencies of the civilian support enabled the unit to function at a high rate of technical and operational proficiency. Complex systems break down and require a specialized and complex set of skills in the workforce to make their continued operations possible. The battlefield innovation process in the 172nd was in part enabled by a complex organizational network of private contractors that provided a task specialization skill set not part of the formal unit structure.[87]

During the twelve months of the 172nd SBCT's deployment to Mosul, the BSB drove 135,635 miles over 787 combat logistical patrols, completed 7,893 direct support maintenance jobs in the motor pool, processed 61,658 parts in the Forward Distribution Point (FDP), produced 3,500,000 gallons of water, issued 1,705,748 gallons of fuel, and treated more than 1,900 patients in thirteen different medical screens.[88]

INFORMATION OPERATIONS

Information Operations (IO) developed into a centerpiece of the 172nd COIN campaign in Ninewa, complementing and feeding the other aspects of the brigade's operations. The brigade integrated IO into its targeting cycle early in its deployment and came to regard it as a vital tool in its COIN campaign. Throughout the deployment in Ninewa, the brigade used radio, television, handbills, loudspeakers, and skillfully positioned press coverage to actively contest the information domain against the insurgents. U.S. units throughout Iraq frequently complained of the cumbersome review and release procedures demanded by higher headquarters before permitting the release of IO products. These procedures meant that U.S. IO efforts lagged those of the insurgency, which dominated the information domain in much of Iraq during the 2004–5 period. This was not the case in northern Iraq, where the 172nd brigade staff assumed release authority for most IO-related products in its battle space and quickly tailored IO products to local events as it sought to drive a wedge between the population and the insurgents. A favorite tactic featured the use of loudspeaker operations in areas where failed IED attacks had occurred to undermine the credibility of the cell prosecuting the attacks. The brigade had the advantage of deploying into an area with a functioning and well-subscribed Iraqi Media Network, or IMN, television station in Mosul. Colonel Shields and his battalion commanders made a determined effort to use the station to publicize the operations of the Iraqi military. Under the direction of the brigade IO coordinator, Major Mike Sullivan, and the public affairs officer, Major Mike Blankartz, local radio stations and the TV station initiated shows in which residents called in to ask questions directly to Iraqi government officials. The staff promoted joint ISF/IP media events whenever possible. A typical press conference included the senior officers of a variety of different units.[89]

The brigade worked to build relationships with the manager of the local TV station and its main engineer. Insurgents had killed three workers from the station. The brigade processed condolence payments to the families of the IMN workers, knowing that the IMN station could not afford it. This gained the brigade traction with the station staff. Other small gestures, such as providing medical care to children in the families that worked at the station, helped to further build a relationship. The IMN station proved very responsive in reporting community events such as school openings and in publicizing insurgent attacks that killed women and children. The relationships developed with local media outlets proved critical in contesting the information domain with the insurgency over the brigade's deployment.[90]

A key feature of the 172nd IO campaign became the "Mosul Most Wanted" list, released every thirty days in handbills and posters and then publicized on the local TV station. As the brigade built momentum with its IO operations, it began refining its TTPs to take advantage of the tool to complement its other COIN activities. By the end of the deployment, the brigade achieved nearly a 50 percent success rate to kill/capture the individuals who were placed on the poster. Placing individuals on the list required concurrence of the brigade and battalion intelligence sections and coordination with other agencies that had reasons to target particular individuals. The brigade carefully vetted the target nomination process and made only one mistake—placing an individual on the poster only to find that he had been detained a month prior and released because of his innocence after interrogation. The brigade IO coordinator, Major

Sullivan, told the S-2 after hearing this: "Tell him to hide for thirty days." After this event, battalion targeteers throughout the brigade began to realize how powerful the product had become.[91] The IO staff then developed the follow-on to the most wanted list, advertising punishments meted out to insurgents by the Iraqi justice system.

The brigade IO coordinators reached out to the battalions in the target co-ordination process and soon realized that more involvement at lower levels in the unit led to greater success rates. As the ISF became integrated into the brigade's targeting cycles, the ISF started providing updates of known locations of the individuals identified on the posters, even to the point of stating who among those listed had already been detained by them. The battalions sub-sequently produced individual "wanted" flyers, which also proved successful, to concentrate on particular areas.[92] Release of the most wanted list evolved into a monthly IO event. Various battalion commanders reported that the local population eagerly awaited the new list each month. The list got released on the first Tuesday of every month—the brigade's ISF targeting meeting day. Lo-cal media outlets such as the television station and the local newspapers were prepared for the stories, making the day a local media blitz day for the product. During this week, the battalions received hundreds of these flyers to give to the ISF for their patrols and checkpoints. They would be posted all over Mosul and broadcast by the television station for the entire week. Later in the brigade's deployment, the most wanted product became the "Ninewa Most Wanted" and was distributed throughout the province.

CIVIL MILITARY OPERATIONS

Execution of civil military operations in northern Iraq occurred through a diverse array of organizations and agencies—not all of which were synchro-nized or coordinated with each other. During its deployment the 172nd estab-lished a CMO coordination cell to synchronize the activities of the two civil affairs battalions (the 401st, later replaced by the 403rd), the U.S. Army Corps of Engineers, and a State Department Provincial Reconstruction Team stood up in November 2005 following a visit by then Secretary of State Condoleezza Rice. As was the case in most areas of Iraq during the period, CMO operations faced a number of hurdles. First, the environment was for the most part non-permissive. The insurgents actively sought to prevent CMO projects from be-ing delivered, and civil affairs units were not combat elements that could both fight and deliver their projects at the same time. Second, the infrastructure was generally in poor condition if it existed at all. In Mosul, for example, the city had taken shape iteratively over centuries with little modern urban planning to integrate central sewage, water, and electrical services. Third, economic activity in general in Iraq had been dominated by state-run activities or, alternatively, the underground, black-market economy. This was certainly the case in northern Iraq. In Ninewa, there were sixteen state-run companies that provided such items as cement, drugs and medical supplies, cotton, sugar and yeast, oil and gas, furniture, and dairy products. Most of these companies operated at less than 30 percent capacity, but served the useful purpose of proving a means for the government to disburse money to local residents that mostly never showed up for work. The notable exception was the pharmaceutical plant located thirty miles outside Mosul, which operated at 100 percent capacity producing a variety of medical products. Despite these hurdles, the 172nd and the organizations executing CMO successfully integrated these projects into the COIN campaign in the north. Weekly targeting meetings throughout the battalion included CMO participation, and the brigade regarded it as a critical nonlethal effect on the battlefield.[93]

When the 172nd arrived, CMO execution at the tactical level fell to the 401st Civil Affairs Battalion. Also present was the Army Corps of Engineers, which focused on larger scale projects such as maintenance of the Mosul dam, located just to the north of the city, and other multimillion dollar projects such as Mosul's electrical substation rehabilitation and the building of a new air traffic control tower at Mosul airport. The Mosul dam provided electricity to the city's residents and needed constant maintenance. The 401st embedded its civil affairs teams with the 172nd battalions and continued to work ongoing projects that had been started under the 1/25's deployment. The 172nd brigade staff exercised oversight over these projects but had no technical authority over the unit, which reported up a separate chain of command to the 11th Armored Cavalry Regiment. Execution of projects occurred through local contractors identified by the 401st teams working in their respective local communities. Each project took shape after consultation with local leadership via the regional security councils set up by the 172nd's battalions throughout the province and provincial government ministries in Mosul. Funding for the projects came through the commander's emergency response funds, or CERP, which were provided to TF Freedom in Tikrit. In November 2005, the State Department created Iraq's first provincial reconstruction team in Mosul, which added yet another organizational entity involved in CMO and which had its own source of funding.

Since it technically worked for the State Department, the PRT, headed by Ambassador Cameron Munter, had no reporting relationship with any of the U.S. military units and worked mainly with Iraqi national government ministries. Coordination between these entities happened at the Civil-Military Operations Center, or CMOC, located at FOB Marez and other CMOCs located in Dahuk in Iraq's northernmost province along the border with Turkey.[94]

The disparate organizations involved created coordination problems for the 172nd, which had overall control over the battle space. In the spring of 2006, the SBCT created a Ninewa Reconstruction and Development Management Cell to ensure unity of effort in executing governance and economic civil-military operations. The cell tried to synchronize the ongoing civil military operations throughout the province. In May, the 172nd helped coordinate Operation Barnstormer—an Iraqi Agriculture Ministry's program to protect crops in northern Iraq from insect damage. Over a two-week period, wheat and date crops got sprayed with pesticide using helicopters and biplanes.

2-1 INFANTRY IN EASTERN MOSUL

The COIN fight in Mosul proper proved a particularly difficult challenge to the wheeled Stryker units. The dense urban terrain provided insurgents with an ideal environment for conducting operations against the 172nd. Without a well-established, modern road network bisecting the city, insurgents could quickly melt back into densely populated neighborhoods crisscrossed by a series of winding alleyways too narrow for the Strykers to mount easy pursuit. The 2nd Battalion, 1st Infantry, or 2-1, operated on the eastern side of Mosul; its 800 to 900 soldiers divided into two infantry companies, a cavalry troop, and seventy-four Stryker vehicles that conducted COIN operations in dense urban terrain hosting a population of between 750,000 and 800,000 spread over five to six square miles. In addition to the fight in these neighborhoods, the unit exercised responsibility over the area north of Mosul, north to Dahuk, and roughly twenty-two villages to the east of the city. To have described the 2-1's operations as an economy of force mission, given its numbers and responsibilities, would be an extreme understatement. Eastern Mosul was an area the size of the city of Ramadi in Anbar Province—a city that received the attention of an entire U.S. brigade in 2005 and 2006. As detailed earlier in this chapter, the 2-1 operated out of a series of FOBs and COPs in its area called "AO Legion" manned by its own personnel, MiTTs, and Iraqi Army units. The area had three Iraqi police divisions and a number of substations. The police had an advertised strength of approximately 1,500; the daily end strength fluctuated between 600 and 800 per day.[95] Like much of the rest of the city, eastern Mosul had a number of active insurgent cells mounting sniper attacks, IEDs, RPG attacks, and targeted assassinations directed at both the ISF and U.S. units. As noted by its commanding officer Lieutenant Colonel Charles Webster: "There was pretty much someone shooting at you all the time."[96]

Interestingly, the 2-1 was under no illusion that it would decisively defeat the insurgency during its deployment. As noted by Webster, "We [that is, Americans] like to solve things, to finish things, to win. But, unfortunately, that's not what a COIN fight is all about. Defeat is a very definitive term. I believe I stressed to my guys the year prior to deployment and all through the deployment that we would not 'defeat' the insurgency or 'win' this fight on our tour. Our job was to win by improving the ISF and improving security."[97] Indeed, the insurgency during the 2-1's deployment proved to be very resilient and remained so as of this writing in 2010.

Prior to arriving in Mosul, the 2-1 actively participated in brigadewide activities to build knowledge and understanding of COIN. The lack of established joint doctrine presented no hindrance to the unit as it prepared for its deployment. Using inputs from a wide variety of sources, the battalion staff collectively identified a number of desired goals and end states to achieve: a secure populace; established local political institutions; a contributing local government; neutralized insurgent capabilities; and information flows from all sources.[98] In its predeployment training, the battalion organized its operations into four broad categories: security, governance, economics, and information operations. To organize its operations in support of its end states, the battalion staff took the novel approach of organizing its own campaign plan for the deployment. While campaign plans are doctrinally the purview of corps- and division-level units in the Army, Webster wanted a systematic way of relating the unit's operations to the overarching campaign plan built by the brigade. Webster looked to established Army doctrine to help prepare a campaign plan for extended tactical operations that, as he characterized it, could "apply doctrinal solutions to nondoctrinal problems."[99] Webster reached back to Army doctrine in *FM 7.0 Training the Force* for an established methodology of building a campaign plan based on the mission essential task list, or METL.[100] These were core tasks identified by the unit that the unit judged would need to be accomplished during the deployment. Identified METL tasks formed the basis for the unit's predeployment training. Over the course of the year prior to arriving in Iraq, the 2-1 built a METL that fed into a flexible, adaptive campaign plan to nest its operations within the 172nd's overall objectives. The plan detailed and identified the tasks required to achieve the end states and established quarterly reviews over the course of the year for the staff to measure its progress toward fulfilling the campaign objectives. The staff constantly reviewed the plan to allow for adjustments and looked at the plan as an adaptive, living product that could be adjusted whenever necessary. The plan served as the battalion's template to guide its lethal and nonlethal targeting operations in attempting to meet the quarterly desired end-states. The targeting cycle evolved over two-week periods in which the staff evaluated the nonlethal and lethal targets and then formally proposed the target set to the battalion staff for mission planning and execution. The battalion established a reporting system in a series of products for all units to pass over the Stryker's communications network to the senior staff, which maintained a database that tracked the battalion's overall progress on a continuous basis. The campaign plan reflected a systems-based approach to the unit's conduct on the battlefield, giving all the units a common framework for understanding the purpose of their daily operations.[101]

Not surprisingly, the battalion realized early in its deployment that a plan drawn up in Fairbanks, Alaska, the unit's peacetime home, would need adjustment when executed on the ground in Mosul. The need for change emerged after the first three months on the ground saw the battalion build situational awareness, gather reporting data, and begin to apply the targeting methodology to the tactical problems on the ground. The battalion evolved through a three-phased analytical process during the first three months in which it identified as: (1) evaluate the enemy and his TTPs; (2) evaluate the terrain—physical, human, and economic/social makeup; and (3) evaluate the unit performance by examining the application of combat power through TTPs and the use of enablers such as Iraqi police and Iraqi Army commandos. During the first three months, the battalion built a series of databases on insurgent networks based on the reporting from daily patrol records that also carried information on the performance of men and equipment. The battalion's initial assessment of eastern Mosul came from intelligence assessments of the city's neighborhoods compiled by the brigade S-2 staff, which drew heavily on the experiences of the prior unit, the 1/25. The assessments of eastern Mosul showed neighborhoods immediately east of the Tigris River free from direct insurgent control—but surrounded by a series of insurgent support zones influenced primarily by Ansar al-Sunna (AAS) and Al Qaeda in Iraq.

During the October–November 2005 period, the battalion faced an upsurge in violence as the insurgents sought to derail the December 2005 elections. In addition to targeting the Iraqi Army and Iraqi police forces, the insurgents specifically sought to destroy the Stryker vehicles. The insurgents filmed the attacks, using the videos to swing popular support in the city against the United States and the local government. Attack pattern analysis showed that 90 percent of all insurgent attacks occurred between 0900 and 1400 and were focused on Iraqi Army and police units and on the Stryker vehicles themselves with IEDs and suicide vehicle attacks.

Attack trends and pattern analysis revealed that insurgents focused their IED and Suicide Vehicle Borne Improvised Explosive Device, or SVBIED, attacks along the two major roads in eastern Mosul—one of which fell upon the seam of sectors patrolled by the 2-1's companies A and B. The seam had been exploited the insurgents in successful IED attacks on four Strykers during October. The battalion responded to these findings by adjusting its own battlefield framework and tactical patterns. First, the battalion eliminated all traffic along Route Buick that had been used by insurgents to mount attacks on the Strykers. Second, the battalion established a multilayered information, surveillance, and reconnaissance, or ISR, plan to detect the insurgent response to the shutdown of Route Buick. The plan included overhead video surveillance by the brigade's remotely piloted vehicle, beefed up signals intelligence interceptions using the Raven airborne system,[102] and aggressive efforts to improve HUMINT networks in the neighborhoods surrounding the attack areas. Last, the unit eliminated the geographic boundaries between its units—meaning that its companies no longer had sole responsibility for a defined battle space. Instead, eastern Mosul became divided up into a series of noncontiguous "L" designated areas.

The changes adopted by the 2-1 through October allowed the unit to penetrate the insurgents' decision cycle, which began to pay immediate dividends with the roll-up of several insurgent networks that had successfully attacked the battalion during September and October. The battalion further leveraged this tactical evolution with organizational changes to its THTs. The experiences of the 2-1 mirrored those of many other units in Iraq over the period, which realized they needed more robust S-2 sections and better tactical intelligence to drive COIN operations. The 2-1 successfully reoriented its THT capacities to generate useful information, which, in turn, fed into a fused tactical-intelligence-operations-cycle used by the unit for the remainder of its deployment in Mosul. By the end of its deployment, nearly 90 percent of deliberate operations conducted by the battalion were HUMINT-source driven.[103] Webster estimated that the battalion mounted 500-plus directed raids during the unit's deployment that resulted from HUMINT and SIGINT.[104]

Upon starting operations in Mosul in early September, the battalion soon realized that it lacked adequate HUMINT gathered from detainees, tactical questioning of the local populace by patrolling soldiers (hindered by language limitations), and informants. First, the unit began to draw upon HUMINT networks that had been developed by OGA—that is, the CIA—in the city. The CIA had a trained cadre of senior, trained personnel who had more latitude (that is, money) and greater experience in supporting informant networks with funding than did the brigade/battalion THT personnel. The all-source information from OGA networks started being fed into the battalion's databases to build their understanding of the insurgent networks.[105] In addition, the unit immediately cycled through a series of internal steps to address its internal deficiencies. First, the battalion broke up its THTs that were centralized at the battalion level and pushed THT personnel down to the maneuver companies to participate directly in patrols and directed raids. The battalion soon discovered that on-site questioning often was the most productive in generating useful information, which could then be passed in real time to the battalion S-2 for correlation with other known information. Detainees were often at their most vulnerable psychologically immediately after being picked up in cordon and knock operations, or after being pursued after they had been engaged in actual operations. The quality of the information generated from these interrogations also improved as a result of new field questioning and interrogation strategies developed by the battalion with OGA inputs. After pushing the THT teams down into his maneuver companies, Webster placed the battalion executive officer, Lieutenant Colonel Richard Greene, in charge of detainee questioning, in effect bridging what had been a gap and lack of capacity between the operations (S-3) and intelligence sections (S-2) on the battalion staff in the conduct of detainee questioning. The S-2 section focused on building its understanding of the insurgent network, while the S-3 concentrated on the targeting process. Neither organization had the overall vision of what the other organization was doing to inform the questioning process, whereas the executive officer had oversight over both the S-2 and S-3.[106] Detainee questioning represented a critical collection tool, and the throughput of detainees required a systematic approach to the process. Approximately 500 detainees cycled through the 2-1 questioning process over the course of ten months. The battalion started seeing results to the increased role of OGA-sourced networks and the new detainee interrogation supervision system. In mid-September, it had generated little information to populate its link-nodal analysis of the insurgent cell structure. By October, the gaps were starting to get filled in—a process that gathered momentum over the next several months.

Information about the insurgent cell structures in eastern Mosul steadily grew in richness and detail during the fall of 2005, enabling the battalion to begin development of its intelligence-operations fusions cycle and better integrate nonkinetic effects, such as information operations and CMO into the targeting process. Information gleaned from interrogations was greatly aided by the participation of OGA, Special Forces, and the ISF personnel during the fall of 2005. Detainees were well aware that the United States could hold them for only two weeks before their being transferred into the Iraqi national government's detention process, which often resulted in the return of the detainees to the streets in weeks. The detainees most feared the prospect of being transferred to Iraqi police custody. When the battalion introduced ISF personnel into the detainee interrogation process, detainees invariably became much more cooperative in the interrogations.[107] All these changes led to a flood of data that began populating the 2-1 databases, which then led to growing link-analysis charts of the insurgent network in eastern Mosul. The changed TTPs, the ISR collection plan, and the focus on generating better HUMINT led to concrete results by late October and November as the 2-1 actively began to disrupt insurgent cells. The quick turnaround of tactical level intelligence into the operations planning cycle of the unit was facilitated by the placing of an intelligence analyst in the battalion S-2 command post operations unit. The analyst monitored all incoming intelligence and could quickly judge how much of the incoming information might warrant a direct, short-notice operation. Placed on the battalion staff, the analyst could quickly relay the information to the battalion S-3 operations officer and his targeting staff.[108]

A series of successful raids on insurgent cells unfolded in late October and November and continued throughout the 2-1 deployment that drew upon changes in the ways the battalion generated intelligence and then integrated it with its targeting cell. In late October, the battalion successfully targeted a series of insurgent cells that had mounted attacks using IEDs, mortars, and snipers. Using information from the ISR collection plan and HUMINT-developed information, the battalion mounted a simultaneous operation by two Stryker companies and a cavalry troop in the Al Sharkya neighborhood of Mosul. Each company raided five houses and the cavalry troop searched four houses, detaining seven members of the Al Jammasa direct action cell, seven members of the Al Sharkaya AAS cell, and three members of the Garage Shima Saddamist cell. These cells had mounted many successful attacks on 2-1 in the early fall. The ability of the Strykers to mount swarmed, targeted raids became a feature of the 172nd's operations throughout Ninewa. Webster and other commanders called it "moving to the sound of the guns."[109]

Days after the successful raids in the last week of October, detainee questioning by ISF and OGA personnel gave the battalion a critical lead by providing the name of a financer of the so-called Opel gang that had been harassing the 2-1 patrols ever since the unit arrived. Gangs of insurgents driving in small Opel cars had mounted continuous RPG and direct-fire small arms attacks at 2-1 units, escaping with their more maneuverable vehicles into Mosul's neighborhoods. The cell also used SVBIED and mortars to attack ISF and U.S. personnel. The battalion also received critical information on the cell's operations from Special Forces units that the 2-1 had invited to participate in the battalion's targeting operations.

The cell had mounted a series of complex attacks throughout the fall, firing mortars from predetermined firing points. Transportation for the mortars was provided in a series of different vehicles. The cell used a security cell in each of its fire missions of six to eight cars that patrolled the neighborhoods from which the direct attacks were launched. The cell received logistics support from a cell leader, Abu Mustafa, which paid each participant about 75,000 Iraqi dinars ($75) for each mission. All the vehicles were returned to parking garages at the conclusion of the operations. Each SVBEID operation was supported by observation teams that also provided covering fire if necessary and ambushes for recovery forces if the attack succeeded. Over a period of thirty-six hours starting on October 26, the 2-1 rolled up the network using a fused intelligence-operations cycle. At 1030 on the morning of October 26, Iraqi police detained three insurgents—one of which confessed and provided details of Opel cell operations and names of key members of the organization. The next day at 0430, based on tips in the debrief, the 2-1 captured three members of a sniper team and their weapons in a directed raid. At 0930 the same day, Iraqi police exchanged fire with insurgents, injuring what they thought to be an innocent bystander in a blue Oldsmobile. However, after battalion personnel searched the car they found several sets of identification—one of which corresponded with the name of the cell's financer that had just been provided to the unit during detainee questioning less than twenty-four hours earlier. Information provided through the detainee questioning had cycled immediately back to the tactical unit searching the vehicle—information confirmed with the battalion S-2 via the Stryker's encrypted communications suite. The patrol quickly deployed to the hospital, where seven cell participants had assembled to free the cell leader. Over the next day, additional information gleaned from interrogations revealed the names of twenty-seven additional cell members that were quickly rounded up.[110]

Over the thirty-six-hour period, a fused intelligence collection and operations cycle had significantly disrupted an entrenched insurgent cell. The pattern of the fused intelligence-operations cycle characterized operations throughout 172nd operations in Ninewa.[111] The operation had begun with deliberate and detailed target exploitation of detainees that revealed cellular linkages and enemy TTPs. By this period of the 2-1's deployment, the battalion had instituted changes to its THT operations and placed the battalion executive officer in charge of detainee questioning. The avalanche of information gleaned from detainee questioning fed into the overall ISR collection plan that included overhead imagery and signals intelligence interceptions. The links created in the insurgent networks created new targets and permitted the development of still more refined collection plans—plans built from prior doctrinal training and practice. As applied in Mosul, however, this process of fusing collections with operations worked extremely quickly—making the Stryker units agile and flexible within the operations- maneuver cycle. The plan allowed maneuver elements to operate within the insurgent decision cycle.

The growing tactical proficiency of the 2-1, however, did not mean the battalion wasn't vulnerable to insurgents, who were themselves adapting and innovating on the battlefield. On November 19, 2005, amid rumors that Abu Musab Zarqawi was in the city, insurgents successfully ambushed a platoon that had been called in to assist an Iraqi police operation. Iraqi police had called for support after being driven off by gunfire from a house they attempted to search. The platoon arrived and attempted to enter the house, only to be met with insurgents throwing fused mortar shells at the unit. As a squad entered the house, it turned out that the building had been fortified with built-up firing positions that caught the unit in a cross-fire. The squad had entered a prepared ambush site, at close range, and lost twelve wounded soldiers in the space of a few chaotic, violent minutes. The squad finally retreated from the house after a soldier outside the building crashed a Stryker through the side of the house to give the squad a way out of the ambush. Insurgents shot Private Christopher Alcozer in the back of the head as he covered the retreat of his wounded comrades from the house. After rocketing the house from a Kiowa helicopter that had been called in for support, a squad of Iraqi soldiers led by a U.S. Special Forces sergeant attempted another clearing of the house. Insurgents then blew up the building, killing U.S. Special Forces Master Sergeant Anthony Yost and four ISF soldiers—the battalion's heaviest single day of casualties in the deployment.[112]

The development of the battalion's fused intelligence-operations cycle facilitated the integration of deliberate lethal and nonlethal planning in an attempt to "mass" these effects in particularly troublesome neighborhoods. The assessments of the first several months drove the battalion into an expanded data collection and analysis to try to improve the unit's situational awareness on a neighborhood-by-neighborhood basis. Using a software tool called the situational template, or SITEMP, the battalion began delving beneath the data populating its databases coming from SIGACTS reporting, or significant actions, which was composed mostly of data flowing from enemy attacks and the unit's response. The unit set out to populate a Microsoft database of each neighborhood focusing on the following: key political and religious leaders, content being delivered in the mosques, location and capabilities of local medical facilities, public works facilities, mass transit services, information on local businesses, and other details. While the databases did not constitute house-by-house census detail—a process used elsewhere in Iraq by U.S. units—the databases provided a product that could be passed along to the next unit. The neighborhood SITEMPs, as they were called, helped the battalion build situational awareness of the complex dynamics driving or supporting the insurgent violence. Using the SITEMP, the battalion divided up eastern Mosul into disruption zones (areas where insurgents wished to draw U.S. and Iraqi forces into unproductive engagements); battle zones (areas where the insurgents wished to engage coalition forces to demonstrate their effectiveness to the civilian population); and support zones (the areas where the insurgents lived or stockpiled their equipment and planned their missions).[113]

By the late fall of 2005, building ISF capacity represented the brigade's top priority. The 2-1 took responsibility for partnering with two Iraqi Army battalions: the 1st Battalion, 2nd Brigade, 2nd Iraqi Army Division; and the 2nd Battalion, 4th Brigade, 2nd Iraqi Army Division. Assisting in the effort were SFODAs, which conducted training for squads, platoons, and companies. MiTTs focused on higher-level staffs at the battalion, brigade, and division level. The 4th Brigade was 90 percent Kurdish and consisted of either Patriotic Union of Kurdistan or Kurdish Democratic Party personnel that had fought each other at various points. The other major component in the partnering program was the Iraqi police. Eastern Mosul had three Iraqi police district headquarters and two emergency unit response battalions. The police advisory program was administered by the 549th Military Police Company. The training efforts for the Iraqi Army took place at the Al Kindi Training Center in eastern Mosul.

The partnership activities at the brigade and battalion staff levels were operationalized early in the 2-1's deployment first through the observation of the battalion's targeting process by the Iraqi Army units. In late 2005, that observation gradually evolved into active participation in the targeting process—which greatly improved the partnership (particularly in the 4th IA Brigade). While the MiTT teams and SFODAs worked at their levels, the rest of the 2-1 remained unsure of how best to interact at the working level between the platoons and companies conducting daily operations.

The battalion had metaphorically divided up its activities into its "day" and "night" jobs. Night jobs were usually directed raids conducted by battalion personnel, whereas their day job included training the Iraqis and working on creating other battlefield effects. Preparing the Iraqi Army to conduct joint operations fell under the rubric of the battalion's day job.[114] To facilitate the interaction with the Iraqis and build tactical proficiency, the 2-1 formed tactical combat advisor teams, or TCATs, to operationalize its objective of building the ISF capabilities and to fill the void left by the departure of the SFODAs in December. The TCATs subsequently established a small-unit training program for two Iraqi Army battalions commanded by Captain Jason Glemser and Captain Rusty Topf. The TCAT mission was to "train and advise the Iraqi infantry companies and below in order to facilitate their capabilities to conduct unilateral missions and the handover of combat missions from U.S. forces to the Iraqi Army."[115] Each team consisted of five men—a sergeant first class team leader, three junior noncommissioned officers, and a soldier. The TCATs designed and supervised a four-week training cycle focused on basic combat skills for an Iraqi company, with one platoon a week in training. When the training program began, some of the ISF personnel did not know how to operate and maintain their weapons. The TCAT program concentrated on fire and maneuver. In addition to supervising the training, the TCAT personnel accompanied joint patrols, but as the Iraqi Army battalions gradually improved over the spring of 2006, the

TCATs became less directly involved in the operations. In planned joint operations, the TCATs served as the liaison between the IA and the battalion staff.[116]

Improved host-nation capabilities became another "effect" available to the 2-1 to apply on the battlefield.[117] During the spring of 2006, the unit began to develop the mature, integrated targeting packages that had been envisioned in the campaign plan. The battalion drew upon its targeting "wheel of stuff" to build targeting packages to address the SITEMP maps developed for each of the neighborhoods. Those elements—developed out of the campaign plan's lines of operation—included all the assets at the battalion's disposal to create battlefield effects.

The wheel represented tools available in the targeting process that got integrated in the biweekly targeting cycle run by the battalion staff. Each of the effects got aligned with the lines of operation and the desired end states. By the winter of 2005–6, the battalion had developed an integrated targeting process that attempted to mass effects in the most troubled neighborhoods of eastern Mosul. The result was a massing of effects in the L3 sector of the city—the so-called heart of darkness in eastern Mosul.[118] The objective of massing effects represented the attempt to operationalize the "ink spot" strategy used by various military commanders in Iraq during the period to create zones of stability free from insurgent influence and control—seeking gradually to expand those areas over time.

The 2-1 COIN campaign in eastern Mosul demonstrated a systematic attempt to apply effects-based operations in a difficult environment. The battalion built a campaign plan from the ground up to apply a variety of organizational capacities on the environment to reach its end states of a neutralized insurgency and stable local security, an ISF capable of independent operations, and a government capable of supporting the population's basic needs. It is clear that the battalion innovated in the field in its attempt to deliver effects to create that end state. The battalion had its greatest success in the direct action domain of operations conducted against the insurgents. The building of the unit's operations-intelligence fusion cycle created an extremely agile, flexible organization that drove authority down the organizational hierarchy to the units in the field. The brigade's predeployment emphasis on junior leader development successfully created a middle management that accepted and exercised authority and initiative and flourished in the field. It is also clear in 2-1's case that the unit worked hard to use nonlethal effects through information operations and local leader engagement. By the definition used in this book, the battalion demonstrated significant innovative capacity in the field in the absence of overarching joint doctrine.

The battalion succeeded in reducing the effectiveness of insurgent attacks, which continued throughout the deployment at relatively constant levels. Total attacks mounted in eastern Mosul actually increased slightly during the period of the 2-1's deployment. Behind the numbers, however, had been a shift in insurgent tactics during the spring of 2006 and a decreasing lethality over the period. As the ISF steadily gained in competence during the spring of 2006, insurgent attacks increasingly focused on Iraqi Army and police personnel. The ISF was subjected to a concerted insurgent fear and intimidation campaign in the spring of 2006 that mirrored tactics used elsewhere in Iraq as the ISF slowly built its capacities. The growing integration of ISF into the battalion targeting cycle and improved operational capabilities led to a steady roll-up of insurgent cells. The continuous disruption of these cells meant fewer skilled bomb makers were established, and the IEDs and SVBIEDs became less effective. Insurgent TTPs also shifted during the period to fewer direct fire engagements and standoff attacks using IEDs.[119]

The insurgency in eastern Mosul, however, clearly was not defeated during 2-1's deployment—despite an active operational tempo that nine months after arrival totaled 7,300 combat patrols, 192 cordon and search operations, and nearly 400 detainees processed. Insurgents mounted 317 IED attacks and 17 vehicle-IEDs against the battalion. None of the unit's Stryker vehicles were destroyed in the campaign. As various observers commented, however, the insurgency throughout Mosul seemed to have a certain resilience that remains as of this writing (four years later). For every cell that got killed or disrupted, another one sprouted up in a relatively short period. The SITEMPs developed early in 2-1's deployment that described the threat facing the battalion in the different neighborhoods looked remarkably similar to the SITEMPs later in the deployment—although the unit showed great proficiency in its targeting methodology and in the translation of that methodology into an effective operations-intelligence fusion cycle.

COMPANY C/1-17 IN WESTERN MOSUL

On the other side of the river, the 1st Battalion, 17th Infantry conducted COIN operations in the western neighborhoods of Mosul—the largely Sunni area of the city that had been the focus of insurgent attacks in November 2004 when the Mosul police force disintegrated.[120] Company C and its 175-odd "on paper" personnel and its 21 Stryker vehicles conducted COIN operations in south-western Mosul from September 2005 to July 2006—an area with a population totaling between 700,000 and 900,000 people. The unit averaged an end strength of 155 people available for duty on a daily basis—significantly below its authorized end strength. By the end of its deployment the unit had received successively greater geographic areas of responsibility. By the summer of 2006, the company had responsibility for policing villages twenty miles to the west of the city. Describing its operations as an economy of force mission would be a charitable description given the number of boots on the ground available for operations in western Mosul. Company C conducted operations in the so-called Old Town part of the city that also hosted most of the Iraqi governmental offices. The Old Town section of western Mosul had only three major roads capable of handling the Strykers, which meant that many operations were fought with soldiers dismounted from their vehicles. The company partnered with the 2nd Battalion, 2nd Brigade, 2nd Infantry Division, turning over primary responsibility for battle space in the city to the unit in January 2006. With this event, Company C ceased to mount independent operations without IA participation.

Upon arrival in its area, the company immediately set about reconfiguring itself to squeeze combat power from the unit. The company's commanding officer, Captain Ed Matthaidess, did away with the traditional Stryker infantry company organizational structure and instead integrated his mortar, fire support, and medical evacuation team into the four existing maneuver elements (three rifle platoons and a mobile gun system platoon). Matthaidess also reconfigured and augmented the dedicated company headquarters element and made it another maneuver force. The configuration of the company into five distinct maneuver elements reflected the embrace of the concept of distributed operations throughout the brigade and drove authority down to the squad leader level.

Also reflecting the brigade's emphasis, the company supported operation of the Northern Iraq Institute Field Training, or NIIFT, and structured a platoon level training program for its partnered IA unit. The program was administered at FOB Marez by the four senior noncommissioned officers in the company, headed by 1st Sergeant Daniel Schoemaker, who received further staffing support by four squad leaders from the company's platoons. The U.S. trainers got augmented by whichever platoon had been assigned force protection duties or were posted as the company's quick reaction force. This meant that different

Troops of Company C, 1-17, on patrol in Mosul's souk in the spring of 2006.

platoons with operational experience all cycled their IA counterparts through the training program. An average of one IA platoon was put through the training every week. The course started with basic rifle marksmanship, maintenance, and weapons safety on a static range. The training evolved to implement "buddy team" movements ranges, and advanced to fire teams moving through shoot houses. Eventually, the IA units all graduated to actual live fire exercises in a facility built by the company to build combat competencies in urban terrain—called a MOUT, or military operations in urban terrain. The average IA soldier fired 1,200 rounds of ammunition per week—more than most soldiers had ever fired in their careers.

The training facility simulated the conditions likely to be encountered in urban combat. The training program emphasized small arms fire discipline to counter the IA tendencies to "spray and pray" in firing their automatic weapons. The course taught the units skills to control their rates of fire and work on target acquisition. The program worked to focus on the IA NCOs learning their roles so that they would be able to make decisions in the absence of their officers. This proved difficult during the program; many senior IA officers opposed the concept, and the IA NCOs were reluctant to take on tactical responsibilities. The curriculum included first aid classes and physical fitness training, which proved difficult in the Iraqi heat. The program integrated rudimentary maintenance classes for the IA weapons and vehicles. The unit worked hard at the program and believed that the tactical proficiency of the IA platoons improved over the course of the training.[121]

Company C conducted nearly all its patrols with IA partnered units—despite continuous frustrations within the company on working with Iraqi units. The unit's After Action Report noted: "When the IA were present they often had poor noise and light discipline, added hours to the execution of the mission . . . and threatened OPSEC. Once the objective they often questioned why people were targets . . . and thought most everyone was innocent."[122] In addition to NIIFT base, company NCOs would conduct "sergeant's time training" at Iraqi Army outposts; company platoon leaders would conduct Troop Leading Procedure classes with IA officers and participated in weekly IA battalion training and targeting meetings.

Working joint patrols with the IA represented one of the unit's lines of operations structured around the brigadewide lines of operation surrounding security, governance, and host nation capacity building.[123] The unit oversaw civil military operations in its sector that included the reconstruction of three schools, two rebuilt parks, two road reconstruction projects and various trash cleanup programs. The unit synchronized CMO and IO, using the Mosul Most Wanted List, and spray painted the names of wanted suspects with contact information using stencils in public places. The IO tools proved extremely useful to the company in generating local tips to the company commander's cell phone, further leveraging the benefits of drawing upon the OGA HUMINT networks in the sector, and in the gradually growing competence of the unit's tactical HUMINT team. The unit did not develop the same sort of tactical operations-intelligence fusion cycle that worked for the 2-1 on the other side of the city. Instead, the unit maintained its own databases of information gleaned from THT debriefs and tips from a growing number of sources in the patrolled neighborhoods. The unit sometimes conducted as many as eight to nine raids a night. The unit also used female U.S. soldiers that had been provided by a neighboring combat support battalion to help in cordon and knock operations and raids. Using female soldiers helped gather information on these operations and defuse tensions in late-night searches of homes in western Mosul's dense urban neighborhoods.[124]

The unit played a dangerous cat-and-mouse game with local insurgents and built a variety of new TTPs to combat IEDs, which represented the most serious daily threat to the unit. They relied on nondoctrinal "Small Kill Teams," or SKTs, to ambush insurgents who were themselves seeking to ambush the company's patrols along the three major roads in western Mosul. The use of SKTs evolved in Iraq in 2005 and 2006 and was more widespread in 2007.[125] In Mosul, the 1/25 had used ambush teams in route over-watch positions but had not refined the TTPs to the extent done in the C/1-17. The Company C SKT teams typically were composed of five or six unit personnel that infiltrated under cover into areas of high insurgent IED activity. Each SKT typically included at least one M240B machine gun, one M14 Rifle, and one M203 grenade launcher in addition to normal fire support team weapons. Other favored weapons included the AT-4 or Javelin antiarmor weapon. Prior to an operation, the company gathered data on the houses adjacent to major intersections using Microsoft PowerPoint. Once the data had been gathered, the unit selected houses with good over-watch positions to infiltrate prior to the operation. The unit devised various innovative ways to infiltrate teams into the houses, which it would then secure for up to forty-eight hours, or until their location was compromised. One favored technique was to place the teams on top of the Strykers to infiltrate a house through the second story. The operations involved multiple locations to give the unit different fields of fire over the area under observation. The SKTs proved effective in killing IED emplacement cells when the teams were employed in the fall of 2005 and winter of 2006, which led to a temporary reduction in the attacks.[126]

A variety of means were used by the company to lure insurgents into SKT ambushes. The unit's after action reported: "Cameras, fake cameras, fake satellite dishes and other technical looking device or CF [coalition force] looking like device have been used to bring AIF [anti-Iraq Forces] into SKT engagement areas. This is a useful method to spot AIF because they will often try to destroy these devices, thereby PIDing [positively identifying] the LNs [local nationals] as AIF."[127] In January 2006, the company mounted Operation Devil's Den, placing six SKT teams and two decoy cameras along a route that had been repeatedly attacked by insurgents. In addition to the SKT teams, the unit established a small COP nearby with a quick reaction force ready to pursue fleeing vehicles.

The operation resulted in the killing of an insurgent IED/sniper cell that had been responsible for the wounding of ten coalition soldiers over the previous several months. The cell tried to destroy the decoy cameras and walked right into the ambush. In addition to SKTs the unit used mortar illumination rounds over key road intersections as a further deterrent to IED emplacement. During May, the company mounted a complex operation composed of firing mortar illumination rounds over key city intersections with SKTs inserted to ambush IED emplacement teams. Counter IED operations mounted by Company C were temporarily successful. As noted in the unit's after action report: "SKT Operations worked very well for a while in the beginning, we were putting them out at random. We seemed to be surprising the enemy on several different occasions. As time went on, though, we began putting out SKTs almost on a schedule, oversaturating the zone. . . . While IED emplacement went down, the AIF just went to other areas or ceased operations until CF operations were complete."[128]

Company C demonstrated significant adaptive capacity using its adaptive skills to build new organizational capacities during its deployment—all while operating below its authorized end-strength in dense urban terrain. The unit's flexibility stemmed from trained, confident personnel throughout the organization that had built cross-functional skills before the deployment and that continued to build cross-functional capabilities within the organization while closed with the enemy in Mosul. Stated differently, members of the unit knew how to do each other's job.[129] Circumstance played a role in forcing this upon the unit, which didn't receive its complement of vehicles until just before its major predeployment training exercise at the Joint Readiness Training Center, which limited its ability to build standardized SOPs and TTPs with its vehicles. This meant that the unit had little practice in building TTPs and SOPs for the coming battle in Mosul. Training prior to JRTC emphasized dismounted operations and focused on skills called "close quarters battle" and "battle drills 6A" that focused on clearing buildings and rooms.[130] This training would be used by the unit to build its training program in early 2006 for its partnered Iraqi units. During the unit's final exercise, the scenario subjected the company to a notional COIN environment against an aggressive opposition force at a time when the unit was at just over 50 percent of its authorized end-strength. The training scenarios at JRTC generally stressed units to a point where they were forced into organizational changes and adaptation to accommodate the scenario. A principal way of doing this is to inflict casualties. During the Company C exercise, the notional insurgents used extremely accurate and powerful mortars that damaged Strykers and wounded between five and ten company members with each round. This meant that lower ranking noncommissioned officers had to fill roles performed by more senior leadership—a step made even more necessary by the unit's understrength status. The exercise helped spur junior leader development and diverse, cross-function skill building that built organizational flexibility. For example, exercise casualties forced different unit members to become proficient at driving their vehicles, a process that normally took each Stryker crew a year's worth of training. During the JRTC exercise, the scenarios saw many crew members "wounded," which meant that another soldier had to step up and fill that position. Matthaidess estimated that by the end of his company's JRTC rotation, the unit had double the coverage across the unit's vehicle crews for people with experience manning the vehicles. The skill building during the training got expanded in the friction of actual combat. The crew casualties became real in Mosul (one killed in action; ten wounded), as did other circumstances, such as leave and administrative and training requirements that pulled crewmembers out of their roles. The unit's skills meant that it had a trained manpower pool to immediately step up and ensure that the company never lost combat capability. More important, the unit found out what teams worked best together and gave it the opportunity to assign individuals to tasks for which they had demonstrated specific competency. While the established organizational hierarchy did not become moot during Company C's deployment, the capacities of the workforce allowed authority to be driven down the hierarchy to reside in team-driven operations. This philosophy extended to the senior company leadership, where Matthaidess designated his fire support officer (as opposed to the executive officer) the unit commander in his absence because of the officer's more complete training.[131]

The unit attempted to apply this experience to its IA/IP training partnerships. During engagements with local Iraqis, it tried to replicate the cross-training experience by incorporating junior leaders into combined planning and engagements to build their confidence and ability to operate independently or assume a higher role. The adaptive capacity in the unit combined with a command atmosphere that emphasized junior leader distributed operations drove the company to develop new organizational capacities like the nondoctrinal SKT as one way to fight the insurgents.

4-11 FIELD ARTILLERY, SOUTHERN NINEWA

The 172nd 4-11 Field Artillery conducted COIN operations south of Mosul and to the west of the Tigris River—an area that spanned nearly 5,000 square miles. The area's population consisted of approximately 75 percent Sunni in the western reaches of its area and 25 percent Kurdish immediately to the south of Mosul. The area was aligned with the 3rd Brigade, 2nd Iraqi Army Division. It hosted twenty-one police stations organized into three districts: Kiara, Makmur, and Hadr. Eight of the towns in the area had elected or appointed mayors. In contrast to the urban landscape of Mosul, the area of 4-11's operations featured low population density and comparatively low levels of insurgent violence. As characterized by the 4-11's commanding officer, Lieutenant Colonel Scott Wuestner, the area required "hold" operations in the clear, hold, build sequence of COIN being used by most U.S. units in Iraq.

The 4-11 deployed into three FOBs: Q West, Jaguar North, and Mahkmur. Each of these facilities hosted U.S. and Iraqi forces. In addition to these three FOBs, the Iraqi Army manned three additional COPs at Tal Abtha, Mishraq, and Gware. The Q-West FOB eventually housed an Iraqi Army noncommissioned officer training academy as well as an Iraqi police training academy. The unit's tactical mobility came not from the Stryker but from up-armored HMMWVs.

The 4-11 deployment represents and interesting case in the context of this analysis because it represented a core competency of the 172nd organization—the organic artillery capacity—that would not be needed in the COIN campaign. The battalion realized a year before the deployment that it would be operating as another brigade maneuver/infantry element and set about recasting itself around a new set of core competencies, while still maintaining an ability to be used as an artillery unit should the need arise. To recast itself and build new infantry-oriented TTPs, the unit redesigned its predeployment training cycle and re-educated its workforce to prepare for its new job. Shooting artillery requires a different set of skills and different mindset than fighting as an infantry organization. As noted by Wuestner, the senior noncommissioned officers in the brigade had "engrained the steptology of shooting a canon whereas as an infantryman everything is variable."[132] The unit drew upon instruction from the Center for Enhanced Performance at the U.S. Military Academy at West Point in reorienting the mindset of the unit to its new tasks. The center had been established in 1989 to help the academy's football players improve their mental approach to their sport. By the early 1990s, the program had been expanded to include a variety of other sports activities and then further expanded to more general training activities. The West Point presentations got married up with experts provided by the JRTC at Fort Polk to familiarize the battalion with the TTPs it would need in Iraq.

Like the other battalions in the 172nd, the 4-11 sought to operationalize an approach to the battlefield based on effects-based operations. Wuestner had worked at JRTC earlier in his career when the concepts were first being tested in the field and believed it was important to develop a holistic understanding of the environment. Attempting to understand the different components of the environment led the battalion to develop an "effects wheel" for trying to develop and evaluate courses of action in the field. The battalion took over a battle space with relatively low levels of violence. The Kurdish villages in the eastern part of the sector provided no haven for the collection of Sunni insurgent groups battling the rest of the brigade in Mosul. In the west, the villages had controlled smuggling routes coming in from Syria. Like the Sunni villages in western Anbar in Al Qaim, these tribes had little interest in aligning themselves with insurgents that would disrupt or seek to disrupt their income stream. The area directly to the south of the 4-11 was thought to be a haven for Saddamist insurgents, but the 4-11 was discouraged from operating in the area that was the responsibility of the 101st.

The battalion developed four LOOs around which to structure its operations: (1) AIF neutralized; (2) legitimate Iraqi government; (3) develop Iraqi infrastructure; and (4) develop capable ISF. While insurgents occasionally planted IEDs on several of the major supply routes, the overall security environment was relatively benign. Wuestner oriented the battalion to aggressively move to build partnerships with the IA and IP and mounted a determined effort to build relationships with local village leadership in the small villages throughout its area. The regional security council meetings held each month with the villages became a fixture in the 4-11 area. These gatherings initially featured the 4-11 leadership meeting in public forums with local mayors and police chiefs to discuss issues surrounding local governance.[133] Eventually, the 4-11 reduced its role in these sessions as Iraqi police and army officials also appeared to take questions with the Iraqi mayors and develop agenda items to work with the provincial government in Mosul. Wuestner took advantage of the State Department provincial reconstruction team that got activated in Mosul in November 2005 and used his security council meetings as part of a process to send project requests up to the PRT and Iraqi ministries in Mosul. By the end of its deployment, the battalion had facilitated $18 million in CMO in its area.

The training program featured side-by-side facilities at Q-West for the Iraqi police and Iraqi Army noncommissioned officers. The police training program went through two iterations. The Iraqi Police Proficiency Training program graduated 100 Iraqi police officers, and its successor, the Iraq Police Basic Skills Training, had a throughput of 250 police officers. The battalion consciously integrated the IP into their patrols, and each unit in the battalion had to do one joint patrol a week with an Iraqi police counterpart. Wuestner distributed his platoons to colocate them with the Iraqi Army units at the various sites in the AOR to cycle their Iraqi counterparts through a training cycle designed to build IA proficiency. A squad from B Battery lived at COP Jaguar to train the 2nd IA Battalion; another squad from the same company deployed to Mahkmur to train the 3rd Battalion; and A Company assumed responsibility to train the 1st IA Battalion at Q-West.

Wuestner used an "effects wheel" to evaluate the conditions of the towns in his area of operations. His wheel sought to look at political and economic conditions, media and information operations, essential services provided by local government, as well as the social and tribal issues.

The integrated assessment drove the battalion's targeting process as it sought to fuse kinetic and nonkinetic tools at its disposal to achieve the brigade's desired end state. The unit built a three-week targeting cycle with its Iraqi units and included constant feedback loops by the Iraqi and U.S. units on the degree to which they were meeting the assigned objectives. The targeting cycle attempted to integrate the wheel elements to build a plan that anticipated second and third order effects. The battalion consciously attempted to shape its targeting strategy and supporting courses of action to determine whether or how the battalion could address the region's persistent unemployment by creating jobs through trash removal. The 4-11 staff used the effects wheel to break the problem down into its constituent elements, using the different "frames" of political, military, information, governance, and essential services to drive potential courses of action and to anticipate second and third order effects of these actions. As noted in the wheel, the goal of job creation required an integrated approach that fused information, political analysis and relationships, military and security issues, with an appreciation of hard-headed economics.

The targeting wheel represented an attempt to apply the same sort of systems-based thinking and analysis used by the 2-1 in eastern Mosul—albeit in a different environment using a somewhat less systematic methodology to specifically nest the activity in a structured campaign plan. The approaches, however, were strikingly similar and arrived at independently by each battalion. In the case of the 4-11, however, the intellectual and organizational reorientation from the artilleryman's motto of "pull lanyard: got cookie" to the complexities of trash removal in rural Iraq is particularly striking. The intellectual and organizational framework developed by the 4-11 helped establish the basis for the unit to build capacities specifically tailored to the environment.

SUMMARY OF 172ND WARTIME INNOVATION

The 172nd SBCT demonstrated significant wartime innovations through the development of a variety of at least four new organizational competencies once it arrived in Ninewa. Although the unit had been organized, trained, and equipped to fight on a conventionally oriented battlefield, the unit seamlessly transitioned to the COIN environment and worked hard to develop capacities that were relevant to COIN. First, the units built a fused operations-intelligence cycle that drew upon a flattened, interagency organizational hierarchy that delivered intelligence to the units using the Stryker's digital communications and data backbone. As demonstrated in the 2-1 campaign in eastern Mosul, that cycle proved its worth in many directed raids against a resilient foe. Second, the brigade built an integrated targeting process as battalion staffs sought ways to meld kinetic and nonkinetic effects into mutually supportive activities as it worked to operationalize the "clear, hold, build" strategy. Third, the brigade consciously sought to develop a systems-oriented perspective on its environment and apply the complex concepts of effects-based operations. Fighting in a COIN environment using these concepts represented a powerful organizational innovation in and of itself. In the space of a year, the 4-11 Field Artillery transformed itself from an organization whose purpose was to deliver indirect fire in conventional military operations into an organization attempting to systematically organize local governments and municipal services in rural Iraq. Fourth, the unit developed an integrated partnership program with the ISF that included infrastructure development, curriculums for training programs, and actual routinized exercises to build host nation capabilities.

It was no accident that the organization demonstrated significant flexibility in building new capacities and applying them to the environment in northern Iraq. Preparations during its training cycle sought to build an organization that embraced the concept of distributed operations that empowered junior leaders operating at the tip of the proverbial spear. In the 172nd, that took the form of squad leaders taking the initiative and being backed up by the brigadewide leadership—whether it was development of training programs for the Iraqi Army or short-notice directed raids against insurgent cells using locally generated intelligence. It is clear that the unit also stretched its combat power, drawing upon a cross-functional workforce that proved to be very flexible in the wartime environment. While the 172nd didn't tear up the doctrinal manuals in building its COIN campaign, its doctrine proved to be no hindrance in structuring operations to meet the demands of the tactical environment. In the case of the 2-1, doctrinal principles got usefully applied to construct a flexible and adaptive campaign plan that related means to ends and provided a transparent, common set of assumptions baseline for all members of the organization to draw upon as they did their jobs. Just as the BSB developed a new organizational structure through its Forward Area Support Teams to conduct logistics over the wide areas of northern Iraq, the SKTs developed by C/1-17 similarly grew out of common-sense applications of the organizational capacities to counter the adversary.

As has been noted previously in this chapter, the 172nd did not defeat the insurgency. Indeed this analysis does not argue that wartime innovation produced a "victory" like that which occurred in the fall of 2006 during the battle for Ramadi. But it is clear that the 172nd and its predecessors consciously sought optimal solutions to the complex problems posed by the insurgency in Mosul and developed new organizational capacities in the field that mirrored the environmental complexity it confronted. In the case of the 172nd, it is clear that its network-centric capabilities proved to be an enabler in that process—but technology alone did not produce the flexible, adaptive organization that flattened its hierarchical structure in the wartime environment. That process happened largely as a result of senior leadership that drove authority down the chain of command to the company, platoon, and squad leader.

6 CONCLUSION

This book has examined how a number of units adapted to the insurgency in Anbar and Ninewa Provinces during 2005 through 2007. The evidence presented in its case studies shows that a disparate series of units in a diverse set of operational environments clearly improved their military response to the insurgency over the period. The units adapted by constructing integrated COIN campaigns using a tailored mix of kinetic and nonkinetic tools. The units constructed these campaigns empirically and, as it were, on the fly, based upon experience, and despite the absence of governing joint military COIN doctrine. Evidence from the case studies suggests that the process of tactical adaptation overwhelmingly resided within tactical units, which, in all the instances studied here, gradually built new organizational capacities that were embodied in SOPs over the course of their deployments. I define the development of these new organizational capacities as innovation. The process of innovation drew upon tailored training and intellectual preparation, leadership that apportioned authority throughout a unit's organizational hierarchy in ways not envisioned in doctrine, and junior leaders that accepted authority willingly and seized the initiative in the execution of missions handed down by the organizational leadership. The process of tactical adaptation evolved into organizational innovation in which new SOPs were developed that in turn built new and more generalized organizational capacities.

It is worth re-emphasizing the relationship between the concepts of tactical adaptation and organizational innovation. In this book, they function as mutually supportive concepts and processes. Tactical adaptation occurs when units change organizational procedures on the battlefield in order to address perceived organizational shortfalls, which are generally revealed by their interaction with the adversary. The concept of organizational innovation in turn seeks to capture the process by which tactical adaptation gathers organizational momentum and validation, leading to the generation of new SOPs embodying organizational capacities that did not exist when the units began their deployments. The generality with which these processes can be observed shows that every unit in this study proved in the end to be a learning organization, which continuously sought to improve its performance and tailor its outputs to meet the demands of the environment. Each unit openly adjusted its outputs over time as ideas within the units surfaced to improve performance and address organizational shortfalls. The learning process drew upon steadily increasing knowledge of the environment and, no less crucially, an increasing understanding of the second- and third-order effects of the unit's operations on that environment—a subtle and inferential form of knowledge easily shrouded in the fog of war, but one whose mastery will always prove critical in counterinsurgency.[1] Each unit eagerly sought information about and from the environment, related that information to its TTPs, and worked hard to change those TTPs as required to achieve their objectives. All the units covered in this study demonstrated significant learning capacities.[2]

This is perhaps a surprising conclusion given a number of factors that framed the original U.S. invasion and its overall operations in the period from 2005 to 2007. As documented here, the innovation accomplished by the U.S. military appears all the more remarkable given that it had arguably been set up for failure by its national-level political and military leadership. In 2005 and 2006, no relevant joint doctrine existed for units to draw upon in preparing for their deployments. The word "joint" should be emphasized, since in Iraq all U.S. ground components conducting COIN operations fought as task forces in which they integrated elements from different services and civilian agencies into their schemes of operation. Army officers commanded Marine units and vice versa. All relied on air support from the Navy and Air Force. Special Forces operated in the same areas as their conventional counterparts. The ubiquitous OGAs supported military operations throughout the country. Personnel from a wide variety of civilian agencies served as members of task force operations.

The process of tactical adaptation and organizational innovation happened despite strategic confusion over the war's objectives at the national level. Without a coherent strategic objective, troop leaders in Iraq would have been justified in being confused about how they were supposed to connect their operations to clearly defined political objectives. The initial justification for the war centered on counterproliferation objectives—objectives that lost their relevance when it became clear that Saddam had successfully hoodwinked the world into believing that he remained armed to the teeth with chemical and biological weapons. The Bush administration then cycled through a series of national-level war aims until it finally settled on the idea of establishing a stable, functioning democracy. This objective was not clearly and consistently articulated until two years after the invasion and even then remained conceptually cluttered with persistent and misplaced references asserting a relationship between the Iraq occupation and the so-called war on terror.[3]

National level leadership and coordination of the war effort were further compromised by a broken governmental interagency process, in which feuding cabinet secretaries—Donald Rumsfeld and Colin Powell—and their departments refused to cooperate. Just as important, a weak National Security Advisor proved unwilling or unable to mediate cabinet-level disputes, set the conditions for interagency coordination, or counter the strong influence of the Office of the Vice President in the decision-making process.[4] A strong contributing element to the fiasco was a politicized Joint Staff that could not or would not confront the civilian leadership with demands for more troops when more were clearly needed.[5] During the period of military operations studied here, all these factors prevented a truly unified national governmental effort to support military operations in Iraq.[6]

Without question, military operations were initially hampered by the biases and beliefs of senior civilian leadership, which received no significant opposition from senior military leadership in the Joint Staff. The lack of prior planning for the postinvasion period placed ground commanders in a reactive position virtually from the moment the insurgency appeared in the summer of 2003. There was no systemic plan for postinvasion operations, if for no other reason than that to have conceived such plans would have required the civilian leadership at the Pentagon to concede that such operations might be necessary. Senior military leadership on the Joint Staff and the Central Command, for its part, seemed to accept a vague plan that called for the exit of U.S. troops soon after the toppling of Saddam. The bungled and haphazard way the Coalition Provisional Authority (CPA) finally got cobbled together in the spring of 2003 reflected the confused decision-making process in the Defense Department's civilian secretariat, which merely mirrored the broken national-level interagency process at the time of the invasion. These deficiencies in planning and foresight manifested themselves most catastrophically in the CPA's May 2003 decision to summarily disband the Iraqi Army. This decision, which was appar-

ently never subjected to comprehensive interagency review and analysis,[7] would
have calamitous and enduring consequences for ground commanders in Iraq
by providing the insurgency with a trained pool of unemployed, military-age
males with a grievance against the occupation. While senior Pentagon leaders
like Rumsfeld and his deputies Paul Wolfowitz and Douglas Feith trumpeted
the benefits of effects-based operations, they made little attempt to practice it
themselves, by way of evaluating even the most obvious branches and sequels
that might arise from their preferred policy choices for postwar Iraq.

Finally, it is worth emphasizing that the organizations charged with executing the ground war in Iraq initially evinced little interest in fighting a counterinsurgency. In Iraq (unlike the Afghanistan campaign of 2001–2) combat
operations fell overwhelmingly to the mainstream "regular" military, whose
institutional preferences and instincts have historically favored heavy forces
and conventional operations. While the Defense Department had produced a
dizzying array of documents suggesting that military institutions should build
capacities to fight irregular war, the military departments had not operationalized these requirements by the time of the Iraq invasion sixteen months after
the 9/11 attacks. The development of what would eventually become institu-
tionwide capacities to conduct irregular war (particularly for the Army) was
forced upon these reluctant organizations by the circumstances of war.[8] While
the Rumsfeld-administered Pentagon sought to advertise the "transformation"
of the U.S. military via standoff weapons, precision strike operations, and other
advanced technologies,[9] an alternative process of defense "transformation" indeed did unfold in Iraq within the units studied here. That transformation
process originated in the minds of company, battalion, and brigade leaders,
who then set about restructuring their battlefield operations and building new
organizational capacities to fight an irregular war. In the final analysis, the wartime innovation process operationalized by brigade, battalion, and company
commanders and their seasoned noncommissioned officers helped rescue a
cowed national-level senior military leadership and their feckless civilian masters from an unfolding strategic debacle in 2004 and 2005. As noted in Chapter
1, this book does not argue that improved American military proficiency on
its own reduced the effectiveness of the insurgency during the period of this
study—but it is clear that it played an important role in helping to stabilize
the country. This book argues that this proficiency grew iteratively and literally
from the ground up in the field and proceeded in parallel with the rear-echelon
efforts to produce a new COIN doctrine.

This observation is perhaps unsurprising. It must be emphasized that any learning process in war takes time—time that may be cut short by political processes beyond the control of the armed forces. For the United States, the adaptive and innovative processes of its engaged units could not alter the rapid erosion of public support for the war that occurred during precisely the period when the U.S. counterinsurgency effort was finally finding its legs in 2006.[10]

There is no denying that the often remarkable efforts at tactical adaptation and organizational innovation that have been studied here were made necessary by the strategic obtuseness and comprehensively poor preparation with which the Iraq war was undertaken in the first place. When strategic objectives are clearly defined, military institutions can more easily tailor their operations to achieve those objectives. When objectives shift or are not clearly defined, military institutions, good ones anyway, will do their best to rise to the occasion, and may still fall short of strategic success in the end. In Iraq the U.S. military confronted a range of problems that would have made Carl von Clausewitz turn over in his grave: a shifting series of political objectives, broken national-level decision-making process, weak domestic political support, and problematic civil-military relations. The dialectical innovation process chronicled in this study may have rescued the nation from immediate strategic debacle, but it may well prove insufficient, in the end, to overcome all these systemic shortcomings. If there is an abiding lesson in all this, it is that strategic objectives must be clearly articulated by civilian and military leaders alike and thoroughly infused with a realistic appreciation of the political limits of military power and with an understanding of the capabilities of the organizations charged with its exercise. The fact that this lesson has been learned so many times before in no way diminishes its importance for the future.

WARTIME INNOVATIONS

All the units in this study realized that their primary conventional war-fighting skills would form only one of a variegated set of competencies that would be needed for the Iraq COIN environment. All consciously searched for an appropriate mix of kinetic and nonkinetic tools suggested by COIN theorists,[11] and sought to build the new organizational competencies required by their diverse array of missions. These missions included such activities as: military operations against the insurgents; local political and leader engagement; building host nation military capacities virtually from scratch through training and exercises; building governance capacities through elections and assisting in the establishment of local civic institutions; helping to build local infrastructure through coordinated civil-military operations; using IO, ranging from radio broadcasts and television to posters and flyers, to shape the battle with the insurgents for the local population. As indicated by the variation in the case studies, the innovation process happened in both rural and urban environments, in areas where the insurgency operated at both higher and lower levels of activity, and while in contact with insurgent elements of markedly different political and ideological makeup. The innovation process appeared unhindered by unit type, tables of equipment and organization, or institutional identity—although it is clear that these variables affected the process. Army legacy units, Marine Corps light infantry, and relatively new Army transformational units all engaged in the innovation process. In other words, the innovation process exhibited common characteristics across disparate organizations fighting in different circumstances and with different equipment and organizational structures.

The principal innovations identified in the cases fall under the following three general categories:

1. *New Organizational Activities and Competencies*: All the units demonstrated a pronounced widening of organizational competencies in addition to the primary conventional warfare skills for which the units had been trained, organized, and equipped. These competencies included the standup of local governing organizations to assume responsibility for civic affairs; information operations designed to shape the tactical environment; partnering and training programs created by U.S. units for Iraqi Army and police units; and coordinated outreach to local leaders to enlist their support against the insurgents. While all the units studied here developed these competencies, examples from a few of the cases are particularly noteworthy. In March 2007, the 1-6 Marines in central Ramadi helped stand up a fifteen-member local district council to discuss security, education, employment, local infrastructure issues, and variety of other governance issues. The local district councils later became a mechanism more widely used in the province to facilitate interaction between municipal authorities, citizens, and the security providers. In southern Ninewa, the 4-11 Field Artillery set up a similar series of local leadership councils throughout their entire area. Other battalions in the 172nd created similar local councils for the same purposes. The 1-6 Marines built an IO campaign from scratch in their sector of Ramadi that used radios, loudspeakers, and handbills to deliver its message directly to the residents of its sector. By the end of the unit's deployment, local officials were virtually lining up to get their messages out over the system.[12] In

Mosul, the 172nd SBCT built its own IO campaign using the local television station and other tools. The unit worked assiduously with the local media, and developed an effective "most wanted" poster program that helped publicize its efforts to counter the insurgents. The 3-6 Marines modeled combined Iraqi-U.S. platoons in western Iraq during late 2005 that helped build host-nation capabilities and improved relationships with local tribes and helped draw them into the process of providing local security. In the fall of 2006, the 1/1 in Ramadi built the effective and much publicized local security forces in the aftermath of the Anbar Awakening that helped lead to a dramatic reduction in insurgent violence in and around Ramadi. In Ninewa province, the 172nd SBCT built a systematic training regime for 18,000 Iraqi soldiers throughout the province that included marksmanship, NCO training, maintenance, fire and maneuver training in urban terrain, logistical support, basic combat medical skills, and a police academy to help increase the skills of the local police.

2. Effects-Based Planning and Operations Cycles: The units in this study consciously embraced and attempted to operationalize effects-based operations in the COIN environment. The units built deliberate planning, operations, and targeting cycles that attempted to integrate the kinetic and nonkinetic effects created by their widened number of competencies. The 2-1 Infantry campaign plan in eastern Mosul perhaps represented the most systemic attempt at the process among the units in this study, since it built a formalized, adaptive campaign plan. In the 2-1 plan, each kinetic and nonkinetic target and tactical operation was consciously related to campaign objectives. Other units in the study largely adopted the same approach, though perhaps on a less formalized basis than the 2-1. Such innovation can be regarded as both intellectual and organizational. Embracing effects-based operations intellectually represented an attempt to use systems-based theory and analysis in guiding organizational courses of action and a deliberate attempt to anticipate second- and third-order effects. The planning and operations cycles led to organizations that delivered outputs addressing requirements ranging from the provision of dental clinics and the building of schools in Anbar, on the one end of the nonlethal spectrum, all the way up to precision ambushes of insurgent cells emplacing IEDs on the roads of Mosul. Not surprisingly, some of the units were more successful than others in the integration process, and competence in the diverse array of new capacities varied from unit to unit. The Marine Corps units initially tended to be somewhat more comfortable than the Army in the COIN role, given the institutional background of the Marine Corps as a light infantry force and its experiences in expeditionary operations. By contrast, the Army units, designed primarily to fight a campaign-style conventional ground war, had a more difficult task in innovating, partly as a result of the large equipment and logistical footprint required to support the conventional operations for which they were designed. The gradual evolution in the Army's adaptation to the environment is vividly illustrated in the transition from the 2/28 in Ramadi from July 2005 to the 1/1 in July 2006. The 2/28 went through a wrenching adjustment process as it struggled to adapt to the difficult COIN environment around Ramadi in 2005 and 2006. That adjustment process, however, and the momentum established by the 2/28, prepared the battlefield for the 1/1 COIN campaign of the fall of 2006 that led to the decisive defeat of the Sunni extremist insurgency in the battle for Ramadi.

All the units studied here demonstrated a grasp of COIN principles and sought to build organizational competencies that could be operationalized in plans and operations. Senior leaders in each of the units studied here universally recognized that the ultimate objective in their operations was to secure the support of the local population and isolate the insurgents from local support. In the 172nd, the 2-1 built an integrated, adaptive campaign plan in eastern Mosul, supported by a targeting cycle that included lethal and nonlethal effects. The 4-11 Field Artillery in southern Ninewa used an "effects" wheel as a decision aid in target selection across the full spectrum of operations. The development of these integrated, effects-based approaches to planning and operations fundamentally changed the conduct of these units on the battlefield—turning them from organizations largely prepared for conventional warfare to organizations that conducted irregular warfare.

3. *New COIN-related TTPs.* The units in this study developed a variety of new TTPs that markedly changed the way they fought the insurgents. In all cases, the units de-emphasized conventional warfare capacities in favor of new warfare skills better suited to the COIN environment in Iraq. This generally meant that relatively heavy, large-unit operations were gradually replaced by a variety of different small-unit operations, some kinetic, others not. The process of the tactical reorientation of the units progressed in an iterative, graduated process. These approaches ranged from the adoption of law enforcement TTPs in order to build more effective patrols (the 1-7 in Qaim), to the tailoring of TTPs for precision raids by relatively small tactical teams that minimized collateral damage without compromising the capacity to disrupt insurgent cells (the 4-14 Cavalry in Rawah; the 2-1 Infantry in eastern Mosul). The new TTPs

collectively gained momentum throughout the deployments of these units studied here and had a cumulative effect that fundamentally changed the way the organizations conducted themselves on the battlefield.

One of the most obvious examples of this sort of adaptation was the general de-emphasis on "fire for effect" indirect fire missions by the 2/28 after complaints by local leaders about casualties and needless destruction during their local leader engagement meetings in the summer and fall of 2005. The 172nd virtually abandoned its indirect fire capability and retrained its artillery unit, the 4-11 Artillery, which reorganized and retrained itself as a brigade maneuver unit. The de-emphasis on traditional, conventionally oriented warfare skills occurred as the units adopted a series of new and extremely effective warfare skills to kill insurgents and disrupt their networks. The 172nd built an organizationwide fused intelligence-operations cycle used to great effect in precision raids on insurgent cells as illustrated in 2-1 operations in eastern Mosul. In western Mosul, C Company in the 1-17 developed TTPs for small kill teams that ambushed insurgent IED teams along the road network in its sector.

The 1-7 Marines in Al Qaim applied lessons developed by U.S. law enforcement experts experienced in combating gangs in large cities in the United States. The 1-7 drew upon this expertise to enable it to disrupt insurgent cells along the Iraq-Syrian border. Not only did the 1-7 retrain its workforce to build law-enforcement-related competencies, it made creative use of the COPLINK relational database software and surveillance equipment to support its COIN operations. The 1-7 example of reorienting its tactical outlook and capabilities is not an outlier in this study. Like various other units over the period, the 1-37 Armored in Ramadi developed new tactics surrounding the concept of census operations to create an integrated database using Microsoft Access software that compiled information on the residents of neighborhoods in its sector. The database provided enhanced situational awareness for the unit throughout the sector and successfully helped target the insurgent network in south-central Ramadi. The idea for the database came from one of the unit's company commanders, and subsequently became an organizationwide SOP during the deployment. The 1-37 came to regard its census patrols as one of the most effective tools in its COIN campaign in south central Ramadi. In both examples, the battalions leveraged technology and software that was either new to the organization (the 1-7) or which had not been used before (the 1-37) as an application to support tactical operations.

All the units studied here adopted a deployment scheme featuring a hub-

and-spoke network of operating bases to push their units out into the populations in their areas. The hub-and-spoke network operationalized the concept of distributed operations. This effectively broke their organizations up into smaller components that were better able to conduct small-unit operations and gave small-unit commanders the flexibility to tailor their TTPs to the environment more effectively. The COP construction procedures used in the 1/1 during its "island hopping" campaign to retake Ramadi in the fall of 2006 subsequently became a recommended SOP for all units operating in Anbar. The hub-and-spoke base network was adopted by the 172nd in Ninewa province partly as a necessity to spread its combat power over the wide expanses of the province in addition to the dense urban terrain in Mosul.

WARTIME INNOVATION ENABLING PROCESSES

The wartime organizational innovations summarized above drew upon a number of enabling processes. The cases covered in this study illustrated six general innovation enablers that are listed below.

1. Organizational leadership that carefully delegated and apportioned authority and responsibility to different sectors of the organization, with particular emphasis on empowering tactical-level leadership. This was not simply a matter of pushing authority downward, but rather of strengthening the tactical orientation of the entire organization in all the units studied here. Virtually all levels of the organizations studied here interacted with the environment at the tactical level in some way, shape, and form—meaning that organizational outputs were delivered from a variety of sources and not just from those at the bottom of the command hierarchy. While the operating units mounted their daily patrols, mid- and senior-level leadership also engaged the environment through local leader interaction, meeting with local media and information outlets, and interrogating detainees and developing local intelligence source networks, to name a few of these activities. The battalion commanders of the 172nd, for example, found themselves giving civics lessons and helping to create municipal authorities (in the case of the 4-11) while their maneuver elements cycled through anti-insurgent operations on a round-the-clock basis. Simultaneously, the brigade staff executed an information operations program through work via the local radio and television stations.

The units studied here delivered their diverse array of organizational outputs from different levels of the organizational hierarchy as a result of delegated and apportioned authority. The apportionment and dispersal of authority throughout the organizations flowed from what military officers might describe as a "command atmosphere" that allowed and even encouraged lower level adaptation and initiative in searching for solutions to the complex problems confronting the units on the battlefield. Ideas developed at different organizational levels that proved successful were quickly passed to other parts of the organization and routinized in new SOPs. The units studied here accepted that while hierarchy remained the central organizing principle for their organizations, they also accepted that delegated and apportioned authority had created organizations that were substantially more complex than their "wiring diagrams" suggested. The circumstances of war pushed the units studied here to embrace a flattened structure of organizational authority and informal relationships that dispersed organizational output capacities throughout the hierarchy. The distribution and apportionment of authority throughout the units proved to be an important enabler to the innovations identified in the previous section. To a certain extent, this outcome resulted from the dispersal of units in their operational sectors that spread their commands out over wide geographic areas. In western Anbar province, the wide open spaces created opportunities for company commanders in the 1-7 Marines to build a system of local security using local tribes and combined action platoons that helped reduce the violence in the area. In Ramadi, information operations by the 1-6 Marines got designed and delivered by an ad hoc working group headed by the battalion executive officer—not normally a job associated with the billet. The wartime environment and the demands on scarce combat power within the organization forced all the hierarchical levels to become involved in outputs of various kinds that tried to maximize the efficiencies in a limited labor pool.

2. *Information flow represented a critical building block for organizational innovation.* Hierarchically structured military bureaucracies have a well-deserved peacetime reputation as stove-piped organizations reluctant to share information. The circumstances of war caused the units studied here to abandon this practice. In war, the flow of information passed quickly up and down the organizational hierarchy and, in certain cases, flowed seamlessly into the units from organizations operating outside the unit. In other words, wartime circumstances created conditions for enhanced intra- and interorganizational information flow at various classification levels. This free-form information flow served several different functions. First, it allowed ideas and initiatives from lower to mid levels to bubble to the surface quickly for evaluation and decision by senior leadership. This happened, for example, in the 1-37 Armored in

south central Ramadi with the building of census databases by a company commander, a process that was eventually adopted throughout the unit. The databases became the basis for a whole new scheme of operations, which took the form of battalionwide census patrols. Second, the information flow served as an intraorganizational highway for continuous feedback loops both within the organization and between the organization and the environment. For example, the reporting requirements of the tactical units in the 2-1 Infantry in eastern Mosul served as vital feedback loops for senior leadership to continually monitor the impact of its interactions in the environment. These feedback loops gave leadership the continuous ability to measure and evaluate organizational performance or nonperformance, which, in turn, formed the basis for changes in organizational activities and outputs. The information flows and feedback loops provided the foundation for an organizational decision-making process that produced, changed, or altered organizational outputs. The 2-1 campaign plan in eastern Mosul featured numerous feedback loops from the tactical and senior levels of the organization that provided the basis for the command leadership to change or alter its operations. Early in its deployment, the feedback loops demonstrated that the battalion was generating insufficient human intelligence on the insurgent networks. The feedback loops provided the basis for the battalion to reorient its tactical questioning methodology and to push its tactical HUMINT teams out into its patrolling units that addressed the unit's intelligence shortfall.

3. The units studied here showed immense flexibility in creating suborganizational structures that were either completely new, or that enhanced the capabilities of existing, doctrinally accepted organizational structures. New organizational structures took form on the battlefield. These provided another important enabling component of the innovations identified above. Company C, 1-17 in western Mosul adopted a completely new, nondoctrinal organizational structure to increase its number of maneuver elements in an effort to maximize its scarce combat power. Circumstances drove various logistics units studied here virtually to tear up their doctrinal manuals governing the delivery of logistical support to their far-flung operating elements. The 2/28 brigade support battalion developed a new series of TTPs and delivered support to combat units with ad hoc organizations to overcome this systemic problem. In the case of the 172nd SBCT, the distances between outposts and the strain on limited combat capabilities forced the unit's brigade support battalion to design a whole new support organization, the fast support team, to keep the brigade in beans and bullets.

Many of the units studied here made significant changes to their intelligence support staffs, dramatically expanding the personnel in their intelligence sections and integrating people and expertise from different organizations to support the added demands that the COIN environment placed on intelligence processing and analysis. The 1-7 Marines in Al Qaim built an entirely new S-2 section that leveraged the capacities brought to the unit through the COPLINK program, which used a relational database developed by the Phoenix Police Department. Another example was the 172nd SBCT, which added personnel to each battalion's intelligence section relatively early in its deployment. The 172nd also drew extensively on OGA sources and expertise and the JIATF at Task Force Freedom to flow information from a variety of sources throughout its encrypted intranet communications system. It is again worth noting that the wartime innovation process was supported by organizations that in peacetime have the reputation of lacking organizational flexibility. In wartime, the organizations that to some extent were already organized in informal task forces displayed few of these peacetime tendencies—standing up organizations like the 1-6 Marines nonkinetic effects group in central Ramadi and the larger intelligence support sections relatively easily and quickly with little interference from their chain of command.

4. *The units studied here consciously sought diverse sources of information that resided outside their formal institutional structures.* Both the Army and Marine Corps digitally based lessons learned websites served as an important source of information outside formal, institutionally "blessed" doctrinal products. Members of Army units all drew upon information posted on the Army Center for Lessons Learned website, or CALL, which provided after action reports, new TTPs, and other observations from units that had deployed in Iraq. The digital-age consolidation of knowledge in a well organized, easily accessible format helped shorten the learning cycles for units preparing for deployment. The 172nd SBCT made use of Strykernet, a website serving as a repository for Stryker units serving in Iraq. All the deploying units also made extensive use of video conferencing and the Defense Department's encrypted Secret-level intranet to build situational awareness prior to deployment.

5. *Various units displayed a marked willingness to work through ad hoc organizational structures to support the flow of information and materiel to the war fighter.* The array of different governmental agencies supporting the intelligence operations of the 172nd SBCT formed themselves into ad hoc working groups operating out of Task Force Freedom. These working groups built relationships

with the 172nd staff that facilitated the flow of information between the war fighter and the informal working groups. This information flow helped the brigade become an agile organization that could draw upon a fused operations-intelligence quickly enough to react effectively to new information in the field. The 172nd also included a substantial contractor support organization that helped maintain the vehicles that formed the basis of the unit's combat power. The civilians providing contractor support functioned as de facto members of the units, although they had the flexibility to draw upon sources of both parts and information that lay outside the formal military structure. The support by the contractor network undoubtedly contributed to the wartime innovation process.

6. *Technology undeniably played a role in supporting the innovation process.* For the U.S. military, warfare in the digital age is enabled through advanced data collection and processing technologies. The units studied here drew upon numerous sources of sensors to gather information that included airborne warning and control system aircraft, or AWACS, signals intelligence collection devices, remotely piloted vehicles that allowed units to monitor terrain on a continuous basis using laptop computers, and a family of databases set up by intelligence agencies to support the link-nodal analysis of insurgent cell structures. Other technologies featured in these units included loudspeakers used in information operations and software such as standard Microsoft Office products like Access and PowerPoint, which allowed units to compile census-type databases of their areas of responsibility. In the case of the 172nd, the unit's digital communications and data backbone clearly facilitated its ability to pass encrypted information directly to its operating units, which in turn led to short-notice operations and gathering intelligence from detainees that fed directly into its cycle of operations. In the 2-1 campaign in eastern Mosul, technology provided an important enabling factor in the form of the Information Surveillance and Reconnaissance, or ISR, collection plan, which helped the unit gauge insurgent reactions to its ongoing tactical operations in the fall of 2005. Information gleaned from these collections directly supported the process of tactical adaptation as the unit searched for ways to defeat the insurgents.

IMPLICATIONS FOR THEORY

A diverse set of implications flow from the case study findings presented above. In Chapter 2, this book surveyed a wide spectrum of literature that covered the sources of military innovation, organizational theory, organizational learning, and prior empirically based studies of wartime adaptation. This study argues that the process of organizational innovation in wartime functioned as a dialectical process that drew upon information from a wide variety of sources but ultimately got executed or implemented within the units themselves. I define innovation as the development of new organizational capacities on the field of battle that did not exist when the unit arrived. The argument presented in this book about the sources of military innovation is contrary to prevailing theories of military innovation on several counts. Most of these theories assert that military innovation predominately happens in peacetime circumstances in which the military organization in question sets about reorganizing itself and its approaches to fighting the next war. This process of developing new ways of fighting is thought to happen as a result of a changed threat perception by political or military leadership, which then directs its military institutions to change in response to the new threat. When innovation happens, that change is reflected in new doctrine, which provides the basis for the military to organize and train itself to the new way of fighting.[13] This approach argues that militaries innovate as a result of top-down processes in which leadership directs change, and the organization delivers the desired output.

A variation on this explanation is that peacetime innovation happens through intrabureaucratic debates within military organizations, with the winners of these debates then reorienting the battlefield approach of the organization.[14] As noted in Chapter 2, this argument also points to the importance of top-down forces in hierarchically structured organizations. That is, whichever side prevails in the internal debate on how best to fight then places its stamp on the organization in the form of new equipment or operations and even new military doctrine. A prevailing view in the theoretical literature is that innovation in war is thought to be extremely difficult. As argued by Stephen Peter Rosen, this is in part due to the difficulties experienced by units penetrating through the so-called fog of war to gain accurate information on battlefield performance. Rosen argues that the difficulties of accurately seeing the battlefield make it difficult for organizations to develop metrics to gauge the strategic effectiveness of battlefield operations relative to the overall war objectives.[15] Rosen argues that organizations will change in war only in those circumstances in which they realize that their operations are not achieving the desired strategic effect. The net effect is to make it extremely difficult for military organizations to develop new ways of fighting while closed with the enemy, according to Rosen.[16]

While the findings of this study certainly are specific to the wartime innovation process, they are also germane to the literature addressing peacetime innovation. The political and strategic subtext of the Iraq invasion makes it in some senses a good case from which to examine the applicability of the American battlefield experience to prevailing theories of military innovation. As argued in Chapter 2, these theories of innovation match poorly against the circumstances of the Iraq war. It is clear that the senior political leadership in the United States believed that a new global threat environment necessitated the development of new battlefield competencies in the area of irregular warfare. It is clear, however, that by the time of the Iraq invasion, the military organizations charged with prosecuting the invasion had not developed these capacities. Moreover, it wasn't until two years after the war started that the Army and Marine Corps began to show any interest in changing their battlefield tactics to address the kind of war that had materialized in Iraq from 2003 to 2005. As chronicled in this study, that process of adaptation occurred in spite of and not because of considered top-down direction from either civilian or military authorities.

The findings in this study also suggest that the process of wartime innovation in Iraq suffered from none of the systemic impediments identified by Rosen as noted above. As discussed in the preceding section of this chapter, units were not in fact blinded by the so-called fog of war. If anything, the units were overwhelmed with information about their environment and faced a tall order in processing it. The units studied here all exhibited acute awareness of the environment, their adversary, and the degree to which their tactical operations were achieving their objectives. Technology certainly helped pierce through the wartime fog, with a wide variety of sensors and data-processing equipment to aid in building a comprehensive understanding of the environment and the adversary. But technology alone does not explain the clarity of forceful leadership exhibited at various levels of the organizational hierarchy in the units studied here. That leadership sought conceptual clarity, accepted environmental complexity, and encouraged lower level initiative. The units in this study developed their new organizational capacities without any commonly accepted metrics with which to measure the strategic effectiveness of their operations. The circumstances and experiences of war gave unit commanders and their subordinates an intuitive grasp of what worked and what didn't in their battle with the insurgents.

The findings of this work are relevant to the literature on military innovation and organizational behavior on a number of additional fronts. First, the case studies demonstrate that the absence of a specific, joint COIN doctrine did not impede the innovation process. Innovation happened without the presence of a scheme of operations imposed from outside organizational hierarchies. If anything, the absence of doctrine may have freed unit commanders to come up with their own solutions to the tactical problems imposed on their organizations by the insurgency. That process unfolded largely within the units, which, as previously noted, drew upon myriad sources of information to develop their new organizational capacities.

While noting the organically driven nature of the innovation process, however, it would be a mistake to assert that military doctrine writ large, or other top-down processes, played no role in guiding innovation by field commanders. All the units studied here exhibited a firm grounding in doctrine. Doctrinal building blocks provided unit commanders with a methodology for preparing and organizing their units for combat. In the Army, for example, building the mission-essential task list is a basic doctrinal process that guides predeployment training and was routinely used by Army units prior to arriving in Iraq. Unit leaders clearly understood the tasks required to do their jobs in the Iraq COIN environment and went about building organizational competencies that drew upon doctrinally bound processes. In one particular case, the 2-1 Infantry in eastern Mosul consciously adapted a doctrinally based planning process for its COIN campaign. While it is true that the units developed counterinsurgency TTPs and organizational SOPs in the absence of an overarching doctrinal guide, intimate knowledge and background in doctrinal assumptions guided them in assembling their new organizational capacities.

This suggests that while doctrine need not be a powerful independent variable in the innovation process, doctrinal grounding by senior leaders can provide a supporting framework to devise innovative and nondoctrinal solutions to difficult tactical problems.[17] Top-down direction played a role in the innovation process and clearly helped units draw up logical lines of operations that focused on a number of generic missions: governance, economic development, building up the ISF, and countering the insurgency. These objectives were articulated in national-level documents such as the Bush administration's *National Strategy for Victory in Iraq*, released in November 2005. The operationalization of the objectives in this report was left largely to battlefield commanders, who searched for solutions on their own without direct guidance or undue interference from higher civilian and military authorities.

It also should be noted that institutional leadership did help in one of the cases studied here. The 1-7 Marine COIN campaign in western Anbar benefited by its exposure to law enforcement experts that helped shape its operations over the course of their deployment. The outreach to the law enforcement community happened because the Marine Corps's senior leadership also was searching for ideas on how to solve the tactical problems posed to its units by insurgency in Iraq.

Second, the process of tactical adaptation chronicled in the case studies is consistent with prior empirical studies covered in Chapter 2, which suggest that internally generated adaptation and innovation are not uncommon in war. In the Iraq war, the units studied here demonstrated an iterative and evolving approach to their operations in their quest to master the complexities of full-spectrum operations. In that sense, their behavior mirrored the experiences of militaries in prior wars, such as the German Army in World War I, which also constantly searched for ways to vanquish its opponent on the field of battle.

Third, the units developed new capacities for addressing the requirements of the environment and showed pronounced capability to add new capabilities and adapt their organizational structures over the period studied here. This phenomenon was common to most of the units, suggesting a kind of symbiotic correlation between organizational structure, organizational capacity, and environmental complexity. The organizations in this study clearly sought to develop task specialization and competencies where required, and built suborganizational structures to house that specialization. This process most clearly reflected itself in the intelligence sections of many units, as well as in those ad hoc groups established to integrate nonkinetic effects into operations. This suggests that America's hierarchically bounded military institutions can, under certain conditions, develop into structurally complex and flexible organizations that mirror environmental complexities. As noted in Chapter 2, Chris Demchak's work has found that military organizations show a propensity to develop complex structures that match the technological complexity of their weapons systems.[18] Her conclusion suggested a relationship between the technological complexity of weapons and the complexity of organizations required to support them. This study suggests that over time military organizations can also develop complex capacities to match environmental complexity. More theoretical and empirical work is needed to examine this relationship, but the implications of this study should provide fodder for future study of this issue.

Fourth, the leadership in the units of this study exercised a rational, value-maximizing, decision-making process in vigorous pursuit of optimal outcomes.

The circumstances of war seemed to militate against any tendency to satisfice by unit leaders and follow the path of least resistance. Further, in this study at least, informal relationships proved a hugely important factor in organizational performance. Chester Barnard would be no doubt pleased at such a conclusion. None of the units studied here sought to drop their problems into succeeding units' laps. All exhibited a commitment to solving their tactical problems and were not afraid to innovate in pursuit of optimal solutions. In that sense, the organizational decision-making processes in this study did not reflect a cautious, bureaucratic approach, nor did they seek solely to manage uncertainty. The decision-making approach exhibited by the units in this study is consistent with theories of innovation that point to the paramount role of individuals who engage in problem-solving activities when gaps in organizational performance are identified.[19]

Fifth, it is worth noting that organizational and institutional culture did not prove to be a systematic variable affecting organizational output.[20] In the cases analyzed here, both Army and Marine Corps units delivered similarly structured outputs in spite of their organizational and cultural dissimilarities. This phenomenon clearly exhibited itself in the COIN operations of the 1-37 and 1-6 in Ramadi during the fall of 2006 and spring of 2007. Both battalions were given the mission of building COPs to retake their portions of the city from the insurgents. The 1-6 and 1-37 COP construction and siting procedures were markedly different. The 1-6 COPs, or security stations, consisted of sites surrounded by sandbags, barbed wire, and a security perimeter, while the 1-37 COPs were constructed with a more formalized, systematic, and elaborate set of procedures. The two battalions used different processes in constructing their COPs, but both essentially delivered the organizational output called for in Colonel MacFarland's campaign plan to retake the city.

IMPLICATIONS FOR STRATEGY AND POLICY

This book does not argue that wartime innovation has produced, or will produce, strategic success for the United States in Iraq. It argues only that U.S. military organizations demonstrated significant innovative capacity in conducting COIN operations there—a form of warfare for which these organizations were largely unprepared and for which there was no authoritative joint doctrine during most of the period of this study. Nevertheless, it seems reasonable to conclude that battlefield innovation by U.S. forces clearly had a strategic impact in Iraq, and dramatically affected the provinces examined in this study.

During 2005 and 2006 it seemed clear that the United States was not achieving success in Iraq, and many believed that the insurgency had gainined the upper hand. This study finds that innovation by U.S. military organizations helped prevent a strategic victory by the toxic mix of insurgent groups seeking political control over the country. During the period of this study, Sunni Islamist insurgents loosely affiliated with Al Qaeda had in fact seized control over much of Anbar Province. While the organizational innovation displayed by units in this study did not in and of itself defeat the insurgents in Anbar, that defeat would almost certainly not have occurred without the wartime innovation of American military units.

In some respects, the relatively short lifespan of the insurgency in Anbar (three years) must be considered as a historic anomaly in relation to other historic examples of insurgencies. This suggests that it was not the type of classic revolutionary insurgency that characterized many of the prolonged armed struggles in the post–World War II era. Whatever the particular circumstances of the Anbar insurgency, however, organizational innovation was necessary but not sufficient to achieve strategic success. Local political dynamics clearly played a vital role in Anbar, but with U.S. units becoming more attuned to those issues it is clear that a flexible and enlightened American tactical leadership skillfully exploited those local dynamics to great effect in 2005 and 2006. In Ninewa Province, the COIN campaign of the 172nd helped suppress the insurgency to give time for the building of host-nation economic and military capacities, which may or may not prove successful in the longer term. As of this writing, the insurgents in Ninewa Province and Mosul continue to battle U.S. units that arrived after the 172nd, and continue to challenge the authority of the central government in Baghdad. In both Anbar and Ninewa, wartime organizational innovation prevented the insurgents from achieving immediate success, and to that extent must be seen as a factor that will help determine whether or not Iraq emerges as a stable, peaceful democracy. Counterinsurgency is always about buying time to secure political legitimacy and enact reform, and the tactical-level innovations studied here surely helped with that. But it is too soon to say with any certainty how that larger political process will work itself out.[21]

It is likewise difficult to offer any comprehensive judgment about the ability of U.S. military organizations to adapt and innovate in future combat environments. Just because American ground forces showed themselves capable of adapting to the Iraq insurgency does not necessarily mean that those same organizations can repeat the feat elsewhere. The progress in the COIN campaign in Anbar in 2005 and 2006 was not replicated in Ninewa Province, after all, although, as documented here, U.S. units innovated successfully in both cases. Nor is it clear that the same process of adaptation and innovation displayed by Army and Marine units in Iraq will be replicated in Afghanistan, a simultaneous conflict in which military, social, political, economic, and geographic conditions may be just sufficiently different to confound whatever new confidence may have been gained from experience in Iraq.

There are clearly a host of variables that determine the degree to which conventional militaries can adapt and innovate in COIN environments, just as there are a host of factors that determine whether that innovation will achieve the desired political impact leading to the defeat of the insurgency. Genuine innovation can occur that still falls short of producing tactical and operational success. In addition to the factors cited earlier in this chapter, broader forces—such as local political and military context, physical and social terrain of the conflict, and degree of political commitment by both the occupying power and the insurgents conducting military operations—are but a few of the variables that can determine the ultimate effectiveness of the innovation process.

As noted at the outset of this study, one of the major implications of this work is that scholars and analysts should more closely consider the sources and processes of military innovation in wartime versus those that occur in peacetime. The conclusion of this study must be that military organizations can and do innovate in certain wartime conditions. In this study, the exigencies of wartime prompted a collection of hierarchically structured organizations to become the kind of agile and adaptive structures thought to exist only in certain parts of the private sector. In Iraq, the units studied here exhibited a profound understanding of their "market" and worked tirelessly to produce outputs relevant to their environment. The innovation processes chronicled here are perhaps only the beginning of what can be new avenues of theoretical and empirical research that scholars and military professionals alike can undertake to further enhance our collective understanding of the complex processes at work in the pursuit of building and maintaining innovative military organizations.

NOTES

CHAPTER 1

1. As detailed in Michael R. Gordon and Bernard E. Trainor, *Cobra II: The Inside Story of the Invasion and Occupation of Iraq* (New York: Pantheon Books, 2006).

2. This term was first introduced into the lexicon of public discourse by Harlan K. Ullman and James P. Wade, *Shock and Awe: Achieving Rapid Dominance* (Washington, DC: National Defense University Press, 1996). Then Chairman of the Joint Chiefs of Staff General Richard Myers told reporters in March 2003: "The best way to do that [end the conflict] would be to have such a shock on the system that the Iraqi regime would have to assume early on the end was inevitable." As quoted in Eric Schmitt and Elisabeth Buhmiller, "Attack Strategy; Top General Sees Plan to Shock Iraq into Surrendering," *New York Times*, March 5, 2005.

3. Paul Davis, *Effects Based Operations: A Grand Challenge for the Analytical Community* (Santa Monica, CA: Rand, 2001), 7. He defines the term as: "operations conceived and planned in a systems framework that considers the full range of direct, indirect and cascading effects—which may, with different degrees of probability—be achieved with the application of military, diplomatic, psychological, and economic instruments."

4. The role of advanced "transformational" capabilities in the invasion is interestingly addressed by Steve Biddle, "Speed Kills: Reevaluating the Role of Speed, Precision, and Situation Awareness in the Fall of Saddam," *Journal of Strategic Studies* 30, no. 1 (February 2007): 3–46. Biddle argues that the role of these advanced capabilities has been overstated and that the incompetence of the Iraqis played a significant role in the speed of the U.S. march into Baghdad.

5. As an example, in June 2003 Secretary of Defense Donald Rumsfeld referred to the Iraqi resistance as "pockets of dead ender," and Deputy Secretary of Defense Paul Wolfowitz referred to them as "the last remnants of a dying cause." As quoted in *USA*

Today, "Rumsfeld Blames Iraq Problems on 'Pockets of Dead Enders,'" *Associated Press*, filed June 18, 2003. Rumsfeld used this formulation again in August 25, 2003, when he stated in a speech to the Veterans of Foreign Wars that "the dead enders are still with us." Transcript at http://www.defenselink.mil/speeches/speech.aspx?speechid=513. Bush administration officials refused to describe the resistance as an "insurgency" until November 2003, when the Central Command's General John Abizaid started using the term to describe the Iraqi resistance.

6. Early developments in the Iraq insurgency are summarized in Anthony Cordesman, "The Developing Iraqi Insurgency: Status at the end of 2004," Center for Strategic and International Studies, Washington, DC, December 22, 2004; Ahmed S. Hashim, *Insurgency and Counter-Insurgency in Iraq* (Ithaca, NY: Cornell University Press, 2006); Ahmed S. Hashim, "Iraq's Chaos: Why the Insurgency Won't Go Away," *Boston Review* (October–November 2004); Steven Metz, "Insurgency and Counterinsurgency in Iraq," *Washington Quarterly* 27 (Winter 2004): 25–36; James A. Russell, "Strategic Implications of the Iraq Insurgency," *Middle East Review of International Affairs* 8 (June 2004): 48–55; Michael Knights and Jeffrey White, "Iraqi Resistance Proves Resilient," *Jane's Intelligence Review* (November 2003). The lack of preparation for the insurgency is also referenced in Lieutenant General David H. Petraeus, "Learning Counterinsurgency: Observations from Soldiering in Iraq, *Military Review* 86 (January–February 2006): 2–12; David Hendrickson and Robert W. Tucker, *Revisions in Need of Revising: What Went Wrong in the Iraq War*, Strategic Studies Institute, U.S. Army War College, Carlisle, PA, December 2005; Alistair Finlan, "Trapped in the Dead Ground: U.S. Counterinsurgency Strategy in Iraq," *Small Wars and Insurgencies* 16, no. 1 (March 2005): 1–21.

7. All summarized in Thomas Ricks, *The Gamble: General David Petraeus and the American Military Adventure in Iraq, 2006–2008* (New York: Penguin Press, 2009); Linda Robinson, *Tell How This Ends: General David Petraeus and the Search for a Way Out of Iraq* (New York: Public Affairs Books, 2008); David Ucko, *The New Counterinsurgency Era: Transforming the U.S. Military for Modern Wars* (Washington, DC: Georgetown University Press, 2009). See also Steven Metz, *Learning from Iraq: Counterinsurgency in American Strategy*, Strategic Studies Institute, U.S. Army War College (December 2006).

8. Interview with Lieutenant Colonel Joel Rayburn, USA, October 14, 2009. Rayburn worked on the Central Command theater planning staff from 2005 to 2007, when he deployed to Iraq and served on the Joint Strategic Assessment Team. He was also attached to the 3rd ACR in Tal Afar in 2005–6.

9. Thomas Ricks, "The Dissenter Who Changed the War," *Washington Post*, February 8, 2009. Ricks documents a disagreement between the two senior MNF-I military leaders, General George Casey and General Ray Odierno, over this point. Odierno advocated an increase in troops, while Casey opposed it, according to Ricks. The article is an extract from Ricks, *The Gamble*.

10. As detailed in Ricks, *The Gamble*.

11. Author e-mail with Sarah Sewell, who participated in the preparation of the manual, June 3, 2009. Sewell indicated, however, many informal, ad hoc interactions occurred between the field and the team preparing the manual. It is worth noting that several Iraq experiences are highlighted in the manual. The manual summarizes Colonel H. R. McMaster's campaign in Tal Afar, cited as a successful example of COIN. See *FM 3–24*, 5–22, 5–23. See also references to the 1st Marine Division operations in Anbar in 4–7, 4–8.

12. An inescapable conclusion that emerges from Bob Woodward, *The War Within: A Secret White House History 2006–2008* (New York: Simon and Schuster, 2008). See also Ricks, *The Gamble*.

13. Woodward, *The War Within*, 31–33.

14. Andrew Krepinevich, Jr., "How to Win in Iraq," *Foreign Affairs* 84, no. 5 (September–October 2005): 87–104. http://www.foreignaffairs.org/20050901faessay84508/andrew-f-krepinevich-jr/how-to-win-in-iraq.html. Another account suggests that Rice used the term in reference to the 3rd ACR's COIN campaign in Tal Afar in 2005–6 commanded by Colonel H. R. McMaster. See Ricks, *The Gamble*, 51.

15. Major General Peter W. Chiarelli, USA, and Major Patrick Michaelis, USA, "Winning the Peace: The Requirements for Full Spectrum Operations," *Military Review* 85 (July–August 2005): 4–17. In this piece Chiarelli and Michaelis describe the LOOs used by the 1st Cavalry Division in operations in Baghdad in 2004. These LOOs eventually would form the basis for most unit operations during the period of this study: combat operations, train and employ security forces, essential services, promote governance, and economic pluralism (p. 7). For other early articles suggesting a change in military tactics, see Elliott Cohen, Conrad Crane, Jan Horvath, and John Nagl, "Principles, Imperatives, and Paradoxes of Counterinsurgency," *Military Review* 86, no. 2 (March–April 2006): 49–53; David J. Kilcullen, "Twenty-Eight Articles: Fundamentals of Company-Level Counterinsurgency," *Military Review* 86, no. 3 (May–June 2006): 103–8; Kalev I. Sepp, "Best Practices in Counterinsurgency," *Military Review* 85, no. 3 (May–June 2005): 8–12.

16. Accessed online at http://www.whitehouse.gov/infocus/iraq/iraq_national_strategy_20051130.pdf.

17. As quoted in David E. Sanger, Michael R. Gordon, and John F. Burns, "Chaos Overran Iraq Plan in '06, Bush Team Says," *New York Times*, January 2, 2007.

18. Text of speech on December 14, 2005, http://www.whitehouse.gov/news/releases/2005/12/20051214-1.html.

19. Casey's approach to the war is trenchantly discussed and critiqued in Brian Burton and John Nagl, "Learning as We Go: The U.S. Army Adapts to Counterinsurgency in Iraq July 2004–December 2006," *Small Wars and Insurgencies* 19, no. 3 (September 2008): 303–27.

20. Author interview with Kalev Sepp, October 14, 2009.

21. Ibid.

22. Details in Thomas Ricks, "U.S. Counterinsurgency Academy Giving Officers a New Mindset," *Washington Post*, February 21, 2006, A10. The academy played to mixed reviews, with many officers reluctant to attend the academy because of the time away from their units. Others found the course superficial. For writings on COIN, see David Galula, *Counterinsurgency Warfare: Theory and Practice* (London: Pall Mall, 1964); Robert Thompson, *Revolutionary War in World Strategy* (New York: Taplinger, 1970); Ian F. W. Becket, ed., *Armed Forces and Modern Counterinsurgency* (London: Croom Helm, 1985). See also Ian F. W. Becket, *The Roots of Counterinsurgency: Armies and Guerilla Warfare 1900–1945* (London: Blandford, 1988); Robert Taber, *War of the Flea: The Classic Study of Guerilla Warfare* (New York: L. Stuart, 1965); Robert B. Asprey, *War in the Shadows: The Guerilla in History* (New York: Doubleday, 1975); Alistair Horne, *A Savage War of Peace: Algeria 1954–1962* (New York: New York Review Books, 2006). For an excellent review of COIN theory literature, see David Kilcullen, "Counter-Insurgency Redux," *Survival* 48, no. 4 (December 2006): 111–30; Robert R. Tomes, "Relearning Counterinsurgency Warfare," *Parameters* 34 (Spring 2004): 16–28.

23. See Burton and Nagl, "Learning as We Go"; and Carter Malkasian, "Counterinsurgency in Iraq," in *Counterinsurgency in Modern Warfare*, Carter Malkasian and Daniel Marson, eds. (Oxford: Osprey Publishing, 2008), 241–59.

24. Burton and Nagl, "Learning as We Go," 305.

25. Author interview, December 30, 2008, with USMC Colonel (ret.) Tom Greenwood, who worked in Multi-National Force West staff in Anbar during the period. Staff officers in the field were not the only skeptics. According to accounts provided in Bob Woodward's *The War Within*, estimates produced by MNF-I showing dramatic increases in the numbers of ISF were widely regarded as a joke in the interagency—most particularly by Secretary of State Colin Powell (p. 22).

26. Woodward, *The War Within*, 11.

27. "Casey Iraq Plan Just One Option: White House," *Reuters*, June 26, 2006.

28. Robin Wright and Peter Baker, "Iraq Strategy Focusing on Three Main Options," *Washington Post*, December 9, 2006, A1.

29. *MNC-I In Brief GEN Petraeus*, February 8, 2007, PowerPoint Briefing posted on *Washington Post* website at http://www.washingtonpost.com/wp-srv/nation/thegamble/documents/Odierno_Briefing_Petraeus_February_2007.pdf.

30. See David Ucko's comprehensive discussion of the interim manual and other Defense Department initiatives to reorient the military departments toward irregular warfare and COIN in *The New Counterinsurgency Era*, 65–80.

31. Also covered in Burton and Nagl, "Learning as We Go."

32. Distinctions between these processes are drawn from a combination of works and will be further developed in Chapter 2. See Michael D. Doubler, *Closing with the Enemy: How GIs Fought the War in Europe, 1944–1945* (Lawrence: University of Kansas

Press, 1994), 8; Stephen Peter Rosen, *Winning the Next War: Innovation and the Modern Military* (Ithaca, NY: Cornell University Press, 1991), 1–53; Barry Posen, *Sources of Military Doctrine: France, Britain, and Germany between the Wars* (Ithaca, NY: Cornell University Press, 1984), 34–80; Peter Dombrowski and Eugene Gholz, *Buying Military Transformation: Technological Innovation and the Defense Industry* (New York: Columbia University Press, 2006).

33. Trenchant and searing critique of the early U.S. approach to COIN in Iraq is contained in Brigadier Nigel Aylwin-Foster, "Changing the Army for Counterinsurgency Operations," *Military Review* 85, no. 5 (November–December 2005): 2–15. See also Warren Chin, "Examining the Application of British Counterinsurgency Doctrine by the American Army in Iraq," *Small Wars and Insurgencies* 18, no. 1 (March 2007): 1–26. Chin argues that the reorientation of the U.S. approach to COIN in Iraq started in 2004 and drew heavily upon British expertise at MNF-I. See also Chin's treatment of the British stumbles in southern Iraq in "Why Did It All Go Wrong? Reassessing British Counterinsurgency in Iraq," *Strategic Studies Quarterly* 2, no. 4 (Winter 2008): 119–35; Steven Metz and Lieutenant Colonel Raymond Millen, *Insurgency and Counterinsurgency in the 21st Century: Reconceptualizing Threat and Response*, Strategic Studies Institute, U.S. Army War College (November 2004).

34. As chronicled by Ricks, *The Gamble*; Gordon and Trainor, *Cobra II*; and Bob Woodard, *Plan of Attack* (New York: Simon and Schuster, 2004).

35. U.S. Department of Defense, Joint Publication 1-02, *Department of Defense Dictionary of Military and Associated Terms*, April 12, 2001 (as amended through October 17, 2007), 169.

36. Comprehensive treatment of the evolving definitions in the U.S. military is given by Keith Bickel, *Mars Learning: The Marine Corps Development of Small Wars Doctrine, 1915–1940* (Boulder, CO: Westview Press, 2001), 1–26.

37. Ibid., 4–7.

38. Posen, *Sources of Military Doctrine*.

39. Daniel J. Moran, "A Theory of Strike Warfare," unpublished paper presented at the Monterey Strategy Seminar, Naval Postgraduate School, Monterey, CA, September 21, 2002. Cited with author's permission.

40. For some examples of writing on the Army's doctrine, see John L. Romjue, "The Evolution of the Airland Battle Concept," *Air University Review* (May–June 1984), http://www.airpower.maxwell.af.mil/airchronicles/aureview/1984/may-jun/romjue.html; LTC John Doerful, "Operational Art of the Airland Battle," *Field Artillery Journal* (September–October 1982), http://sill-www.army.mil/famag/1982/SEP_OCT_1982/SEP_OCT_1982_PAGES_32_36.pdf.

41. Steve Biddle, *Military Power: Explaining Victory and Defeat in Modern Battle* (Princeton: Princeton University Press, 2004).

42. Patrick G. Scott and Sanjay K. Pandy, "The Influence of Red Tape on Bureau-

cratic Behavior: An Experimental Simulation," *Journal of Policy Analysis and Management* 19, no. 4 (Autumn 2000): 615–33. The authors offer the following definition on page 616: "Red tape is commonly invoked to describe organizational procedures that are viewed as wasteful, unnecessary, self-serving, and vexing; in fact, it connotes the very worst of bureaucracy." See also Barry Bozeman, "A Theory of Government 'Red Tape,'" *Journal of Public Administration Research and Theory: J Part 3*, no. 3 (July 1993): 272–303; Herbert Kaufman, *Red Tape: Its Origins, Uses and Abuses* (Washington, DC: Brookings, 1977).

43. Thomas Ricks and Karen De Young, "Al Qaeda Reported Crippled," *Washington Post*, October 15, 2007, A1. The article notes: "There is widespread agreement that AQI has suffered major blows over the past three months. Among the indicators cited is a sharp drop in suicide bombings, the group's signature attack, from more than 60 in January to around 30 a month since July. Captures and interrogations of AQI leaders over the summer had what a senior military intelligence official called a 'cascade effect,' leading to other killings and captures. The flow of foreign fighters through Syria into Iraq has also diminished, although officials are unsure of the reason and are concerned that the broader Al Qaeda network may be diverting new recruits to Afghanistan and elsewhere." Much of the press reporting starting in August and September 2007 mirrors this assessment.

44. John Nagl, *Learning to Eat Soup with a Knife* (Chicago: University of Chicago Press, 2005), and Andrew Krepinevich, *The Army and Vietnam* (Baltimore: Johns Hopkins University Press, 1986).

45. As discussed in Robert Komer, *Bureaucracy at War: U.S. Performance in the Vietnam Conflict* (Boulder, CO: Westview Press, 1986), 111–29.

46. *The National Security Strategy of the United States of America,* The White House, Washington, DC, February 2006 and 2001; *The National Strategy to Combat Weapons of Mass Destruction,* The White House, Washington, DC, December 2002; *The National Strategy for Homeland Security,* The White House, Washington, DC, July 2002; *The National Strategy for Combating Terrorism,* The White House, Washington, DC, February 2003; *National Military Strategy,* Joint Chiefs of Staff, Washington, DC 2004; *National Defense Strategy,* Department of Defense, Washington, DC, March 2005; *The National Strategy for Maritime Security,* The White House, Washington, DC, September 2005. This list is by no means exhaustive but provides a flavor of the unprecedented attention paid by the Bush administration to the release of public documents dealing with various aspects of strategy and strategic priorities.

47. John Lewis Gaddis, "A Grand Strategy of Transformation," *Foreign Policy* 33 (2002): 50–57.

48. *Transition To and From Hostilities,* Defense Science Board 2004 Summer Study, Department of Defense, Washington, DC, December 2004; http://www.acq.osd.mil/dsb/reports/2004-12-DSB_SS_Report_Final.pdf.

49. Text of the directive can be accessed online at the Federation of American Scientists website at http://www.fas.org/irp/offdocs/nspd/nspd-44.html.

50. Richard Neustadt, *Presidential Power: The Politics of Leadership* (New York: John Wiley, 1970); Louis Fisher, *Presidential War Power* (Lawrence: University of Kansas Press, 2004); William G. Howell, *Power without Persuasion: The Politics of Direct Presidential Action* (Princeton: Princeton University Press, 2003); Michael Sherry, *In the Shadow of War: The United States since the 1930s* (New Haven: Yale University Press, 1994); John Lewis Gaddis, *The United States and the Origins of the Cold War* (New York: Columbia University Press, 2000); Arthur Schlesinger, *The Imperial Presidency* (New York: First Mariner Books, 2004).

51. Thomas Ricks, *Fiasco: The American Military Adventure in Iraq* (New York: Penguin, 2006).

52. U.S. Army *Field Manual (FM) 3-0, Operations*, Department of the Army, Washington, DC, June 14, 2001.

53. Ibid., 4–31, 4–32.

54. Robert E. Stake, *The Art of Case Study Research* (New York: Sage Publications, 1995); Robert Yin, *Applications of Case Study Research*, 3rd ed. (New York: Sage Publications, 2003); Kathleen M. Eisenhardt, "Building Theory from Case Study Research," *Academy of Management Review* 14, no. 4 (October 1989): 532–50.

55. Hashim, *Insurgency and Counter-Insurgency*, 1–59.

56. Carter Malkasian, "Did the Coalition Need More Forces in Iraq? Evidence from Al Anbar," *Joint Forces Quarterly* 46, no. 3 (2007): 120–26.

57. Carter Malkasian, "Signaling Resolve, Democratization and the First Battle of Fallujah," *Journal of Strategic Studies* 29, no. 3 (June 2006): 423–52. See also Malkasian's additional excellent analysis on other aspects of the U.S. counterinsurgency campaign in Al Anbar: "A Thin Blue Line in the Sand," *Democracy Journal*, no. 5 (Summer 2007): 48–58; "The Role of Perceptions and Political Reform: The Case of Western Iraq, 2004–2005," *Small Wars and Insurgencies* 17, no. 3 (September 2006): 367–94.

58. Bing West, *No True Glory: A Frontline Account of the Battle for Fallujah* (New York: Bantam Books, 2005).

59. Author interview with Brigadier General John Gronski [Commanding Officer 2/28], October 5, 2007.

60. Interview conducted by the author with Colonel Sean MacFarland, USA, [Former brigade commander of 1/1], October 15, 2007, in the Pentagon, Washington, DC.

61. David Kilcullen, "Anatomy of a Tribal Revolt," *Small Wars Journal*, August 29, 2007, http://www.smallwarsjournal.com/blog/2007/08/anatomy-of-a-tribal-revolt/; Michael Eisenstadt, "Tribal Engagement Lessons Learned," *Military Review* 87, no. 5 (September–October 2007): 16–31; Marie Colvin, "Sunni Sheiks Turn Their Sights from U.S. Forces to Al Qaeda," *Sunday Times*, September 9, 2007, http://www.timesonline.co.uk/tol/news/world/iraq/article2414588.ece.

62. For an example, see Max Boot, "An Iraq Success Story," *Los Angeles Times*, April 24, 2007, http://www.latimes.com/news/opinion/la-oe-boot24apr24,0,6844465.column?coll=la-news-columns. See also Michael O'Hanlon and Kenneth Pollack, "A War We Might Just Win," *New York Times*, July 30, 2007, http://www.nytimes.com/2007/07/30/opinion/30pollack.html.

63. Interview with MacFarland.

64. For early reporting on the background of the U.S. counterinsurgency campaign in Mosul, see Robert D. Kaplan, "The Coming Normalcy," *Atlantic* (April 2006): 72–81.

65. See, for example, Anthony Shadid, "Troops Move to Quell Insurgency in Mosul," *Washington Post*, November 17, 2004, A1.

66. Interview conducted by the author with Colonel Michael Shields, USA, [former brigade commander, 172nd SBCT], October 15, 2007, in the Pentagon, Washington, DC.

67. For example, see Steve Fainaru, "In Mosul, a Battle 'Beyond Ruthless,'" *Washington Post*, April 13, 2005, A01; Nelson Hernandez, "Mosul Makes Gains against Chaos," *Washington Post*, February 2, 2006, A14.

68. For early details of the SBCT performance in Mosul, see Ren Angeles, "Examining the SBCT Concept and Insurgency in Mosul, Iraq," *Infantry Magazine* (May–June 2005).

CHAPTER 2

1. See citations in Chapter 1, note 15.

2. Samuel Huntington, *The Soldier and the State: The Theory and Politics of Civil-Military Relations* (Cambridge: Belknap Press of Harvard University Press, 1957).

3. For statements on realist thought, see Hans Morgenthau, *Politics among Nations* (New York: Knopf, 1966); E. H. Carr, *Twenty Years' Crisis: 1919–1939* (New York: Perennial Press, April 1964); George Kennan, *American Diplomacy, 1900–1950* (New York: New American Library, 1951); and George Kennan, *Realities of American Foreign Policy* (Princeton: Princeton University Press, 1954). For more recent treatments of realism and neorealism, see the scholarship of Kenneth Waltz, *Theory of International Politics* (New York: McGraw Hill, 1979). See also Kenneth Waltz, *Man, the State and War* (New York: Columbia University Press, 2001); John J. Mearsheimer, *The Tragedy of Great Power Politics* (New York: W. W. Norton, 2003); Stephen M. Walt, *The Origins of Alliances* (Ithaca, NY: Cornell University Press, 1990); for a constructivist critique, see Alexander Wendt, *Social Theory of International Politics* (Cambridge, England: Cambridge University Press, 1979).

4. Graham Allison and Philip Zelikow, *Essence of Decision: Explaining the Cuban Missile Crisis*, 2nd ed. (New York: Longman, 1999); Graham Allison and Morton Halperin, "Bureaucratic Politics: A Paradigm and Some Policy Implications," *World Politics* 24 (1972): 40–79; Francis E. Rourke, *Bureaucracy and Foreign Policy* (Baltimore, MD:

Johns Hopkins University Press, 1972); Jerel A. Rosati, "Developing a Systematic Decision-Making Framework: Bureaucratic Politics in Perspective," *World Politics* 33 (1981): 234–52; Jack Levy, "Organizational Routines and the Causes of War," *International Studies Quarterly* 30 (1986): 193–222; Roger Hilsman, *The Politics of Policy Making in Defense and Foreign Affairs*, 3rd ed. (Englewood Cliffs, NJ: Prentice Hall, 1993). A negative critique of the Allison-Halperin argument is provided in Robert Art, "Bureaucratic Politics and American Foreign Policy: A Critique," *Policy Sciences* 4 (1973): 467–90; Steven D. Krasner, "Are Bureaucracies Important? Or Allison Wonderland," *Foreign Policy* 7 (1972): 159–79. More recent treatment of these issues are in David A. Welch, "The Organizational Process and Bureaucratic Politics Paradigms: Retrospect and Prospect," *International Security* 17, no. 2 (1992): 112–46; Paul T. Hart and Uriel Rosenthal, "Reappraising Bureaucratic Politics," *Mershon International Studies Review* 42 (1998): 233–40; J. Garry Clifford, "Bureaucratic Politics," *Journal of American History* 77 (1990): 161–68; Edward Rhodes, "Do Bureaucratic Politics Matter? Some Disconfirming Findings from the Case of the U.S. Navy," *World Politics* 47, no. 1 (October 1994): 1–41; Daniel Drezner, "Ideas, Bureaucratic Politics, and the Crafting of Foreign Policy," *American Journal of Political Science* 44 (2000): 733–49.

5. Halperin and Allison, *Essence of Decision.*

6. Stephen Peter Rosen, *Winning the Next War: Innovation and the Modern Military* (Ithaca, NY: Cornell University Press, 1991), 2.

7. The Marine Corps is technically part of the Navy—not its own military department. Most observers would agree, however, that the Marine Corps effectively constitutes its own distinct organizational entity not unlike its sister military departments.

8. As an example of the evolution of bureaucratic behavior in the U.S. Air Force, see Walter J. Boyne, *Beyond the Wild Blue: A History of the U.S. Air Force* (New York: St. Martin's Press, 1997).

9. Morton Halperin, *Bureaucratic Politics and Foreign Policy* (Washington, DC: Brookings, 1974), 26–63; David C. Kozak and James M. Keagle, eds., *Bureaucratic Politics and National Security: Theory and Practice* (Boulder, CO: Lynne Rienner 1988). The same principles are believed to apply to most public and private bureaucracies. See James Q. Wilson, *Bureaucracy: What Government Agencies Do and Why They Do It* (New York: Basic Books, 1989); Anthony Downs, *Inside Bureaucracy* (Boston: Little Brown, 1967); Michel Crozier, *The Bureaucratic Phenomenon* (Chicago: University of Chicago Press, 1964); and Richard Cyert and James March, *A Behavioral Theory of the Firm* (Englewood Cliffs, NJ: Prentice Hall, 1963).

10. Kurt Lang, "Military Organizations," in James G. March, *Handbook of Organizations* (Chicago: Rand McNally and Co., 1965), 838–78.

11. In the Air Force's case, it has essentially given "early out" to 40,000 young officers—paying them to leave the service early in order to save money to pay for the F-22. The Navy is also letting officers retire prematurely to pay for hardware. See Scott

Canon, "Air Force, Navy Downsizing to Pay for Hardware," *Kansas City Star*, November 14, 2007, http://www.freerepublic.com/focus/f-news/1925589/posts.

12. The V-22 tilt rotor aircraft used by the Marine Corps is a classic example of that phenomenon. It exists to this day only because Congress forced it down the throats of the Marine Corps and Defense Department, over the opposition of both those organizations.

13. Frederick M. Downy and Steven Metz, "The American Political Culture and Strategic Planning," *Parameters* 18 (1988): 34–42; Steven Casey, "Selling NSC-68: The Truman Administration, Public Opinion, and the Politics of Mobilization," *Diplomatic History* 29 (2005): 655–90; Allan C. Stamm III, *Win, Lose or Draw: Domestic Politics and the Crucible of War* (Ann Arbor: University of Michigan Press, 1999).

14. Michael E. Brown, *Flying Blind: The Politics of the U.S. Strategic Bomber Program* (Ithaca, NY: Cornell University Press, 1992); Daniel Wirls, *Buildup: The Politics of Defense in the Reagan Era* (Ithaca, NY: Cornell University Press, 1992); Thomas McNaugher, *New Weapons, Old Politics: America's Military Procurement Muddle* (Washington, DC: Brookings, 1989), 123–50; Thomas McNaugher, "Weapons Procurement: The Futility of Reform," *International Security* 12, no. 2 (1987): 63–104; Morton Halperin and Arnold Kanter, eds., *Readings in American Foreign Policy: A Bureaucratic Perspective* (Boston: Little and Brown, 1973); James H. Lebovic, "Riding Waves or Making Waves: The Services and the U.S. Defense Budget, 1981–1993," *American Political Science Review* 88 (1994): 839–52; Philip A. Odeen, "Organizing for National Security," *International Security* 5, no. 1 (1980): 111–29.

15. As argued by Barry Posen, *Sources of Military Doctrine: France, Britain, and Germany between the Wars* (Ithaca, NY: Cornell University Press, 1984).

16. Elizabeth Kier, *Imagining War: French and British Military Doctrine between the Wars* (Princeton: Princeton University Press, 1999); Kimberly Martin Zisk, *Engaging the Enemy: Organization Theory and Soviet Military Innovation, 1955–1991* (Princeton: Princeton University Press, 1993); and Deborah Avant, *Political Institutions and Military Change: Lessons from Peripheral Wars* (Ithaca, NY: Cornell University Press, 1994), all emphasize the role of internal factors in shaping the character of the state's military institutions and the resultant military doctrine that structures how these institutions fight. Zisk (*Engaging the Enemy*, 1–10) forcefully argues that military institutions *are* attuned to the external environment and do engage in doctrinal development and change in search of the best method of fighting adversaries. She argues that the case of the Soviet military suggests that military institutions will explore changes to doctrine internally when the institution believes it necessary to counter changes in the doctrine of its adversaries. Kier (*Imagining War*, 21–37) emphasizes the role that organizational culture can play in shaping military doctrine.

17. Rosen, *Winning the Next War*; Posen, *Sources of Military Doctrine*; Kier, *Imagining War*; Avant, *Political Institutions and Military Change*; Colin Gray, "Irregular Enemies and the Essence of Strategy: Can the American Way of War Adapt?" Strategic

Studies Institute, U.S. Army War College, Carlisle, PA, March 2006; Zisk, *Engaging the Enemy*; Theo Farrell and Terry Terriff, eds., *The Sources of Military Change: Culture, Politics and Technology* (Boulder, CO: Lynne Rienner, 2002); Theo Farrell, "Figuring Out Fighting Organizations: The New Organizational Analysis in Strategic Studies," *Journal of Strategic Studies* 19 (1996): 122–35; Theo Farrell, "Culture and Military Power," *Review of International Studies* 24 (1998): 407–16; Jack L. Snyder, *The Ideology of the Offensive: Military Decision Making in the Disasters of 1914* (Ithaca, NY: Cornell University Press, 1984); Jeffrey W. Legro, "Culture and Cooperation in the International Cooperation Two-Step," *American Political Science Review* 90 (1996): 118–37; Allen R. Millett, Williamson Murray, and Kenneth H. Watman, "The Effectiveness of Military Organizations," *International Security* 11, no. 1 (1986): 37–71; Colin S. Gray, "National Style in Strategy: The American Example," *International Security* 6, no. 2 (1981): 21–47; Dan Reiter and Allan C. Stamm III, "Democracy and Battlefield Military Effectiveness," *Journal of Conflict Resolution* 42 (1988): 259–77; David R. Segal and Mady Wechsler Segal, "Change in Military Organization," *Annual Review of Sociology* 9 (1983): 151–70; Deborah Avant, "The Institutional Sources of Military Doctrine: Hegemons in Peripheral Wars," *International Studies Quarterly* 37 (1993): 409–30; David Jablonskly, "U.S. Military Doctrine and the Revolution in Military Affairs," *Parameters* 24 (1994): 18–36; Williamson Murray and R. Allen Millett, eds., *Military Innovation in the Interwar Period* (Cambridge: Cambridge University Press, 1996); Jeffrey A. Isaacson, Christopher Layne, and John Arquila, *Predicting Military Innovation* (Santa Monica, CA: Rand, 1999); John Nagl, *Learning to Eat Soup with a Knife* (Chicago: University of Chicago Press, 2005); Jeremy Black, "Military Organisations and Military Change in Historical Perspective," *Journal of Military History* 62 (October 1988): 871–93; Richard Duncan Downie, *Learning from Conflict: The U.S. Military in Vietnam, El Salvador, and the Drug War* (Westport, CT: Praeger, 1998).

18. For distinctions between these concepts, see Edward Luttwak, "The Operational Level of War," *International Security* 5, no. 3 (Winter 1980–81): 61–79.

19. Stephen Peter Rosen, "New Ways of War: Understanding Military Innovation," *International Security* 13, no. 1 (1988): 134.

20. Rosen, *Winning the Next War*, 1–53.

21. Theo Farrell, "Innovation in Military Organizations without Enemies," unpublished paper presented at the International Studies Association Annual Convention, San Diego, CA, April 16–20, 1996, as cited in Farrell and Terriff, *The Sources of Military Change*, 5.

22. Isaacson, et al., *Predicting Military Innovation* 8.

23. For a good summary of the application of complexity theory to organizations, see Philip Anderson, "Complexity Theory and Organizational Science," *Organization Science* 10, no. 3 (May–June 1999): 216–32; Heinz Otto-Peitgen, Hartmut Jurgens, and Dietmar Saupe, *Chaos and Fractals: New Frontiers of Science*, 2nd ed. (New York:

Springer, 2004); David Byrne, *Complexity Theory and the Social Science* (London: Routledge, 1998); Todd R. LaPorte, ed., *Organized Social Complexity* (Princeton: Princeton University Press, 1975); John Steinbruner, *The Cybernetic Theory of Decision* (Princeton: Princeton University Press, 1974).

24. Alan Beyerchen, "From Radio to Radar: Interwar Military Adaptation to Technological Change in Germany, the United Kingdom, and the United States," in *Military Innovation in the Interwar Period,* Murray and Millet, eds., 266–69. Beyerchen cites Thomas P. Hughes, "The Development Phase of Technological Change," *Technology and Culture* 17, no. 3 (July 1976): 423–31 on these points.

25. Beyerchen, "From Radio to Radar," 267.

26. Williamson Murray, "Innovation: Past and Future," in *Military Innovation in the Interwar Period,* Murray and Millet, eds., 303.

27. Ibid., 305.

28. Ibid., 304–12.

29. James G. March and Herbert A. Simon, *Organizations* (New York: John Wiley and Sons, 1985), 177–86.

30. Ibid., 183.

31. Several of the best empirical works addressing wartime innovation are Bruce I. Gudmundsson, *Stormtroop Tactics: Innovation in the German Army, 1914–1918* (Westport, CT: Praeger, 1989); Timothy T. Lupfer, *The Dynamics of Doctrine: The Change in German Tactical Doctrine during the First World War* (Leavenworth, KS: U.S. Army Combat Studies Institute, 1981); Thomas Alexander Hughes, *Overlord: General Pete Quesada and the Triumph of Tactical Air Power in World War II* (New York: Free Press, 1995); Geoffrey Parker, *The Military Revolution: Military Innovation and the Rise of the West* (Cambridge: Cambridge University Press, 1988); Jeremy Black, *A Military Revolution? Military Change and European Society 1550–1800* (London: Macmillan, 1991).

32. Carl von Clausewitz, *On War,* ed. and trans. by Michael Howard and Peter Paret (Princeton: Princeton University Press, 1976), 117.

33. Ibid., 121.

34. Ibid., 101. For an excellent critique of the uses and misuses of this famous metaphor in popular culture, see Michael J. Shapiro, "The Fog of War," *Security Dialogue* 36, no. 2 (June 2005): 233–46; Alan Beyerchen interestingly argues that Clausewitz's metaphor suggested an embrace of modern theories of complexity and the nonlinear nature of warfare. See Alan Beyerchen, "Clausewitz, Nonlinearity, and the Unpredictability of War," *International Security* 17, no. 3 (Winter 1992/1993): 59–90.

35. Rosen, *Winning the Next War,* 35.

36. Ibid.

37. Rosen, *Winning the Next War,* 1–76; Segal and Segal, "Change in Military Organization"; Joseph Harris, "Wartime Currents and Peacetime Trends," *American Political Science Review* 40 (December 1946): 1137–54; Chris Demchak, *Military Organizations,*

Complex Machines: Modernization in the U.S. Armed Forces (Ithaca, NY: Cornell University Press, 1991).

38. Posen, *Sources of Military Doctrine*; Kier, *Imagining War,* Avant, *Political Institutions and Military Change.*

39. Posen, *Sources of Military Doctrine.*

40. Ibid., 224.

41. See note 2 in this chapter for some of the foundational works in realism.

42. Posen, *Sources of Military Doctrine,* 171–76.

43. Avant, *Political Institutions and Military Change,* 1–20.

44. James G. March and Johan P. Olsen summarize the field comprehensively in "The New Institutionalism: Organizational Factors in Political Life," *American Political Science Review* 78 (1984): 734–49; Terry M. Moe and Scott A. Wilson, "Presidents and the Politics of Structure," *Law and Contemporary Problems* 57 (1994): 1–44; Terry M. Moe, "Politics and the Theory of Organization," *Journal of Law, Economics and Organization* 17 (1991): 106–29; Terry M. Moe, "The New Economics of Organization," *American Journal of Political Science* 28 (1984): 739–77.

45. Stephen A. Ross, "The Economic Theory of Agency: The Principal's Problem," *American Economic Review* 63 (1973): 134–39; William Rogerson, "The First Order Approach to Principal-Agent Problems," *Econometrica* 53 (1985): 1357–67; Kathleen M. Eisenhardt, "Agency Theory: An Assessment and Review," *Academy of Management Review* 14 (1989): 57–74; David Sappington, "Incentives in Principal Agent Relationships," *Journal of Economic Perspectives* 5 (1991): 45–66; Richard M. Watterman and Kenneth J. Meier, "Principal Agent Models: An Expansion?" *Journal of Public Administration Research and Theory* 8 (1998): 173–202; V. Nilakant and Hayagreeva Rao, "Agency Theory and Organizations: An Evaluation," *Organization Studies* 15 (1994): 649–72.

46. See for example Mancur Olson, *The Logic of Collective Action* (Cambridge: Harvard University Press, 1971).

47. Avant, *Political Institutions and Military Change,* 49–75.

48. Lang, "Military Organizations," 852.

49. As also argued by Zisk, *Engaging the Enemy.*

50. *Quadrennial Defense Review Report,* Department of Defense, Washington, DC, February 6, 2006, 1.

51. Ibid.

52. Ibid., 63–73.

53. James J. Wirtz and James A. Russell, "U.S. Policy on Preventive War and Preemption," *Nonproliferation Review* 10, no. 1 (Spring 2003): 113–23.

54. Defined as "a form of warfare that has as its objective the credibility and/or legitimacy of the relevant political authority with the goal of undermining or supporting that authority. Irregular warfare favors indirect approaches, though it may employ the full range of military and other capabilities to seek asymmetric advantages, in order to erode

an adversary's power, influence and will." The definition comes from *The Quadrennial Defense Review Irregular Warfare Roadmap* cited in the statement by Brigadier General Otis G. Mannon, USAF, Deputy Director J-3., Joint Staff, Testimony before the 109th Congress, Committee on Armed Services Subcommittee on Terrorism, Unconventional Threats and Capabilities, U.S. House of Representatives, September 27, 2006, 4.

55. As covered in Bob Woodward, *Plan of Attack* (New York: Simon and Schuster, 2004).

56. The Joint Forces Command also released the *Stability Operations Joint Operating Concept* in September 2004. JFCOM had no real means to operationalize the JOC in the field.

57. James A. Russell, "Strategy, Security, and the War in Iraq: The United States and the Gulf in the 21st Century," *Cambridge Review of International Affairs* 18, no. 2 (July 2005): 283–301.

58. Statement of Ambassador Ryan Crocker, U.S. ambassador to Iraq before a Joint Hearing of the Committee on Foreign Affairs and the Committee on Armed Services, September 10, 2007; Report to Congress on the Situation in Iraq, General David H. Petraeus Commander, Multi-National Force-Iraq September 10–11, 2007. Petraeus presented a briefing during his testimony titled "Multinational-Force Iraq: Charts to Accompany the Testimony of General David H. Petraeus." The flavor of the debate over measures of effectiveness is captured in Karen De Young and Thomas Ricks, "The General's Long View Could Cut Debate Short," *Washington Post*, September 11, 2007.

59. Summarized by Seymour Hersh, "Offense and Defense: The Battle between Donald Rumsfeld and the Pentagon," *The New Yorker*, April 7, 2003, http://www.newyorker.com/archive/2003/04/07/030407fa_fact1?currentPage=all.

60. As argued by Adam Grissom, "The Future of Military Innovation Studies," *Journal of Strategic Studies* 29, no. 5 (October 2006): 920–21.

61. Gudmundsson, *Stormtroop Tactics*.

62. Paddy Griffiths, *Battle Tactics on the Western Front: The British Army's Art of Attack, 1916–1918* (New Haven: Yale University Press, 1996).

63. Ibid., 171–79.

64. Germany's war of mechanized maneuver in World War II is chronicled in John Erickson's masterful works *The Road to Stalingrad* (Boulder, CO: Westview Press, 1983) and its companion volume, *The Road to Berlin* (Boulder, CO: Westview Press, 1983).

65. As covered by Max Hastings in *Armageddon: The Battle for Germany, 1944–1945* (New York: Knopf, 2004), 22.

66. Hughes, *Overlord*.

67. Keith Bickel, *Mars Learning: The Marine Corps Development of Small Wars Doctrine, 1915–1940* (Boulder, CO: Westview Press, 2001).

68. Started as a privately run website, subsequently taken over by the Army.

69. Downie, *Learning from Conflict*; Nagl, *Learning to Eat Soup with a Knife*.

70. Downie, *Learning from Conflict,* 22.

71. Doubler, *Closing with The Enemy: How GIs Fought the War in Europe, 1944–1945* (Lawrence: University of Kansas Press, 1994). See also Michael D. Doubler, "Busting the Bocage: America's Combined Arms Operations in France 6 June–31 July 1944," Combat Studies Institute, Fort Leavenworth, KS, 1988, http://www-cgsc.army.mil/carl/resources/csi/doubler/doubler.asp. Doubler's mostly laudatory assessment of the Army's performance in Europe after D-Day is not universally shared. See Max Hastings, *Armageddon,* for an alternative view. Hastings argues throughout his excellent book that the Western armies were plagued with the interrelated and systemic problems of poor senior leadership and mediocre battlefield performance that repeatedly let the Wehrmacht off the hook and unnecessarily prolonged the war.

72. Doubler, *Closing with The Enemy,* 57–62.

73. Ibid., 58.

74. Ibid., 31–62.

75. Lynn Eden, *Whole World on Fire: Organizations, Knowledge, & Nuclear Weapons Devastation* (Ithaca, NY: Cornell University Press, 2004), 37–60. Some of the same ground is covered in Scott Sagan, *The Limits of Safety: Organizations, Accidents and Nuclear Weapons* (Princeton: Princeton University Press, 1993), 204–49.

76. Eden, *Whole World on Fire,* 50.

77. Demchak, *Military Organizations, Complex Machines.* See also Chris Demchak, "Complexity, Rogue Outcomes and Weapon Systems," *Public Administration Review* 52, no. 4 (July–August 1992): 347–55; Chris Demchak, "Complexity and Theory of Networked Militaries," in *The Sources of Military Change,* Farrell and Terriff, eds., 221–62.

78. Demchak, *Military Organizations, Complex Machines,* 18.

79. Ibid., 103–31.

80. Ibid., 103–4.

81. Ibid., 132–62.

82. Dwight Waldo, "What Is Public Administration?" in *Classics of Public Administration,* Jay M. Shafritz and Albert C. Hyde, eds. (Oak Park, IL: Moore Publishing Co., 1978), 171.

83. Max Weber, *The Theory of Social and Economic Organization,* trans. by A. M. Henerson and Talcott Parsons (New York: Free Press, 1964), 337.

84. Ibid.

85. Ibid.

86. Ibid.

87. List also derived from Max Weber, *Essays in Sociology,* ed. by H. Gerth and C. Wright Mills (Oxford: Oxford University Press, 1946). See also Peter M. Blau and Marshall Meyer, *Bureaucracy in Modern Society,* 3rd ed. (New York: Random House, 1987), 18–25; Charles Perrow, *Complex Organizations: A Critical Essay,* 3rd ed. (New York: McGraw Hill, 1986), 3; William G. Scott, Terence R. Mitchell, and Philip H. Birnbaum,

Organizational Theory: A Structural and Behavioral Analysis, 4th ed. (Homewood, IL: Richard D. Irwin, 1981), 4–7.

88. As argued by Rosen, *Winning the Next War,* 2. See Karl W. Deutsch, "On Theory and Research in Innovation," in *Innovation in the Public Sector,* Richard L. Merritt and Anna J. Merrit, eds. (Beverly Hills, CA: Sage, 1985), 20; Marshall Meyer, *Change in Public Bureaucracies* (London: Cambridge University Press, 1979), 99. Cited by Rosen, *Winning the Next War,* ch. 1, note 3.

89. Robert Merton, "Bureaucratic Structure and Personality," *Social Forces* 18, no. 4 (May 1940): 560–68.

90. Ibid., 562.

91. Ibid., 563.

92. Chester Barnard, *The Function of the Executive* (Cambridge: Harvard University Press, 1939).

93. As argued by Perrow, *Complex Organizations,* 63.

94. F. J. Roethlisberger, "The Hawthorne Experiments," reprinted in Shafritz and Hyde, *Classics of Public Administration,* 67–77.

95. A. H. Maslow, "A Theory of Human Motivation," *Psychological Review* 50 (1943): 370–96.

96. Some of Simon's initial thinking is addressed in "The Proverbs of Administration," *Public Administration Review* 6 (Winter 1946): 53–67.

97. Ibid., 64–65. See also March and Simon, *Organizations,* 136–71. Simon's initial thinking in this piece provided fodder for a range of works that appeared over the next fifty years. See Herbert Simon: *Administrative Behavior,* 3rd ed. (New York: Free Press, 1976); "A Behavioral Model of Rational Choice," *Quarterly Journal of Economics* 69, no. 1 (February 1955): 99–115; "Bounded Rationality and Organizational Learning," *Organization Science* 2, no. 1 (1991): 125–34; *Models of Bounded Rationality* (Cambridge: MIT Press, 1997).

98. March and Simon, *Organizations,* 140–41.

99. Ibid., 141.

100. As observed by Perrow, *Complex Organizations,* 122.

101. Steinbruner, *The Cybernetic Theory of Decision.*

102. Ibid., 56.

103. Ibid.

104. Ibid., 55.

105. Ibid., 78–79. Also cited by Sagan, *The Limits of Safety,* in note 4, 205.

CHAPTER 3

1. Thomas E. Ricks, "Situation Called Dire in West Iraq, Anbar Is Lost Politically, Marine Analyst Says," *Washington Post,* September 11, 2006; Michael Gordon, "Grim Outlook Seen in West Iraq without More Troops and Aid," *New York Times,* September 12, 2006.

2. Ricks, "Situation Called Dire in West Iraq."

3. See *State of the Insurgency in al-Anbar, I MEF G-2, SECRET//REL MCFI//20310816*, http://media.washingtonpost.com/wp-srv/nation/documents/marines_iraq_document_020707.pdf.

4. Gordon, "Grim Outlook Seen in West Iraq."

5. As quoted in Patrick J. McDonnell and Julie E. Barnes, "The Conflict in Iraq," *Los Angeles Times*, September 13, 2007, 10.

6. Leo Shane III, "Commander Fears Impact of Anbar Report's Release," *Stars and Stripes*, September 16, 2006.

7. Pamela Hess, "Analysis: Anbar Troops Moved to Baghdad," *UPI*, September 15, 2006.

8. Arguments summarized in Kenneth Pollack, "The Seven Deadly Sins of Failure in Iraq: A Retrospective Analysis of the Reconstruction," *Middle East Review of International Affairs* 10, no. 4 (December 2006), http://meria.idc.ac.il/journal/2006/issue4/jv10no4a1.html.

9. Summarized in Thomas Ricks, *The Gamble: General David Petraeus and the American Military Adventure in Iraq, 2006–2008* (New York: Penguin Books, 2009), 12–13.

10. Ricks, "Situation Called Dire in West Iraq."

11. Ibid.

12. Senator John McCain used the term during an exchange with the Central Command's General John Abizaid in the summer of 2006 in a hearing held by the Senate Armed Services Committee. McCain expanded on the metaphor in an August 20, 2006, appearance on "Meet the Press"; transcript at http://www.msnbc.msn.com/id/14390980/.

13. Bob Woodward, *The War Within: A Secret White House History 2006–2008* (New York: Simon and Schuster, 2008).

14. Kirk Semple, "Uneasy Alliance Is Taming One Insurgent Bastion," *New York Times*, April 29, 2007.

15. Anthony Cordesman, "Success or Failure? Iraq's Insurgency and Civil Violence and US Strategy: Developments through June 2007," *Center for Strategic and International Studies*, July 9, 2007, http://www.csis.org/media/csis/pubs/070709_iraqinsurgupdate.pdf.

16. Ambassador Zalmay Khalilzad, "Statement on the Situation Concerning Iraq: Remarks in the Security Council Chamber," *U.S. Department of State*, October 19, 2007, http://www.state.gov/p/io/rls/rm/93729.htm.

17. Presentation titled "Best Practices in al-Anbar" by Kelly Musick, Joint Center for Operational Analysis, Joint Forces Command, Naval Postgraduate School, September 13, 2007; presentation titled "Studying Insurgency in Al Anbar," by Carter Malkasion, Center for Naval Analyses, Naval Postgraduate School, November 28, 2007.

18. As noted by David Kilcullen, "Anatomy of a Tribal Revolt," *Small Wars Journal*, August 29, 2007, http://www.smallwarsjournal.com/blog/2007/08/anatomy-of-a-tribal-revolt/.

19. Lieutenant Evan Lopez, stationed in the region in 2004 and 2005, as quoted in David Cloud, "Recovery and War Vie in Iraq," *International Herald Tribune*, April 6, 2006.

20. See, for example, Sabrina Tavernise and Dexter Filkins, "Local Insurgents Tell of Clashes with Al Qaeda's Forces in Iraq," *New York Times,* January 11, 2006. See also details in Steve Negus, "Border Region Offers Glimmer of Hope for Post Insurgency Peace," *Financial Times*, May 6, 2006; Mark Mazzetti and Solomon Moore, "Insurgents Flourish in Iraq's Wild West," *Los Angeles Times*, May 24, 2005.

21. Hannah Allam and Mohammed al Dulaimy, "Iraqis Lament Call for Help," *Philadelphia Inquirer*, May 17, 2005.

22. Ahmed Hashim, "Iraq's Civil War," *Current History* (January 2007): 2–10; Carter Malkasian, "Did the Coalition Need More Forces in Iraq? Evidence from Al Anbar," *Joint Forces Quarterly* 46, no. 3 (2007), 123. See also Christopher Allbritton: "Making Tribal War Work for the U.S. in Iraq," *Time*, November 8, 2005; "Iraq's Desert Protection Force at War," StrategyPage, January 1, 2006, http://www.strategypage.com/htmw/htworld/articles/20060101.aspx.

23. Christian T. Miller, "Marines Are Cracking Down on Insurgent Stronghold of Ramadi," *Los Angeles Times*, February 21, 2005.

24. Tony Perry, "After Fallujah, Marines' Mission Shifts Northwest," *Los Angeles Times*, February 18, 2005.

25. Ellen Knickmeyer, "Zarqawi Followers Clash with Local Sunnis," *Washington Post*, May 29, 2005; Mazzetti and Moore, "Insurgents Flourish in Iraq's Wild West," *Los Angeles Times*, May 24, 2005; Dan Murphy, "After Temporary Gains, Marines Leave Iraqi Cities," *Christian Science Monitor*, March 3, 2005.

26. Murphy, "After Temporary Gains."

27. Carol J. Williams, "The World; U.S. Troops Pour into Rebel-Held Iraqi Town," *Los Angeles Times*, May 26, 2005.

28. Patrick J. McDonnel, "Attacks Mar Anniversary of Return to Iraqi Rule," *Los Angeles Times*, June 29, 2005.

29. Dahr Jamail, "Operation Matador: Claims over US Siege Challenged," *Inter Press Service*, May 19, 2005.

30. As quoted in Allam and al Dulaimy, "Iraqis Lament Call for Help."

31. Ellen Knickmeyer and Caryle Murphy, "U.S. Ends Iraqi Border Offensive," *Washington Post*, May 15, 2005, A24.

32. As quoted in Mazzetti and Moore, "Insurgents Flourish in Iraq's Wild West."

33. As noted by Malkasian, "Did the Coalition Need More Forces in Anbar?" 120–21.

34. LTC Philip Skuta: "Introduction to 2/7 CAP Platoon Actions in Iraq," *Marine Corps Gazette* (April 2005): 35; "Partnering with the Iraqi Security Forces," *Marine Corps Gazette* (April 2005): 36–38; Lieutenant Jason Goodale and Lieutenant Jon Webre, "The Combined Action Platoon in Iraq," *Marine Corps Gazette* (April 2005): 40–42.

35. Malkasian, "Did the Coalition Need More Forces in Anbar?" 123.

36. Jill Carroll, "Evolution in Iraq's Insurgency; Attacks on U.S. troops Are Down 22 percent since January," *Christian Science Monitor*, April 7, 2005.

37. Mark Mazzetti, "Insurgency Is Waning, a Top U.S. General Says," *Los Angeles Times*, March 2, 2005.

38. Jill Carroll and Dan Murphy, "Iraqi Insurgents Are a Moving Target," *Christian Science Monitor*, September 15, 2005.

39. Mazzetti and Moore, "Insurgents Flourish in Iraq's Wild West."

40. John F. Burns, "Iraq's Ho Chi Minh Trail," *New York Times*, June 5, 2005.

41. Carroll and Murphy, "Iraqi Insurgents Are a Moving Target"; Mazzetti and Moore, "Insurgents Flourish in Iraq's Wild West."

42. Burns, "Iraq's Ho Chi Minh Trail."

43. Solomon Moore, "Rebels in Western Iraq Under Siege," *Los Angeles Times*, May 10, 2005.

44. Ellen Knickmeyer, "Zarqawi Followers Clash with Local Sunnis," *Washington Post*, May 29, 2005.

45. Jeffrey Fleishman, "U.S. Ponders Iraq Fight After Zarqawi;," *Los Angeles Times*, May 28, 2005.

46. Ibid.

47. Craig S. Smith and Eric Schmitt, "U.S. Contends Campaign Has Cut Suicide Attacks," *New York Times*, August 5, 2005; John Hendren, "8 U.S. Troops Killed in Battle for Border;" *Los Angeles Times*, August 3, 2005.

48. Edward Wong and John F. Burns, "Marines and Iraqi Troops Start Push against Rebels," *New York Times*, July 10, 2005.

49. Jonathan Finer and Saad Sarhan, "U.S., Iraq Strike Volatile Area; Politicians Stall Constitution Writing to Resolve Central Issues," *Washington Post*, August 7, 2005.

50. Bradley Graham, "Forces Bolstered In Western Iraq; Commanders Hope to Block Infiltration," *Washington Post*, September 21, 2005.

51. Louise Roug, "The World; 6 Marines Slain by Bombs in Western Iraq Offensive; U.S. and government troops mounted two operations against suspected foreign fighters in advance of the constitutional vote," *Los Angeles Times*, October 8, 2005.

52. Craig S. Smith, "U.S. and Iraq Step up Effort to Block Insurgents' Routes," *New York Times*, October 3, 2005; Wong and Burns, "Marines and Iraqi Troops Start Push against Rebels."

53. Richard Boudreaux, "The World; U.S. and Iraqi Forces Mount Offensive," *Los Angeles Times*, October 5, 2005.

54. "Operation Steel Curtain (al Hajip Elfulathi)," 2nd Marine Division/Regimental Combat Team 2 briefing, undated.

55. Interview conducted by the author with Lieutenant Colonel Dale Alford, then Commanding Officer of 3rd Battalion, 6th Marine Regiment, 2nd Marine Division, February 29, 2008.

56. Ibid.

57. Ibid.

58. 3/6 PowerPoint presentation titled "Command Brief," undated.

59. Ibid.

60. 3/6 PowerPoint presentation titled "Al Qaim August 05–March 06."

61. Author interview with Alford.

62. 3/6 PowerPointBrief titled "Al Qaim August 05–March 06."

63. For details of one round of meetings in December 2005, see Bill Roggio, "The Sulemani," *Long War Journal*, December 1, 2005, http://www.longwarjournal.org/archives/2005/12/the_sulemani_1-print.php.

64. Interview with Colonel Nicholas Marano, 1/7 Commanding Officer, conducted by the author on April 17, 2008.

65. Ibid.

66. Ibid.

67. Andrew Tilghman, "Marines Living 'Outside the Wire' on Syrian Border See Progress," *Stars and Stripes*, June 12, 2006.

68. 1/7 Brief.

69. John Koopman, "Marines Helping to Line up Sunnis for Iraq's Army," *San Francisco Chronicle*, March 27, 2006. The article quotes Captain Todd Pillo, the 1/7 intelligence officer, who gives this number.

70. Author interview with Marano.

71. Results of one workshop are summarized in an unpublished white paper titled "Confidence of the Community: Law Enforcement Support to Counterinsurgency," dated June 27, 2005.

72. Author interview with Marano.

73. Morten conducted numerous training seminars for deploying troops on suicide bombings and improvised explosive devices. See H. G. Reza, "Arming Marines with Know-How for Staying Alive," *Los Angeles Times*, October 24, 2005.

74. Matt Hilburn, "Policing the Insurgents," *Seapower Magazine*, March 2006, http://www.navyleague.org/sea_power/mar06-44.php.

75. Author interview with Marano.

76. See details of GBOSS in Richard Tomkins, "U.S. Troops Deploy New Weapon

in Iraq," *Middle East Times*, November 20, 2007, http://www.metimes.com/International/2007/11/20/us_troops_deploy_new_weapon_in_iraq/5560/.

77. According to Hilburn, "Policing the Insurgents."

78. Memorandum from 1/7 Marines Intelligence Section to Lockheed Martin, October 2, 2006.

79. Memorandum from Commanding Officer, Baker Company [Captain C. A. Wolfenbarger, USMC], 1/7 to Commanding General 1st Marine Expeditionary Force, Subject: OIF 05-07 Lessons Learned in Regards to Training Provided by Mr. Ralph. Morten, LAPD, October 4, 2006.

80. Matt Hilburn, "Combat Hunter," *Seapower Magazine*, October 2007; Rick Rogers, "Teaching Marines to Be Like Hunters," *San Diego Union-Tribune*, February 29, 2008, http://www.signonsandiego.com/uniontrib/20080229/news_1n29hunter.html; Molly Dewitt, "Insurgents Beware; Marines are Ready," *jdnews.com*, March 22, 2008, http://www.jdnews.com/news/marines_55612___article.html/training_combat.html.

81. John Koopman, "Marines Helping to Line up Sunnis for Iraq's Army."

82. Charles Crain, "Marines on the Beat in Iraq," *Asia Times Online*, June 7, 2006, http://wwwatimes.come/atimes/Middle_East/HF07Ak02.html.

83. As quoted by Bing West in "Streetwise," *Atlantic*, January–February 2007, http://www.theatlantic.com/doc/print/200701/west-iraq.

84. Background from Ulrike Putz, "An Iraq Town Shrugs off Terror," *Spiegelonline*, December 14, 2007.

85. Author interview with Lieutenant Colonel Mark Freitag, Commanding Officer, TF 4-14, May 15, 2008.

86. As quoted in "Coalition Announces Capture of Zarqawi 'Key Associate,'" *American Forces Press Service News Articles*, May 7, 2005.

87. As quoted in Sean Naylor, "Rawah and Baghdad," *Army Times*, August 28, 2006.

88. Sean Naylor, "Liberating Anah," *Army Times*, August 26, 2006.

89. Putz, "An Iraqi Town Shrugs off Terror."

90. These capabilities introduced new, complex workloads for the SBCT fire support officers. See 1st Lieutenant Jeffrey J. Bouldin, "The FSO's AO Database for the Stryker Company," *Field Artillery Magazine* (January–February 2006): 40–41.

91. Interview with Major Joseph Blanding, 4-14, S-3, brigade support group, conducted as part of the Operational Leadership Experiences Project, Combat Studies Institute, Fort Leavenworth, KS, September 17, 2007.

92. Author interview with Freitag.

93. *FM 3-21.31, The Stryker Brigade Combat Team*, Headquarters, Department of Army (March 2003), http://www.globalsecurity.org/military/library/policy/army/fm/3-21-31/index.html.

94. Ibid., ch. 1, para. 1-19.

95. Author interview with 172nd SBCT Commanding Officer Colonel Michael Shields, December 3, 2008.

96. Author e-mail exchange with Lieutenant Colonel Freitag, November 6, 2008.

97. Author interview with Freitag.

98. Background in this paragraph drawn from author interview with 172nd SBCT Commanding Officer Colonel Michael Shields, May 15, 2008.

99. Author interviews with Freitag and Shields.

100. The experiences of 3/2 and 1/25 SBCT are captured in *Networked Forces in Stability Operations* (Santa Monica, CA: Rand Corporation, 2007).

101. Interview with Major Douglas Merritt, Operational Leadership Experiences Interview Collection, Combat Studies Institute, Fort Leavenworth, KS, August 22, 2007.

102. Drawn from PowerPoint briefing slide, "4-14 Commander's Intent," undated.

103. Author interview with Freitag.

104. As described in John Hendren, "Base Set Up to Curb Rebels," *Los Angeles Times*, July 31, 2005, A-1. For details of supporting the operation of COP Rawah, see, Pfc Spencer Case, "129th Forward Logistics Element Supports Rawah," *Anaconda Times*, September 25, 2005, 4.

105. Author interview with Freitag.

106. Ibid.

107. Author interview with Merritt.

108. *Center for Army Lessons Learned Newsletter No. 01-04*, Joint Readiness Training Center Training Program Observations, ch. 3, Intelligence, http://www.globalsecurity.org/military/library/report/call/call_01-4_ch3.htm.

109. Details in "Troops from Alaska Find Huge Weapons Cache behind Chicken Coop Using Hotwired Backhoe," *Anchorage Daily News*, October 17, 2005.

110. Author interview with Freitag.

111. Ibid.

112. As detailed by Naylor, "Liberating Anah"; additional information from author interview with Freitag; author interview with Major Mattew Albertus, March 12, 2009. Albertus was promoted from captain to major during the research for this book.

113. Ibid.

114. As quoted in Naylor, "Liberating Anah."

115. Ibid.

116. Author interview with Merritt.

117. Ibid.

118. Ibid.

119. Sources for the 4-14 police training program are author interview with Freitag and 4-14 Storyboard PowerPoint briefings.

CHAPTER 4

1. Interview conducted by the author with Colonel Sean MacFarland, USA, [Former brigade commander of 1/1], October 15, 2007, in the Pentagon, Washington, DC.

2. As quoted in Tom Lasseter, "Insurgents Have Changed U.S. Ideas about Winning," *Philadelphia Inquirer*, August 28, 2005, A1.

3. "Insurgents Hamper U.S., Iraqi Forces in Ramadi," *Associated Press*, May 22, 2006.

4. Ibid.

5. Major Niel Smith and Colonel Sean MacFarland, "Anbar Awakens: The Tipping Point," *Military Review* 88, no. 2 (March–April 2008): 42.

6. The breakdown in the insurgent groups in and around Ramadi is drawn from Brigadier General John Gronski, "Setting the Conditions in Ramadi," July 2007, unpublished paper used with permission of the author.

7. Michel Moss, "Bloodied Marines Sound Off about Want of Armor and Want of Men," *New York Times*, April 25, 2005.

8. As quoted in Lasseter, "Insurgents Have Changed U.S. Ideas about Winning."

9. Rory Carroll, "Gunmen Take over Ramadi as Bomb Kills Five Marines," *Guardian.co.uk*, June 17, 2005.

10. Anny Scott Tyson, "To the Dismay of Local Sunnis, Shiites Arrive to Police Ramadi," *Washington Post*, May 7, 2005, A13.

11. See, for example, Jackie Spinner, "Marines, Iraqi Forces Launch Offensive in Ramadi," *Washington Post*, February 21, 2005, A21; T. Christian Miller, "Marines are Cracking Down on Insurgent Stronghold of Ramadi," *Los Angeles Times*, February 21, 2005, A4.

12. "Insurgents Hamper U.S., Iraqi Operations in Ramadi."

13. Quoted in Moss, "Bloodied Marines Sound Off about Want of Armor and Want of Men."

14. Ibid.

15. Author interview with Major Mark Pike, 2/28 logistics officer, January 17, 2008.

16. Ibid.

17. Author interview with Brigadier General John Gronski [Commanding Officer 2/28], October 5, 2007.

18. *2/28 After Action Review Report on Iraq Deployment*, undated, [provided to author by General John Gronski], 1.

19. Interview with Brigadier General John Gronski, December 20, 2007, by the Contemporary Operations Study Team, Combat Studies Institute, Fort Leavenworth, KS.

20. Ibid.

21. Author interview with Gronski.

22. Ibid.

23. As detailed by Major Mark D. Pike, "BCT Logistics in Anbar Province," *Army Logistician* (May–June 2008): 22–28.

24. Ibid., 26.

25. Ibid., 24.

26. The cat and mouse game—with the exact roles of who was hunting whom—is captured in Sabrina Tavernise, "Unseen Enemy Is at Its Fiercest in a Sunni City," *New York Times*, October 23, 2005, 1. Insurgents equipped with Russian-made Dragunov sniper rifles were particularly feared adversaries.

27. Ibid.

28. As quoted in Sabrina Tavernise, "U.S. Battles to Control Insurgents in Ramadi," *New York Times*, October 24, 2005, 6.

29. Press reporting over the period chronicles the nearly continuous battles between insurgents and 2/28. See, for example: Steven Hurst, "Fighting in Ramadi as U.S. Reports Two More Deaths," *Associated Press*, September 24, 2005; "New Offensive Begins in Anbar Capital," *United Press International*, November 23, 2005; Sabrina Tavernise, "Scores Are Killed by American Airstrikes in Sunni Insurgent Stronghold West of Baghdad," *New York Times*, October 18, 2005; Jonathan Finer, "Insurgent Attacks Repelled," *Washington Post*, January 26, 2006, A18; Todd Pitman, "U.S., Iraqi Forces Fight Ramadi Insurgents," *Associated Press*, April 22, 2006; Todd Pitman, "U.S., Iraqi Troops Frustrated by Insurgent Hunt in War-Ravaged City," *Associated Press*, May 8, 2006.

30. Press Release 6-08, Camp Blue Diamond, Ar Ramadi, Iraq, January 16, 2006.

31. Press Release 06-011, Camp Blue Diamond, Ar Ramadi, January 23, 2006.

32. Interview with Gronski, Fort Leavenworth.

33. Author interview with Gronski.

34. Interview with Gronski, Fort Leavenworth.

35. Author interview with Gronski.

36. For details on the November 29, 2005, meeting in Ramadi's city auditorium, see Ellen Knickmeyer, Jonathan Finer, and Omar Fekeiki, "U.S. Debate on Pullout Resonates as Troops Engage Sunnis in Talks," *Washington Post*, November 30, 2005, A1.

37. Interview with Gronski, Fort Leavenworth.

38. Ibid.

39. Catherine Philip, "Insurgents Stage Show of Strength on City Streets," *London Times*, December 2, 2005, 45.

40. "Citizens Turn over 'Butcher of Ramadi' to Iraqi, U.S. Troops," *Armed Forces Press Service*, December 9, 2005. Fighting in Ramadi between insurgent groups was reported as early as the summer of 2005. See Ellen Knickmeyer and Jonathan Finer, "Iraqi Sunnis Battle to Defend Shiites," *Washington Post*, August 14, 2005, A1. The piece provides the

following quotation from Sheik Ahmad Khanjor, leader of the Albu ali clan: "We have had enough of his nonsense. We don't accept that a non-Iraqi [Zarqawi] should try to enforce his control over Iraqis, regardless of their sect—whether Sunnis, Shiites, Arabs or Kurds."

41. Interview by author with 2/28 public affairs officer Major Todd Poole, USMC, May 3, 2008.

42. Details of the attack in Monte Morin, "Suicide Bomb Kills Dozens of Iraqi Police Recruits, 2 Americans," *Stars and Stripes*, January 6, 2006, http://www.stripes.com/article.asp?section=104&article=33278&archive=true. See also Monte Morin, "Officer Killed by Suicide Bomb Had High Hopes for Ramadi," *Stars and Stripes*, January 9, 2006, http://www.stripes.com/article.asp?section=104&article=34193.

43. Louise Roug, "Iraq Sunnis Seek Police Jobs after Attack," *Los Angeles Times*, January 13, 2006, http://articles.latimes.com/2006/jan/13/world/fg-sunnis13.

44. "Homegrown Ramadi Police Prepare to Patrol Iraqi Streets," *Agence France Presse*, February 26, 2006.

45. Tim McGirk, "A Rebel Crack-Up?" *Time Magazine*, January 22, 2006, http://www.time.com/time/magazine/article/0,9171,1151790,00.html.

46. "Iraq's Sunni Tribes Fight to Expel Al Zarqawi Supporters," *BBC Worldwide Monitoring*, January 26, 2006.

47. Hala Jaber, "Sunni Leader Killed after Violence Talks," *Australian*, February 7, 2006, 7.

48. Anthony Lloyd, "Murder of Sheikh Provokes Sunnis to Turn on Al Qaeda," *London Times*, February 10, 2006, 43.

49. Ibid.

50. As quoted in John Ward Anderson, "Iraq Tribes Strike Back at Insurgents," *Washington Post*, March 7, 2006, A12.

51. As quoted in Ellen Knickmeyer, "U.S. Will Reinforce Troops in Western Iraq," *Washington Post*, May 30, 2006, A1.

52. Ibid.

53. Ramadi was extremely dangerous in the late spring 2006. See Michael Ware, "The Most Dangerous Place," *Time Magazine*, May 29, 2006, 45, for a particularly harrowing account of the experiences of 3rd Battalion, 8th Marine Regiment in Ramadi in April–May 2006.

54. Detail from author interview with Pike.

55. *After Action Review Report*, 6.

56. Todd Pitman, "Iraqi Troops Start Rolling out in Armored HMMWVs in Restive Iraqi City," *Associated Press*, April 10, 2006.

57. Author interview with Gronsky.

58. For example, see Corporal Jeremy Gadrow, "6th Civil Affairs Group Organized Delivery of $500,000 in Medical Supplies," *Department of Defense Marine Corps News*,

November 6, 2005; Captain Julianne Sohn, "Reserve Marines Help Transform Electricity in Ramadi," *Department of Defense Marine Corps News*, August 17, 2005.

59. List consolidated from Gronski Fort Leavenworth interview, which references *Final Report of 2BCT, 28th Infantry Division (Mechanized) Operations in Operation Iraqi Freedom 4 January 2005 to 24 June 2006*, 2 BCT Headquarters, 28th Infantry Division (Mechanized) 125 Goodridge Lane, Washington, PA 15301, February 25, 2008.

60. Author interview with MacFarland.

61. Bryan Bender, "Insurgent Attacks in Iraq at Highest Levels in 2 Years," *Boston Globe*, May 31, 2006, http://www.boston.com/news/world/middleeast/articles/2006/05/31/insurgent_attacks_in_iraq_at_highest_level_in_2_years/.

62. The balancing process in 1st Brigade, 1st Armored Division is described in *1st Brigade 1st Armored Division CAAT Initial Impressions Report*, undated, posted online at http://209.85.141.104/search?q=cache:SL8sBIcBo8UJ:www.usm.edu/armyrotc/402classes/6a_FOUO_COP.pdf+Ramadi+CMO&hl=en&ct=clnk&cd=25.

63. Author interview with MacFarland, USA, Commanding Officer of 1/1.

64. Ibid.

65. Author interview with MacFarland.

66. As detailed by Major Niel Smith, "Retaking Sa'ad: Successful Counterinsurgency in Tal Afar," *Armor Magazine* (July–August 2007): 26–35. See also David R. McCone, Wilbur J. Scott, and George R. Mastroianni, "The 3rd ACR in Tal'Afar: Challenges and Adaptations," Strategic Studies Institute, U.S. Army War College, Carlisle, PA, January 8, 2008; Lawrence Kaplan, "Centripetal Force: The Case for Staying in Iraq," *New Republic*, March 6, 2006, 19, for other details on the 3rd ACR operations in Tal Afar.

67. As quoted in Jim Michaels, "An Army Colonel's Gamble Pays Off in Iraq," *USA Today*, May 30, 2007, http://www.usatoday.com/news/world/iraq/2007-04-30-ramadi-colonel_n.htm.

68. Megan K. Stack and Louise Roug, "Fear of Big Battle Panics Iraqi City," *Los Angeles Times*, A1.

69. The 1/1's overall campaign plan is also summarized in Smith and MacFarland, "Anbar Awakens: The Tipping Point," 41–52; Alex Rodriguez, "Retaking Ramadi, One District at a Time," *Chicago Tribune*, July 9, 2006.

70. Smith and MacFarland, "Anbar Awakens: The Tipping Point," 46.

71. Initial reporting of 1/1's campaign in Wade Zirkle, "In Ramadi, A Test of Iraqi Forces," *Philadelphia Inquirer*, July 6, 2006, A17.

72. Special forces played an important role in the battle in support of the conventional forces as detailed by Dick Couch, *Sheriff of Ramadi* (Annapolis, MD: Naval Institute Press, 2008).

73. Author interview with Colonel V. J. Tedesco III, Commanding Officer of TF 1-37 in Ramadi, May 17, 2008.

74. *1st Brigade 1st Armored Division CAAT Initial Impressions Report*.

75. Paper titled "Combat Outposts," Multi-National Forces Iraq, Counterinsurgency Center for Excellence, Baghdad, Iraq, March 21, 2007.

76. Author interview with MacFarland.

77. As quoted in Michaels, "An Army Colonel's Gamble Pays Off in Iraq."

78. Author interviews with MacFarland and Tedesco.

79. Smith and MacFarland, "Anbar Awakens: The Tipping Point," 44.

80. Author interview with MacFarland. Also as summarized in Michaels, "An Army Colonel's Gamble Pays Off in Iraq."

81. Author interview with MacFarland.

82. Ibid.

83. For a breakdown of the insurgent groups in Ramadi, see Lydia Khalil, "Who's Who in Ramadi among the Insurgent Groups," *Terrorism Focus* 3, no. 24 (June 20, 2006): 2, http://www.jamestown.org/terrorism/news/article.php?articleid=2370035.

84. For background on the halting efforts to engage Sunni tribal leaders in Anbar in 2004 and 2005, see David Rose, "Heads in the Sand," *Vanity Fair* (May 12, 2009); posted online at http://www.vanityfair.com/politics/features/2009/05/iraqi-insurgents200905.

85. Michael Fumento, "Return to Ramadi," *Weekly Standard*, November 27, 2006.

86. Author interview with MacFarland; attack details drawn from Monte Morin, "After Attack, Iraqi Police Stand Up to Insurgents," *Stars and Stripes*, September 3, 2006, http://www.stripes.com/article.asp?section=104&article=38853&archive=true. Efforts of the engineers to stand up the outpost and repair it following the attack are detailed in Captain Samuel Dallas, Jr., 1st Lieutenant Jonathan E. Rushin, and 2nd Lieutenant Kevin W. Wooster, "Construction Engineers: Committed to Making a Difference," *Professional Bulletin of Army Engineers*, October–November 2006, 10–11.

87. As detailed in Steven Simon, "The Price of the Surge: How U.S. Strategy Is Hastening Iraq's Demise," *Foreign Affairs* 87, no. 3 (May–June 2008): 63. See also Martin Fletcher, "Fighting Back: The City Determined Not to Become Al Qaeda's Capital," *Times Online*, November 20, 2006, http://www.timesonline.co.uk/tol/news/world/iraq/article642374.ece.

88. Khalid Al Ansary and Al Adeeb, "Most Tribes in Anbar Agree to Unite against Insurgents," *New York Times*, September 18, 2006, http://nytimes.com/2006/09/18/world/middleeast/18iraq.html; Peter Beaumont, "Iraqi Tribes Launch Battle to Drive al-Qaida out of Troubled Province," *Guardian*, October 3, 2006, http://guardian.co.uk./world/2006/oct/03/alqaida.iraq/; Smith and MacFarland, "Anbar Awakens: The Tipping Point," 48, report Sittar reached agreement with tribal leaders on September 9, 2006; Some feared the consequences of the new militias; see Joshua Partlow, "Sheik's Help Curb Violence in Iraq's West; Others See Peril in Tribal Confederation," *Washington Post*, January 27, 2007, A13.

89. Smith and MacFarland, "Anbar Awakens: The Tipping Point," 43.

90. Ibid., 44; Rowan Scarborough, "Sunnis in Anbar Cooperate with Security Effort," *Washington Times*, January 30, 2007, A5.

91. For background on this group, see Lydia Khalil, "Leader of 1920s Revolutionary Brigades Killed by Al Qeada," *Terrorism Focus* 4, no. 9 (April 2007): http://www.james-town.org/terrorism/news/article.php?articleid=2373310; Bill Roggio, "1920s Revolution Brigade Turns on al Qaeda in Diyala," *Long War Journal*, July 12, 2007. Both pieces report on the split between the 1920s Revolution Brigade and Al Qaeda, as well as fissures within the group itself, which led to the creation of Iraqi Hamas in March 2007.

92. Author interview with MacFarland.

93. Ibid.

94. Details in Smith and MacFarland, "Anbar Awakens: The Tipping Point," 49–50. See also Bill Roggio, "Anbar: The Abu Soda Tribe vs. al Qaeda," November 26, 2006, *Long War Journal* at http://www.longwarjournal.org/archives/2006/11/anbar_the_abu_soda_t.php.

95. Author interview with Colonel V. J. Tedesco, June 8, 2009.

96. Dexter Filkins, "U.S. and Iraq Retake Ramadi One Neighborhood at a Time," *New York Times*, June 27, 2006, http://www.nytimes.com/2006/06/27/world/middleeast/27ramadi.html?_r=1&oref=slogin; Monte Morin, "Taking up Residence in Insurgent Havens," *Stars and Stripes*, August 13, 2006, http://www.stripes.com/article.asp?section=104&article=38367&archive=true; Monte Morin, "Unexpected Neighbors Bring Hope in Ramadi," *Stars and Stripes*, August 24, 2006; Julian Barnes, "A Suspect Iraqi: Do You Fire?" *Los Angeles Times*, August 15, 2006, http://articles.latimes.com/2006/aug/15/world/fg-choices15; Monte Morin, "Ramadi Checkpoints Allowing U.S. Troops to Isolate the Enemy," *Stars and Stripes*, August 29, 2006, http://www.stripes.com/article.asp?section=104&article=38747&archive=true.

97. Author interviews with Tedesco.

98. TF 1/37 "Bandits' Coin Operations in Ramadi," PowerPoint Briefing.

99. Fighting around COP Falcon in early August 2006 is detailed in Monte Morin, "1st AD Units Hit Insurgents Hard in Largest Battle of New Campaign," *Stars and Stripes*, August 3, 2006, http://www.stripes.com/article.asp?section=104&article=38138&archive=true.

100. As quoted in Morin, "Unexpected Neighbors Bring Hope in Ramadi."

101. A photo essay on COP construction by the 40th Engineer Battalion in Ramadi is detailed by Monte Morin, "DIY Base Construction in Ramadi," *Stars and Stripes*, August 21, 2006, http://www.stripes.com/article.asp?section=104&article=38545&archive=true.

102. Ibid.

103. Author interview with MacFarland.

104. As recalled by Colonel Tedesco in author correspondence and confirmed by Captain Greg Pavlichko, USA, Commanding Officer of Company C, 1-37, in author

interview, May 13, 2008. Many units in Ramadi developed census patrols, building databases of the neighborhoods. See, for example, Monte Morin, "Surveying the Situation in Volatile Ramadi," *Stars and Stripes*, August 16, 2006, http://www.stripes.com/article.asp?section=104&article=38436&archive=true. Morin's article details the conduct of census patrols of the 2nd Battalion, 6th Infantry Regiment in western Ramadi.

105. Author interview with Captain Pavlichko.

106. Ibid.

107. Information on TF 1-37's census activities was derived from a variety of different sources: (1) Author interview with Tedesco; (2) Powerpoint briefing titled *TF 1/37 COIN Operations in Ramadi*; (3) unpublished paper by Captain Dave Black, Captain Jon-Paul Hart, and Lieutenant Colonel V. J. Tedesco III, "Sun-Tzu and BeanieBabies: Census Operations in Urban Counterinsurgency." Paper cited with permission of Colonel Tedesco; and (4) author interview with Pavlichko.

108. TF 1-37 cordon and search operations are chronicled in Monte Morin's photo essay, "Photo Gallery: Cordon and Search Operation in Ramadi," *Stars and Stripes*, August 3, 2006, http://www.stripes.com/article.asp?section=104&article=38139&archive=true.

109. Ibid.

110. Ibid.

111. Ibid.

112. As noted by Andrew Lubin, "Ramadi From Caliphate to Capitalism," *Naval Institute Proceedings* 134 (April 2008).

113. Mindset of the Marines in the campaign is discussed in Terry Boyd, "For Marines in Anbar, the Key Is to Patrol Often and Keep it Personal," *Stars and Stripes*, September 24, 2006, http://www.stripes.com/article.asp?section=104&article=39339&archive=true.

114. Ibid.

115. 1-6 worked under RFCT 1 commanded by Colonel MacFarland.

116. Author interview with Jurney, May 15. 2008.

117. Ibid.

118. Ibid.

119. As quoted in Andrew Lubin, "With the Marines in Ramadi," *Military.com*, October 27, 2006, http://www.military.com/forums/0,15240,117941,00.html.

120. Ibid.

121. Author interview with 1-6 Executive Officer, Major Dan Zappa, June 18, 2008.

122. PowerPoint Brief titled "Commander's Intent: TF 1/6 Making a Difference," undated. This one-page document was widely disseminated throughout 1-6.

123. Untitled paper provided to the author that conveyed the 1-6 plan throughout the unit for conducting operations starting on September 23, 2006, through January 2007.

124. Author interviews with Zappa and Jurney.

125. Author interview with Zappa.

126. For reporting on the battles surrounding the government center, see Dexter Filkins, "In Ramadi, Fetid Quarters and Unrelenting Battles," *New York Times*, July 6, 2006, http://www.nytimes.com/2006/07/05/world/middleeast/05ramadi.html?n=T op%2FReference%2FTimes%20Topics%2FPeople%2FF%2FFilkins%2C%20Dexter; Julian Barnes, "A Summer of Discontent in Iraq," *Los Angeles Times*, August 12, 2006, posted at http://www.leatherneck.com/forums/archive/index.php/t-33293.html; "US Troops Fend off Coordinated Attacks on Sites in Ramadi," *Associated Press*, May 17, 2006; Fumento, "Return to Ramadi"; Neil Shea, "Ramadi Nights," *Virginia Quarterly Review* (Winter 2008): 6–29, http://www.vqronline.org/articles/2008/winter/shea-ramadi-nights/.

127. Jim Michaels, "In Ramadi, the Force Isn't Huge but the Task Is," *USA Today*, August 28, 2006, http://www.usatoday.com/news/world/iraq/2006-08-28-iraq-usat_ x.htm.

128. Monte Morin, "U.S. Troops Razing Ramadi Buildings to Renew Security," *Stars and Stripes*, September 2, 2006, http://www.stripes.com/article.asp?section=104&articl e=38831&archive=true.

129. Author interview with Jurney.

130. Details in Lubin, "Ramadi from the Caliphate to Capitalism."

131. Author interview with Zappa.

132. For a snapshot of life in the 17th St. Station in the spring of 2007, see Moni Basu, "Bullets, Braves and Boiled Peanuts," *Atlanta Journal-Constitution*, April 18, 2007, http:// www.ajc.com/metro/content/shared-blogs/ajc/georgiansatwar/entries/2007/04/18/ georgia_marines_bond_together.html.

133. Rick Jervis, "Police in Iraq See Jump in Recruits," *USA Today*, January 14, 2007, http://www.usatoday.com/news/world/iraq/2007-01-14-police-recruits_x.htm; Joint patrols in Ramadi's Albu Faraj neighborhood are described in Michelle Tan, "On the Ground in Iraq: A Ride-Along with Soldiers Training Iraqi Police," *Army Times*, January 23, 2007, http://www.armytimes.com/news/2007/01/atramadi.training070122hold/.

134. Andrew Lubin, "The Tide Turns in Ramadi," *On Point, Military.com*, May 4, 2007, http://www.military.com/forums/0,15240,134629,00.html.

135. Pamela Hess, "Tribal Militia Policing Ramadi," *UPI*, February 20, 2007.

136. Author interview with Zappa.

137. Author interview with Jurney.

138. Multi-National Force West Public Affairs Office, "Transition of Authority Ceremony Marks Progress of Iraqi Battalion," January 22, 2007, Release No. 200702122-13.

139. Author interviews with Jurney and Zappa.

140. Ibid.

141. Author interview with Jurney.

142. Author interview with Zappa.

143. Lance Corporal David A. Weikle, "Lejeune, Marines, Iraqis Work Together to Take Census in Ramadi," November 6, 2006, http://www.munciefreepress.com/node/18111.

144. Author interview with Jurney.

145. Author interview with Zappa.

146. Author interview with Jurney.

147. Statement of Commander's Intent.

148. Ibid.

149. Author interview with Jurney.

150. Author interviews with Jurney and Zappa.

151. Ibid.

152. Department of Defense Bloggers Roundtable with Colonel Richard Simcock, commander of Regimental Combat Team Six, June 13, 2007, http://www.defendamerica.mil/specials/2007/blog/docs/Simcock_Transcript.pdf. Simcock, commander of RCT-6, noted that his unit had sent liaison officers to examine Jurney's use of district councils and neighborhood watches and had decided to replicate those practices in Fallujah; see pages 1–15 of transcript. See also Teri Weaver, "Iraqi Town Grows Calm after Fed Up Citizens Form Informal Security Team," *Stars and Stripes*, May 24, 2007, http://www.stripes.com/article.asp?section=104&article=53708&archive=true. The article details the stand up of neighborhood watch/local militia in Habbaniyah in the spring of 2007.

153. Teri Weaver, "U.S. Stations Keeping Ramadi Calm," *Stars and Stripes*, May 17, 2007, http://www.stripes.com/article.asp?section=104&article=53514&archive=true.

154. Author interview with Zappa.

155. Ibid.

156. Ibid.

157. Pamela Hess, "Loudspeaker Diplomacy Comes to Iraq," *UPI*, February 17, 2007.

158. Teri Weaver, "Voice of Ramadi Speaks for Police, City Leaders," *Stars and Stripes*, May 13, 2007.

159. Author interview with Jurney.

160. Author interviews with Jurney and Zappa.

161. Ibid.

162. Author interview with MacFarland.

CHAPTER 5

1. Details of the plan are in *Posture of the United States Army 2007*, February 14, 2007, submitted by the Honorable Francis J. Harvey and General Peter J. Schoomaker to the U.S. Senate and House of Representatives, 1st session, 110th Congress.

2. The universal opinion of the brigade's senior staff in author interviews.

3. Covered in David McDowall, *A Modern History of the Kurds*, 3rd ed. (London: I. B. Taurus, 2004); Charles Tripp, *A History of Iraq* (Cambridge: Cambridge University Press, 2000); Phebe Marr, *The Modern History of Iraq*, 2nd ed. (Boulder, CO: Westview Press, 2004).

4. "Iraqi Arabs—Kurds Clash in Mosul," *Middle East News Agency*, Cairo, April 12, 2003.

5. Paul Salopek, "Ethnic Tensions in Mosul Could Trap U.S. Forces in a Crossfire," *Chicago Tribune*, April 13, 2003.

6. Details summarized in Thomas Ricks, "The Lessons of Counterinsurgency: US Unit Praised for Tactics against Iraqi Fighters, Treatment of Detainees," *Washington Post*, February 16, 2006, A14. See also George Packer, "The Lesson of Tal Afar," *New Yorker*, April 10, 2006; David R. McCone, Wilbur J. Scott, and George R. Mastroianni, "The 3rd ACR in Tal'Afar: Challenges and Adaptations," *Of Interest Series*, Strategic Studies Institute, U.S. Army War College, January 8, 2008; Lieutenant Colonel Chris Gibson, "Battlefield Victories and Strategic Success: The Path Forward in Iraq," *Military Review* 86, no. 5 (September–October 2006): 47–59.

7. Author e-mail exchange with Lieutenant Colonel Mitchell Rambin, then operations officer of the 172nd SBCT, March 23, 2009.

8. Luke Harding, "War in the Gulf: Mosul Descends into Chaos as Even the Museum Is Looted of Treasures," *Guardian*, April 12, 2003.

9. A resident named Ahad, quoted in Daniel Williams, "Rampant Looting Sweeps Iraq," *Washington Post*, April 11, 2003, A1.

10. Margaret Neighbor, "U.S. Troops Kill Four Fighters in Mosul Gun Battle," *Scotsman*, April 29, 2003, 12.

11. Richard Oppel, "3 U.S. Soldiers Killed in Attack Near Mosul," *New York Times*, July 25, 2003.

12. Michael R. Gordon, "The Struggle for Iraq: Reconstruction; 101st Scores Success in Northern Iraq," *New York Times*, September 4, 2003, A1.

13. Reported by Kurdish Satellite TV in Salah-al-Din, November 5, 2003.

14. Charles Levinson, "Iraq's 'Terps' Face Suspicion from Both Sides," *Christian Science Monitor*, April 17, 2006.

15. Seb Walker, "Black Hawk Attack Kills 17 Soldiers," *Washington Post*, November 17, 2003, A6.

16. Rory McCarthy, "Bombs Shatter Iraq's Brief Calm," *Guardian Online*.

17. Jason Burke, "Nine Killed in Attack on Iraqi Police," *Observer*, February 1, 2004.

18. As quoted in Daniel Williams, "Violence in Iraq Overtakes an Oasis of Relative Calm," *Washington Post*, November 16, 2003, A24.

19. Ibid.

20. Ibid.

21. Ibid.

22. See http://www.globalsecurity.org/military/world/para/ansar-al-sunna.htm (accessed March 4, 2009).

23. Aqeel Hussein, "Militants Force Women to Wed Local Jihadists," *Sunday Telegraph*, October 10, 2004.

24. Edward Wong, "Insurgents Attack Fiercely in the North, Storming Police Stations in Mosul," *New York Times*, November 12, 2004.

25. Richard Oppel and James Glanz, "More Iraqi Army Found Dead, Two Clerics Slain," *New York Times*, November 23, 2004.

26. Developments covered in C. Mark Brinkley, "Mosul's Militants Fight Mostly from the Shadows," *Army Times*, November 29, 2004.

27. Michael Knights, "Northern Iraq Faces Increased Instability in 2005," *Jane's Intelligence Review* (February 2005): 31.

28. Richard Oppel, "U.S. and Iraqi Troops Capture a Top Militant Leader in Mosul," *New York Times*, June 17, 2005; Eric Hamilton, "The Fight for Mosul," Backgrounder no. 31, Institute for the Study of War, April 2008.

29. Richard Oppel, "In Northern Iraq, the Insurgency Has Two Faces, Secular and Jihad, but a Common Goal," *New York Times*, December 19, 2004.

30. As noted by Colonel Robert Brown, Commanding Officer in 1/25 SBCT in Mosul, "Special Defense Department Operational Update Briefing on Operations in Northwest Iraq," Department of Defense, Washington, DC, September 14, 2005.

31. Edward Wong, "Attacks by Militant Groups Rise in Mosul," *New York Times*, February 22, 2005;

32. "Ba'athists Reportedly Direct Attacks from Syrian Border Town," Elaph Website, March 8, 2005. The report identified Muhammad Yunis al-Ahmad as a key Baathist leader directing operations from the Syrian border town of Al-Qamishli.

33. "Two Brothers in Arms: Two Faces of the Same Uprising," *Irish Times*, May 26, 2005.

34. Brown, Defense Department Briefing, September 14, 2005.

35. Ibid.

36. Annia Ciezadlo, "Fragmented Leadership of the Iraqi Insurgency," *Christian Science Monitor*, December 21, 2004.

37. Robert Enders and Edward Wong, "Bombing at Shiite Mosque in Mosul Leaves 30 Dead," *New York Times*, March 11, 2005. See also David Enders, "Suicide Bomber Kills 36 at Shiite Funeral," *Independent,* March 11, 2005.

38. Drawn from Lieutenant Colonel Robert Hulslander, "The Operations of Task Force Freedom in Mosul, Iraq: A Best Practice in Joint Operations," *Joint Center for Operational Analysis Journal,* Joint Forces Command, Norfolk, VA (September 2007), 18.

39. Tom Lasseter, "Hard Lessons for High Tech Force: Some Stryker Brigade Sol-

diers Blame Violence in Mosul on Insufficient Numbers of U.S. Troops," *Philadelphia Inquirer*, January 23, 2005.

40. Richard Oppel and Eric Schmitt, "Bombing Attacks on Iraqi Forces Leave 38 Dead in North," *New York Times*, June 27, 2005.

41. Dlovan Brwari and Ellen Knickmeyer, "Suicide Bomber Targets Army Recruits," *Washington Post*, July 31, 2005.

42. David Axe, "U.S. Forces Rebuild Ragged Police Force," *Washington Times*, April 13, 2005; Steve Fainaru, "Handoff to Iraqi Forces Being Tested in Mosul," *Washington Post*, April 7, 2005. Details of 1/25's COIN campaign are also summarized in Ren Angeles, "Examining the SBCT Concept and Insurgency in Mosul, Iraq," *Infantry Magazine*, May 1, 2005. See also Major David M. Hamilton and Captain Ryan C. Gist, "Synchronizing Lethal and Nonlethal Effects in 1/25 SBCT," *Field Artillery Journal* (July–August 2004): 17–23.

43. Brown, Defense Department Briefing, September 14, 2005.

44. Ibid. Also noted in Robert Kaplan, "The Coming Normalcy," *Atlantic* (April 2006): 72–81.

45. Brown, Defense Department Briefing, September 14, 2005.

46. See *FM 3-21.31 Stryker Brigade Combat Team (SBCT) Operations Doctrine Field Manual.*

47. Author interview with Colonel Michael Shields, 172nd SBCT Commanding Officer, June 10, 2008. Shields was subsequently promoted to brigadier general.

48. Ibid.

49. Ibid.

50. This preparation to focus on the provision of municipal services proved its worth in the field, see Tataboline Brant, "Alaskans' Tour Passes Midpoint: Brigade Loses 14 While Training Iraqi Troops to Battle Insurgents," *Anchorage Daily News*, May 15, 2006.

51. Margaret Friedenauer, "Stryker Soldiers Get Battlefield, Cultural Training," *Fairbanks Daily News-Miner*, June 6, 2005.

52. Ibid.

53. PowerPoint Presentation titled "172nd SBCT Operations," dated November 26, 2006.

54. PowerPoint Presentation titled "Fighting COIN: 'It's All Connected': TF 2-1 Leader Assessment," Mosul Iraq, undated. The brief specifically references the 172nd campaign plan as documented in 172nd Fragmentary Order 63 and Operational Order 05-101 (Campaign SOVEREIGN QUEST), November 9, 2005.

55. PowerPoint Briefing, "Fighting COIN: 'It's All Connected': TF 2-1 Leader Assessment," Mosul Iraq, undated, with author adaptations.

56. Evolution of the brigade's mission is covered in Nelson Hernandez, "Mosul Makes Gains against Chaos," *Washington Post*, February 2, 2006.

57. For background on this effort in 2006–7, see *SFA Case Study—Mosul, Iraq*, Joint Center for International Security Force Assistance, Joint Chiefs of Staff, Washington, DC, undated.

58. Author interview with Shields.

59. Details of the NIRTC opening are in Margaret Friedenauer, "Officer Training Center Rises from Former Terrorist Stronghold," *Fairbanks Daily News-Miner*, December 17, 2005.

60. Author interview with Colonel Mark Mitchell, Commanding Officer of the 1st Battalion, 5th Regiment, March 24, 2009.

61. Author interview with Major Seth Wheeler, who served as a company executive officer in 1-5 in western Ninewa, March 28, 2009.

62. Author interview with Mitchell.

63. Ibid.

64. U.S. Federal News, "Iraqi Security Forces Take on the Insurgency in Nineveh," July 21, 2006.

65. Also a common problem in the ISF units being trained in Anbar in 2005–6, as detailed in Chapters 3 and 4.

66. Kaplan, "The Coming Normalcy," 72–81.

67. Principles summarized by Hulslander, "The Operations of Task Force Freedom in Mosul, Iraq," 18–21.

68. The JIATF had been initially stood up by the 101st Airborne division immediately after the invasion. See Donald P. Wright and Colonel Timothy R. Reese with the Contemporary Operations Study Team, *On Point II—Transition to the New Campaign: The United States Army in Operation Iraqi Freedom May 2003 to January 2005* (Fort Leavenworth, KS: Combat Studies Institute Press, 2008), http://www.globalsecurity.org/military/library/report/2008/onpoint/index.html. Details in Chapter 5, Intelligence and High Value Target Operations.

69. Hulslander, "The Operations of Task Force Freedom in Mosul, Iraq," 19.

70. Author interview with Shields.

71. Hulslander, "The Operations of Task Force Freedom in Mosul, Iraq," 18–21.

72. Author interview with Shields and Colonel Charles Webster, Commanding Officer of 2nd Battalion, 1st Regiment.

73. Examples will be provided later in this chapter.

74. Author interview with Major Ed Matthaidess, Commander of "C" Company, 1st Battalion, 17th Infantry. Company C conducted COIN operations in south-west Mosul over the period.

75. Ibid.

76. Hulslander, "The Operations of Task Force Freedom in Mosul, Iraq," 20.

77. Author interview with Shields.

78. Major Dwayne M. Butler and Captain Eric J. Van De Hey, "The Logistics Sup-

port Team: SBCT Combat Multiplier," *Army Logistician* 37, no. 6 (November–December 2005), https://www.almc.army.mil/alog/issues/NovDec05/sbct_multiplier.html.

79. Information drawn from author interviews with Colonel Bill Keyes, April 8, 2009, and Major Jeffrey Dayton, Forward Maintenance Company Commander, 172nd BSB, 172nd SBCT.

80. Ibid.

81. Ibid.

82. Ibid.

83. Ibid.

84. Ibid.

85. Ibid.

86. Ibid.

87. Ibid.

88. Much of the information in this section is distilled from an author interview with Colonel William Keyes, Commanding Officer of the 172nd Brigade Support Battalion, as well as background papers on BSB operations provided by Colonel Keyes.

89. Author interview with Shields and with Lieutenant Colonel Rambin, March 23, 2009 and e-mail exchanges with Major Michael Sullivan, March 28, 2009.

90. Author interviews with Shields and Rambin, and e-mail exchanges with Major Michael Sullivan, March 28, 2009.

91. Author interview with Sullivan, March 20, 2009.

92. Ibid.

93. Author interview with Lieutenant Colonel Rick Somers, March 27, 2009. Somers served as the brigade's civil affairs officer during the 172nd deployment in Ninewa.

94. Author interview with Somers.

95. Author interview with Webster, March 7, 2009.

96. Ibid.

97. Ibid.

98. Ibid. Ideas further fleshed out in Lieutenant Colonel Wayne Brewster, 1-25 S3, and Lieutenant Colonel Charles Webster, TF 2 Senior JRTC Operations Group, "Task Force Adaptive Planning: Everything Is Connected," *A Battalion Task Force in COIN*, CALL Newsletter no. 08-25 (July 2008), Center for Army Lessons Learned, Fort Leavenworth, KS, 4.

99. Author interview with Webster.

100. *Field Manual 7-0, Training the Force*, Department of Army, Washington, DC (October 22, 2002).

101. Author interview with Webster.

102. Details of the Raven system components at http://www.telemus.com/datasheets/s-eagle.pdf; http://www.telemus.com/datasheets/raven.pdf.

103. Author interview with Webster. See also LTC Richard G. Green, Jr. TF XO, and

CPT Mark N. Awad, TF 2-1, "Optimizing Intelligence Collection and Analysis: The Key to Battalion-level Intelligence Operations in Counterinsurgency Warfare," *A Battalion Task Force in COIN*, CALL Newsletter no. 08-25, 17–32.

104. Author interview with Webster.

105. Ibid.

106. Ibid.

107. Green and Awad, TF 2-1, "Optimizing Intelligence Collection and Analysis," 17–32; author interview with Webster.

108. Green and Awad, TF 2-1, "Optimizing Intelligence Collection and Analysis," 25.

109. Author interview with Webster, and with Lieutenant Colonel Mark Freitag, Commanding Officer, TF 4-14, conducted at the Pentagon, Washington, DC, May 15, 2008.

110. Details of the operation from author interview with Webster; Linda Robinson, "The Shadow Warriors," *U.S. News and World Report*, August 28, 2006; Margaret Friedenauer, "Strykers Make a Difference in Mosul," *Fairbanks Daily News-Miner*, November 11, 2005.

111. Also detailed in 4-14 operation in Anbar in Chapter 3.

112. Details of the violent encounter in Rachel D'Oro, "Army Makes Clearer How Soldier Died," Associated Press, November 23, 2005; Doug O'Harra, "Terrorist's Blind Fire Killed Stryker Soldier," *Anchorage Daily News*, November 23, 2005.

113. An example of a patrol in a battle zone is detailed in Margaret Friedenauer, "Soldiers Employ Daring Tactic," *Fairbanks Daily News-Miner*, December 21, 2005.

114. Author interview with Webster.

115. Major Jason Glemser, "Task Force Partnership," A Battalion Task Force in COIN, CALL Newsletter no. 08-25, July 2008.

116. Ibid.; author interview with Webster.

117. Details of one such joint operation in Charles Levinson, "In Iraq, U.S. Troops Widen Role as Soldier Teacher," *Christian Science Monitor*, April 4, 2006.

118. As characterized by Webster in author interview.

119. Ibid.

120. Details of operations in western Mosul in early 2006 are in Julian Barnes, "Cracking an Insurgent Cell," *U.S. News and World Report*, January 9, 2006; Shawn Macomber, "Preparing to Transition," *American Spectator*, January 13, 2006.

121. Information distilled from author interview with Master Sergeant Daniel Schoemaker, April 29, 2009; author interview with Matthaidess, March 12, 2009.

122. After Action Comments for C/1-17 IN During OIF 2005–2006, Memorandum for the Record, Camp Taji Iraq, November 15, 2006.

123. Examples of joint patrols in early 2006 are covered in Shawn Macomber, "They Shoot Litter Bugs, Don't They?" *American Spectator*, January 10, 2006; Shawn Macomber, "Night Raid!" *American Spectator*, January 5, 2006.

124. Author interview with Matthaidess.

125. Use of SKTs in Diyala, for example, is detailed in Spc. Ryan Stroud, "6-9 SKT's Dominate the Enemy in Diyala Province," NewsBlaze.com, July 31, 2007. The article details SKT operations by 1st Platoon, B Troop, 6-9 Armored Reconnaissance Squadron, 3rd Brigade Combat Team, 1st Cavalry Division.

126. The use of these teams has been controversial. See Josh White and Joshua Partlow, "U.S. Aims to Lure Insurgents with Bait," *Washington Post*, September 24, 2007.

127. After Action Comments for C/1-17 IN During OIF 2005–2006, Memorandum for the Record, Camp Taji Iraq, November 15, 2006.

128. Ibid.

129. Author interviews with Matthaidess and Schoemaker.

130. Standard Army training in accordance with *FM 7-1, Battle Focused Training*, Headquarters Department of Army, Washington, DC, September 15, 2003; posted online at http://35.8.109.2/resources/FM7-1BattleFocusedTraining.pdf.

131. Author interview with Matthaidess and Schoemaker.

132. Author interview with 4-11 Commanding Officer, Colonel Scott Wuestner, April 2, 2009.

133. An example of one meeting detailed in Kaplan, "The Coming Normalcy," 72–81.

CHAPTER 6

1. See discussion in Chapter 2, with reference to Lynn Eden's research on the roles of knowledge frames and knowledge-laden organizational routines in *Whole World on Fire: Organizations, Knowledge, & Nuclear Weapons Devastation* (Ithaca, NY: Cornell University Press, 2004).

2. As noted in Chapter 2, see definition offered by Richard Duncan Downie that is applicable here: "A process by which an organization (such as the U.S. Army) uses new knowledge or understanding gained from experience or study to adjust institutional norms, doctrine, and procedures in ways designed to minimize previous gaps in performance and maximize future successes." See *Learning from Conflict: The U.S. Military in Vietnam, El Salvador, and the Drug War* (Westport, CT: Praeger, 1998), 22.

3. Articulated in the White House's *National Strategy for Victory in Iraq*, released in November 2005. As one of three "long-term" wartime objectives, the report notes that U.S. objectives are: "An Iraq that is peaceful, united, stable, democratic, and secure, where Iraqis have the institutions and resources they need to govern themselves justly and provide security for their country" (p. 3). Even this document, however, is confusing in its verbiage, in which it conflates the "war on terror" with the myriad, complex problems faced by tactical commanders throughout the country. For a summary of the constantly shifting war objectives of the United States, see Associated Press, "AP Charts Shifting Justifications for Iraq War," October 14, 2006.

4. As documented by David L. Phillips, *Losing Iraq: Inside the Postwar Reconstruction Fiasco* (New York: Westview Press, 2005). See also Ron Suskind, *The One Percent Doctrine* (New York: Simon and Schuster, 2006); Bob Woodward, *State of Denial: Bush at War, Part III.*

5. It is also worth noting that the MNF-I Commander, General Casey, believed that more troops were neither desirable nor necessary. See the account in Bob Woodward, *State of Denial: Bush at War Part III,* 75–76.

6. The British effort suffered from some of the same maladies. See Anthony King, "Britain's Vietnam: Learning the Lessons of Operation Telic," *Commentary,* Royal United Services Institute, April 30, 2009, http://www.rusi.org/research/militarysciences/uk/commentary/ref:C49F9BEE224FA0/.

7. Background covered in Michael Gordon, "Debate Lingering on Decision to Dissolve the Iraqi Military," *New York Times,* October 21, 2004. Then Vice Chairman of the Joint Chiefs, General Peter Pace, claimed that the Joint Staff had never been consulted in the decision. See AFP, "Joint Chiefs Bypassed in Decision to Disband the Iraqi Army," February 18, 2004. Secretary of State Colin Powell later claimed not to have been consulted in the decision, according to the account in Bob Woodward, *The War Within: A Secret White House History 2006–2008* (New York: Simon and Schuster, 2008), 49; President Bush later said he did not recall reviewing the decision, an account disputed by the CPA's Paul Bremer. See Edmund Andrews, "Envoy's Letter Counters Bush on Dismantling of Iraqi Army," *New York Times,* September 4, 2007.

8. As noted by Thomas Ricks in *Fiasco: The American Military Adventure in Iraq* (New York: Penguin, 2006); also as poignantly documented in Dexter Filkins, *The Forever War* (New York: Alfred A. Knopf, 2008).

9. Detailed in a stream of press releases posted on the homepage of the Defense Department's Office of Force Transformation created by Rumsfeld in October 2001. The office was closed in September 2006.

10. For polling that charts the decline in U.S. public support for the war during the period studied here, see "Pessimism Grows as Iraq War Enters Its 4th Year," Pew Research Center for the People and the Press, March 16, 2006, http://people-press.org/report/272/pessimism-grows-as-iraq-war-enters-fourth-year.

11. One of the most widely cited COIN theorists is David Galula, *Counterinsurgency Warfare: Theory and Practice* (London: Pall Mall, 1964); see also Robert Thompson, *Revolutionary War in World Strategy* (New York: Taplinger, 1970); Ian F. W. Becket, ed., *Armed Forces and Modern Counterinsurgency* (London: Croom Helm, 1985). In addition, see F. W. Becket, *The Roots of Counterinsurgency: Armies and Guerilla Warfare 1900–1945* (London: Blandford, 1988). For an excellent review of COIN theory literature, see David Kilcullen, "Counter-Insurgency Redux," *Survival* 48, no. 4 (December 2006): 111–30; Robert R. Tomes, "Relearning Counterinsurgency Warfare," *Parameters* 36 (Spring 2004): 16–28.

12. Author interviews with Colonel William Jurney, 1-6 Commanding Officer, and Major Daniel Zappa, Battalion Executive Officer and head of battalion nonkinetic effects working group.

13. Barry Posen, *Sources of Military Doctrine: France, Britain, and Germany between the Wars* (Ithaca, NY: Cornell University Press, 1984). As noted in Chapter 2, Deborah Avant offers a variation on Posen's argument by drawing upon principal-agent theory. Avant argues in *Political Institutions and Military Change: Lessons from Peripheral Wars* (Ithaca, NY: Cornell University Press, 1994) that in democracies military institutions develop customer-type relationships with legislatures, which control the purse strings for the military. She argues that change can also be driven by the need to satisfy the demand from this important customer.

14. Stephen Peter Rosen, *Winning the Next War: Innovation and the Modern Military* (Ithaca, NY: Cornell University Press, 1991).

15. Ibid., 22–38.

16. Rosen, *Winning the Next War*, 1991.

17. I am indebted to the insights of Colonel Charles Webster (Commanding Officer of 2-1 in Mosul) on this particular point.

18. See note 37 in Chapter 2, Chris C. Demchak, *Military Organizations, Complex Machines: Modernization in the U.S. Armed Forces* (Ithaca, NY: Cornell University Press, 1991).

19. See note 20 in Chapter 2, James G. March and Herbert A. Simon, *Organizations* (New York: John Wiley and Sons Inc., 1985), 177–86.

20. For a survey of the field, see Edgar Schein, "Culture, the Missing Concept in Organizational Studies," *Administrative Science Quarterly* 41 (1996); Geert Hofstede, Bram Neuijen, Denise Daval Ohayv, and Geert Sanders, "Measuring Organizational Cultures: A Qualitative and Quantitative Study across 20 Cases," *Administrative Science Quarterly* 35 (1990).

21. A sobering assessment of these prospects is provided by Thomas Ricks, "An Interview with Thomas Ricks," *Proceedings Magazine* 135, no. 5 (May 2009): 20–24.

APPENDIX

The following figures may be found at http://www.sup.org/itw

INDEX

AAS, *see* Ansar al-Sunna
Abizaid, John, 5–6
Abu Hamza, 86, 88
Abu Zubayr, 156
ACR, *see* Armored: Cavalry Regiment
Ad hoc organizations, 70, 202
Adaptation, 8–9, 19, 21, 27–28, 43–44, 46, 74, 128, 135, 184, 199, 206, 211; iterative process of, 95
Adaptive organizations, 10, 149, 190
Adversaries, 1, 32, 36, 190–91, 206
Affairs, civil, 66–67
AIF (anti-Iraq forces), 90, 150, 183–84, 187
Air Force, 25, 41, 44, 84
Aircraft carriers, 25
Al-Anbar Province, 54, 58
Al Qaeda in Iraq, 20, 54, 57–63, 76, 87–88, 95–96, 103–6, 114–17, 127, 133, 170
Albu Fahad, 106
Albu Mahals, 60–61, 76
Albu Soda, 116
Alford, Lieutenant Colonel Dale, 65–68, 74
Alil, 143, 152
Alternatives, 50
Ambushes, 41, 174, 176, 183–84
Anah, 76–78, 82–84, 86–87, 90–92, 139
Analysts, 69, 156, 173, 211
Anbar, 2, 8, 19–21, 54–62, 64–65, 76–77, 79, 81–83, 85, 87–88, 91, 94–9104, 106, 114–16, 132–33, 210–11; Governor, 103, 127; insurgency, 77, 210, Province, 2–3, 6, 14, 61, 68, 84, 86, 104, 108, 145, 168, 201, 210. *See also* Western Anbar
Ansar, 143–45
Ansar al-Sunna (AAS), 143, 145, 170
Anti-Iraq forces, *see* AIF
Anuman Brigade, 105
AQI, *see* Al Qaeda in Iraq
Armored: Battalion, 97, 111; brigade, 17, 98, 111; Cavalry Regiment, 112, 137, 167; Regiment, 97, 111, 113, 115–17
Arms caches, 38, 85, 92, 102
Army: Air Corps, 41; battalions, 56; multiple Iraqi, 160; brigades, 17, 154; active-duty, 17; reconstituted Iraq, 61; Corps of Engineers, 166–67; doctrine, 161, 169; infantry brigade, 78; infantry units, 134–35; light infantry units, 17
Artillery brigade, 141
Asad Air Base, 76–77
Assault, 6, 19, 56, 59, 107, 115
Attacks, 15, 19–20, 36–38, 57, 61–62, 71, 73, 87, 95, 100–101, 115–16, 131–32, 142–44, 146–47, 171, 174; coordinated insurgent unit, 125; glass factory, 105–6; preferred insurgent, 145
Authority, 3, 23, 31, 33–34, 48, 68, 113–14,